Lexical
Relations

STANFORD MONOGRAPHS IN LINGUISTICS

The aim of this series is to make exploratory work
that employs new linguistic data, extending the scope or domain
of current theoretical proposals, available to a wide audience.
These monographs will provide an insightful generalization of the
problem and data in question which will be of
interest to people working in a variety of frameworks.

STANFORD MONOGRAPHS IN LINGUISTICS

LEXICAL RELATIONS

Jean-Pierre Koenig

CSLI
PUBLICATIONS
Center for the Study of
Language and Information
Stanford, California

Copyright © 1999
CSLI Publications
Center for the Study of Language and Information
Leland Stanford Junior University
Printed in the United States
03 02 01 00 99   5 4 3 2 1

Library of Congress Cataloging-in-Publication Data

Koenig, Jean-Pierre.
Lexical relations / Jean-Pierre Koenig.
p.   cm.
Based on the first three chapters of the author's thesis (Ph. D.—University of California at Berkeley).
Includes bibliographical references (p.) and index.
ISBN 1-57586-177-1 (alk. paper).
ISBN 1-57586-176-3 (pbk. : alk. paper)

1. Lexicology. 2. Grammar, Comparative and general. I. Title.
P326.K567   1999
413′.028—dc21   98-45562
CIP

"Ancienne Manier de Bender avec le Tentoir les Rouleaux des Metiers", the drawing on the cover of the paperback edition of this book, is from *Encyclopédie ou Dictionnaire Raisonné des Sciences des Arts et des Métiers*, edited by Diderot. Première Édition de 1751–1780.

∞ The acid-free paper used in this book meets the minimum requirements of the American National Standard for Information Sciences—Permanence of Paper for Printed Library Materials, ANSI Z39.48-1984.

CSLI was founded early in 1983 by researchers from Stanford University, SRI International, and Xerox PARC to further research and development of integrated theories of language, information, and computation. CSLI headquarters and CSLI Publications are located on the campus of Stanford University.

CSLI Publications reports new developments in the study of language, information, and computation. In addition to monographs, our publications include lecture notes, working papers, revised dissertations, and conference proceedings. Our aim is to make new results, ideas, and approaches available as quickly as possible. Please visit our web site at
http://csli-publications.stanford.edu/
for comments on this and other titles, as well as for changes and corrections by the author and publisher.

To Alfred and Yolande Koenig

Contents

Acknowledgements

This book grew out of the first three chapters of my PhD thesis, completed at the University of California at Berkeley. Too many people deserve credit for the ideas contained in this book for any list to be complete. Let me briefly mention the obvious ones. First and foremost, I would like to thank my thesis advisors, Paul Kay and George Lakoff. Each in their own way provided all a student can ask for: a challenging ear and constant intellectual stimulation. Thanks also to the Berkeley and Buffalo Linguistics communities for their intellectual openness, their theoretical diversity, and their communal spirit. Special thanks go to Charles Fillmore for his gentle guidance. I would have erred much more without his incisive hints. Many thanks also to Larry Hyman for always leaving his door open and introducing me to much of what linguistics is about outside of Berkeley, to Eve Sweetser for her support and interest in my work, and especially to Robert Wilensky for providing a different perspective on language and changing my way of looking at linguistics. A special thanks to Ivan Sag for being an enthusiastic guide.

I also owe a lot to my former fellow graduate students and my current students and colleagues. They helped shape my ideas in so many ways, often simply by listening as if I had a clear vision of what I wanted to say, sometimes by being critics or guides through previous literature. Their own work influenced much of this book. I hope the final product is not undeserving of their help. Thanks in particular to Tony Davis, Adele Goldberg, Hana Filip, David Houghton, Dan Jurafsky, Knud Lambrecht, Gail Mauner, Alissa Melinger, Karin Michelson, Laura Michaelis, Orhan Orgun, Eric Pederson, Len Talmy, and Robert Van Valin.

I owe a special debt to David Houghton and Alissa Melinger. Their numerous comments on a draft of this book was invaluable; thanks also to David for the great work on the index and to Cori Grimm for her proof-reading. Many thanks are also due to the people of California

ix

and the United States of America for being so generous and open to half-foreigners. They made financially possible the initial research that developed into this book.

Finally, thanks to all my family for supporting me throughout the years, even when it was from far away. Thanks, Alisa, Mom, Dad, Papi, Mami, and Michel.

1

Introduction

1.1 Lexical Knowledge

What is the nature of the lexicon and lexical knowledge? According to an early view within modern linguistics (see Bloomfield 1933, Chomsky 1965) the lexicon consists of a theoretically uninteresting repository of idiosyncrasies— what Di Sciullo and Williams 1987 call a listeme. This view meshes well with the experience of language learners; learning a language consists in part in the memorization of idiosyncratic properties of words and morphemes. From a more theoretical perspective, linguists often distinguish between the universal aspects of language— syntax being the clearest locus of such universality— and the inescapable idiosyncratic left-overs, what lexical knowledge is about. The lexicon is, then, a place where the (theoretical) linguist's job ends. This view is unsatisfactory in at least two respects. For one thing, in more recent years, linguists have transferred more and more of the structure of grammatical systems to the lexicon and have let syntax take its lead from lexical entries (in technical terms, syntax is projected from the lexicon). As the grammatical burden has shifted progressively to words and morphemes, lexical structure has been more and more endowed with the regularity and productivity which was once the sole province of syntax. The traditional notion of the lexicon as 'a prison for the lawless' (Di Sciullo and Williams, op.cit.) does not capture those productive aspects of lexical knowledge which are not simply the result of rote memorization.

Furthermore, by letting lexical knowledge be the repository of all idiosyncrasies, we are forced into a false dichotomy— a language consists of universal principles (often conceived of as a set of parameter values in a list of innate universal properties) and a list of (lexical) idiosyncratic facts. What this dichotomy leaves out is *medium-size generalizations*— facts that are neither particular to individual lexical items, nor conse-

quences of universal properties of the human language capacity. Much
of lexical knowledge resides in such medium-size properties. By con-
struing the lexicon as an unorganized repository of idiosyncrasies, we
ignore a large portion of it. To illustrate, let's consider an example from
Williams 1994. Williams notes that nouns which refer to 'lower trunk
wear' in English are all *pluralia tantum* (witness, 'pants', 'jeans', 'shorts',
and so forth). He introduces the following informal rule to account for
this fact.

(1)   Ns ←: 'lower trunk wear'

Any word whose meaning can be characterized by the expression
on the right hand side of the arrow must be a plural noun. Now, this
rule is particular to English. French, for example, does not have such a
rule; its lexicon contains 'pantalon' ('pants (sg)'), 'short' ('shorts' (sg)),
and so forth. What kind of linguistic knowledge, then, does the rule
in (1) illustrate? Clearly not the value of an innate parameter. There
is no "pants" parameter for which English would be marked [+plural]
and French [+singular]. Nor is it an idiosyncrasy of a single lexical entry or an idiomatic fact on a par with the idiomatic meaning of 'kick
the bucket', as Williams points out. The "pants" rule illustrates well
what I call medium-size generalizations— descriptive generalizations
that are not plausibly the consequences of universal principles, however
parametrized, but do not constitute idiosyncrasies of individual lexical
items either. What the traditional view of the lexicon misses is not only
the productive, non-idiosyncratic aspects of lexical knowledge, but also
the medium-size nature of some of this knowledge.

The thrust of this book is to provide a model of lexical relations
which reconciles the lexicon's idiosyncratic and productive traits. Building on work in Head-driven Phrase Structure Grammar, an organization
of lexical knowledge is proposed— called the Type Underspecified Hierarchical Lexicon— which provides a unified model for partial regularities, medium-size generalizations, and truly productive processes. The
intuitive ideas and tools behind this architecture are simple.

- A language's lexicon consists of a multidimensional taxonomy of
  word or lexeme categories.[1]
- Lexical entries are stored underspecified.
- Lexical processes reduce to category intersection.

The use of inheritance networks or underspecification to model linguistic knowledge is not new. Inheritance networks have been used

---

[1] Throughout this book, I use the word 'lexeme' to refer to the class of roots, stems,
and words.

in Natural Language Processing systems to flexibly and efficiently encode human knowledge since at least the late 60's (see Quillian 1968, Bobrow and Webber 1980, Brachman and Schmolze 1985, among others). Furthermore, several linguistic frameworks which can be characterized as category-based, to borrow a term from Pullum and Zwicky 1991, already make extensive use of category networks in their descriptions of grammatical knowledge. It is illustrated by work in Construction Grammar (hereafter CG, Lakoff 1987 and Fillmore and Kay (Forthcoming)), Head-driven Phrase Structure Grammar (Pollard and Sag 1994) (hereafter HPSG), and Cognitive Grammar (hereafter COGGR, Langacker 1987, Langacker 1991).

Underspecification, moreover, has been widely used in (lexical) phonology since at least the mid 80's (see among others Archangeli 1984 and Kiparsky 1985, as well as Steriade 1995 for a recent survey). More recently, Lexical-Functional Grammar's (hereafter LFG) Lexical Mapping Theory makes a limited appeal to underspecification (see *inter alia* Bresnan and Kanerva 1989). But, the combination of these two tools is new and allows for a unified account of the idiosyncratic and productive aspects of lexical knowledge.

By letting lexical entries be underspecified, the model proposed in this book departs from other architectures based on the notion of a taxonomic hierarchy of categories— be they unification-based frameworks such as HPSG or strictly usage-based models, such as COGGR. In both approaches, stored entries contain (directly or indirectly) all information needed for their use in a particular sentence. By contrast, in the lexical architecture proposed in this book, lexical entries may be stored stripped of all information which varies across their syntactic contexts of occurrence. Stored entries are abstract blue-prints, so to speak. Actual words used in uttering and interpreting sentences result from intersecting these underspecified objects with various lexeme classes that fill in information left out of stored entries. Applying lexical processes simply means filling in information.[2]

---

[2] Two caveats are in order. Firstly, lexical entries *may* be stored underspecified; they do not have to be. The Type Underspecified Hierarchical Lexicon does not require lexical storage to be minimally redundant. What is crucial for its account of lexical productivity is that entries are allowed to be stored without some of their contextually determined information. Because Type Underspecification does not require minimal redundancy, it can account for well-known psycholinguistic results that show that the mental lexicon contains redundancies (Lukatela et al. 1980).

Secondly, in current HPSG Hierarchical Lexicons, information contained in an entry need not be directly stipulated as part of this entry's definition. Much of the information associated with entries is indirectly inferred from the properties of the superclasses to which they belong. Moreover, the stipulated information might be

Lexical knowledge, as I argue for in this book, thus differs markedly from what is traditionally assumed. It is not a mere enumeration of idiosyncratic, fully specified entries. It consists of a set of underspecified entries organized taxonomically into lexeme classes which capture generalizations that are true of (potentially open) sets of entries. The dual aspects of lexical knowledge reconcile the two views of the lexicon mentioned at the outset. The set of *minimal* entries is indeed a repository of idiosyncrasies; but the set of *lexeme classes* the lexicon broadly construed also contains explains the fact that much of the productive patterning of grammars is lexical in nature. Four major advantages, I argue, accrue to a Type Underspecified Hierarchical Lexicon (hereafter TUHL). One stems from the hierarchical organization of lexical information it borrows from HPSG's Hierarchical Lexicon. Three are specific to the TUHL architecture.

Firstly, we can directly account for lexical productivity: we do not need to use lexical rules or any other ancillary devices. We thus avoid all difficulties attached to lexical rules I discuss in chapter 2. Productivity results from category abstraction, the fundamental structuring tool of hierarchical grammars. Furthermore, by reducing rule application to independently needed notions such as category abstraction and intersection, we provide an account of rule-like behavior without relying on rules, which are often criticized by psychologists as implausible. Rules reduce to abstract lexical categories filling in information in underspecified entries. Rule application reduces to category intersection or, more generally, boolean operations on categories.

Secondly, many salient properties of morphological processes find a natural explanation once lexical processes reduce to category intersection.

Thirdly, because the account of productivity the TUHL proposes is category-based, it does not run afoul of the well-known idiosyncrasies of lexical behavior. Lexical exceptions can be modeled without added machinery: their exceptional behavior stems from the inclusion of additional information which regular (minimal) entries leave underspecified. Any added information reduces the combinatorial potential of lexemes by restricting the set of categories with which they are compatible and can therefore combine. Exceptionality thus becomes relative and is naturally measured by the amount of information we need to specify in an

---

partly underspecified, as when a language neutralizes particular case distinctions (see Pollard and Sag 1994, chapter 2). But lexical entries are still crucially completely specified with respect to their category membership (or type). What sets the Type Underspecified Hierarchical Lexicon apart is the presence of *type* underspecification in the definition of stored entries, as explained in detail in chapters 2 and 3.

entry. It does not require new structure or formal apparatus. Exceptionality is the limiting case of general principles of knowledge organization.

Finally, medium-size or language-specific generalizations receive an adequate model. Many lexical generalizations are to a large extent language-specific (see Wasow 1977). They do not fall in either the universal or idiosyncratic dichotomy; they are general, often productive, but cannot be reduced to a small set of parametrized universals, even when cross-linguistic patterns are discernible. Moreover, lexical processes are typically organized taxonomically; one needs to distinguish various subcases of a particular process, some more productive than others, each sharing some common structure as well as including particular properties. Because lexical productivity stems from the organization of a hierarchical lexicon, which is well suited to capturing medium-size generalizations, the TUHL architecture directly accounts for this defining property of lexical processes.

1.2   Sign-based, category-based grammars

To better understand the overall model of lexical knowledge proposed in this book, it is useful to put the proposal within the larger context of grammatical theories. At an abstract level, grammars may be viewed as transducers associating phonological strings, semantic, and contextual representations. The linguist's task is then to characterize the general architecture of these transducers as well as how native speakers acquire it. An important task of Linguistics as a Cognitive Science is thus the construction of a computational device that accounts for the set of well-formed string-meaning-context triplets. Of course, just as important as finding out their general architecture, is finding out how much these transducers can vary across languages. The general architecture of the "transducer" I assume in this book is based on four leading ideas (outlined in this section) that are shared by frameworks as diverse as Langacker's Cognitive Grammar, Lakoff or Fillmore and Kay's Construction Grammar, and Head-Driven Phrase-Structure Grammar.[3] Even though the analyses I present are stated within HPSG, they can all be translated into Construction Grammar, and most into Cognitive Grammar.

---

[3]Construction Grammar is best seen as a research program rather than a specific theory. Scholars who call themselves construction grammarians often differ in the specifics of their grammatical theories. See Brugman 1988b, Fillmore et al. 1988, Fillmore and Kay (Forthcoming), Goldberg 1991, Goldberg 1995, Jurafsky 1991, Jurafsky 1996, Koenig 1993, Koenig 1994, Lambrecht 1994, Lakoff 1987, Michaelis 1993, Michaelis and Lambrecht 1996, and Zwicky 1989 for recent studies within this research program.

1. Grammars are sign-based. They consist of direct associations between form and meaning. In that sense, the approach I take in this book conforms to the rule-to-rule hypothesis of Bach 1976, according to which each syntactic rule is directly paired with a semantic rule.[4] It also conforms to the idea of linguistic gestalts introduced in Lakoff 1977, another early precursor to sign-based grammars. By locally pairing semantic and syntactic information in single rules or constructions, sign-based grammars are antithetic to the "pipeline" model familiar from work in Extended Standard Theory according to which syntax and semantics proceed independently of each other and are associated globally as separate modules (see Chomsky 1981). As a consequence, cross-module mappings between form and meaning are expected: part of linguistic knowledge consists of cross-domain associations between pieces of conceptual structure, pieces of syntactic information, and pieces of phonological information (see Lakoff 1993 among others). Sign-based theories thus also differ from theories of linguistic knowledge that follow Fodor 1983's notion of informationally encapsulated modules, which precludes construction-specific cross-domain associations.

2. Grammars are richly articulated systems of categories. Consequently, no principled difference exists between the lexicon and other parts of a language's grammar. Although phrase-structure schemata may be considered more abstract than typical lexical entries, no ontological difference between the two is presumed to exist. They bear very similar kinds of properties and are modeled via the same logic, simplifying somewhat, the logic of classes. Grammars are thus "big lexicons" or "constructicons." But this single constructicon has more structure than grammars and lexicons in traditional generative studies. Whereas grammars and lexicons traditionally consist of a set of unordered rules or principles and a collection of entries, hierarchical sign-based grammars are not flat. Grammatical signs (and linguistic objects, more generally) form a system of categories within a structured inheritance network, in a manner very similar to models of other kinds of knowledge in Artificial Intelligence.[5] Because of this hierarchical organization, relationships

---

[4]The semantic side of signs or constructions differs among sign-based grammars. In particular, it is more inclusive in CG than typically assumed in classical model-theoretic semantics. It includes (at least) information-structure notions such as Topic or Focus (see Lambrecht 1994), pragmatic variables (see Fillmore et al. 1988), illocutionary force (see Lakoff 1987), and construal or frame-based semantics (Fillmore 1982, Fillmore 1985, Langacker 1987, Talmy 1985).

[5]I assume the strongest version of this claim— that grammatical knowledge is organized like any other kind of knowledge. Note that this question is in principle independent of whether the content of linguistic knowledge is different from other kinds of knowledge, and in particular, is the result of a particular language faculty.

between patterns are not modeled derivationally, through the transformation of one structure into another, but through the specification of the common classes to which patterns belong and through which they share a set of properties.

3. Grammars are constraint-satisfaction systems. String interpretation or production is not accomplished via derivations, but by simultaneous satisfaction of sets of constraints (intuitively speaking, by superimposing constructions or signs). This idea dates back in part to Generative Semantics and McCawley 1968, but its more general implementation is the hallmark of several modern approaches to grammatical theory, from CG to HPSG, or some versions of the Principles and Parameters approach (see Berwick 1991).

4. All grammatical facts belong to a single grammar common to both competence and performance. This claim encompasses two slightly different hypotheses. Firstly, no *a priori* distinction is recognized between a grammatical core and a grammatical periphery. Generalizations as well as true substantive universals are captured by positing more and more abstract objects; idiosyncratic patterns are simply objects low in the hierarchy of signs.[6] Secondly, the strong competence hypothesis of Bresnan and Kaplan 1982 (anticipated in the cognitive grammar of Lakoff and Thompson 1975) is assumed: grammars described by linguists as constituting native speakers' knowledge of their language are the same grammars used by speakers to interpret and produce utterances. For reasons made abundantly clear in Bresnan and Kaplan 1982, Shieber 1986, Sag 1991, and others, this last assumption leads sign-based grammarians to prefer monotonic, declarative representations of grammatical knowledge: such representations allow for an easy modeling of partial interpretations of substrings, the integration of knowledge from various sources at any point during interpretation/production, and

---

Claiming that the organization of linguistic knowledge parallels that of other kinds of knowledge does not commit oneself to any hypothesis as to its content.

[6]A word of caution is in order. Although universal distinctions are high in the hierarchy of linguistic objects and language-specific distinctions will be further divisions of the universal classes, determining a cut-off point above which only universal categories occur is not easy. To that extent, category hierarchies do not by themselves separate universal classifications from general, cross-linguistic frequent ones. In the specific representational scheme I adopt for this book (Typed Feature Structures), the only universals are (i) formal universals induced by the representational scheme itself; (ii) universals that follow from the particular "feature geometry" one chooses; (iii) stipulated universal principles, such as the subcategorization principle of Pollard and Sag 1994. I leave open the question of the existence of abstract, universal types as well as the relationship between such hypothetical universal types and language-specific types. See Green 1996 for some suggestions concerning universal types.

the construction of a single model of grammatical knowledge for both interpretation and production.[7]

1.3 The psychological reality of grammars

Ideally, grammars of natural languages as linguists describe them should correspond to individual speakers' internal grammars. One must therefore partly evaluate the former on how well they reflect what is known about the cognitive systems within which the latter are embedded. Most of my discussion in this book, though, does not focus on such "cognitive" issues. In fact, to "cognitively"-oriented linguists, there might seem to be very little cognition in the pages to follow. Two remarks should suffice to clarify the cognitive status of the grammatical descriptions included in this book. Firstly, the representational scheme I use to state grammatical descriptions is somewhat minimalist. I make use of very few properties of cognitive systems. I only rely upon three tools: the ability to generalize over instances, the ability to organize categories along several taxonomic schemes, and the ability to identify two (sub)structures. None of these abilities seems particularly controversial. As such, the general mechanisms underlying the grammar fragments I present are cognitively plausible. In fact, some cognitive psychologists recently have independently proposed psychological models of linguistic productivity very similar to the one proposed here (see for example Barsalou 1993 and Barsalou and Prinz 1997). Such unexpected convergence suggests the initial cognitive plausibility of the model of lexical knowledge for which I argue.

Secondly, the gist of the book lies in the description of some general properties of grammars and the logic of their organizations. It is these properties which are claimed to have a cognitive equivalent, not the representational scheme used to describe them. The formalism that I use should not therefore be directly interpreted in cognitive terms. Although I assume that the grammatical structures being formally represented are (in the best of all cases) isomorphic to the actual implementation of grammatical systems in the brain/mind, no claim is made

---

[7]This monotonic and declarative stance is slightly bent in those versions of CG that use default inheritance schemes, such as Lakoff 1987, Goldberg 1992. But, as George Lakoff pointed out to me (p.c.), this alteration only concerns the representation of grammatical information, not its use: once a construction is chosen in interpreting or producing an utterance, the information structure it contributes to the analysis of the string cannot be altered. Moreover, Lascarides et al. 1996's recent approach to the logic of defaults in unification grammars can be applied so as to make Lakoff's and Goldberg's theories conform to the desideratum of order-independence intimately tied to the strong competence hypothesis.

as to the actual mechanisms by which they are cognitively realized. To borrow freely from Marr 1982's terminology, what is being described is merely some of the properties of *what* is computed by the brain when interpreting or producing sentences.

To illustrate this point with an example, the classification of linguistic categories into cross-cutting inheritance hierarchies is claimed to be part of the structure of people's actual internal grammars. But the formalism used to make the idea precise does not commit us to any particular realization. What corresponds to the type hierarchy psycholinguistically or neuro-physiologically is left completely open. The only cognitive hypothesis I make is that the realization of grammars obeys the logic of types and the relations between types discussed in this book. In other words, the grammatical descriptions included in this book are merely abstract characterizations of certain properties of the "machines" ("transducers") which underly people's grammars. They are not descriptions of the machines themselves. There might be many (linguistically equivalent) ways to build a machine meeting these design requirements. The same is true of my major claim— that lexical entries are stored underspecified. This property of lexical organization is intended to reflect a property of the psychological/neurological implementation of individual speakers' grammars, but no assumption is made as to how this property is implemented.

Such a minimal cognitivism seems to be the most linguistic methodologies can hope for. As Gupta and Touretzky 1994 show, the inner workings of particular implementations of a grammatical theory can differ significantly from the mechanisms foreseen by the linguistic theory which underlies them. Given the looseness of the connection between grammatical and actual cognitive modeling, such broad cognitivism is, for the moment, the only game in town. What linguists describe are sets of properties grammars obey, which they model with a certain description language provided with a logic. What attributes of the brain/mind correspond to these properties and implement this logic— while ultimately the goal of a theory of language— is beyond the scope of linguistic methodology. This book is no exception.

2

Two kinds of lexical relations

Lexical knowledge can be divided into knowledge of individual words and knowledge of relations between words. It is the study of the latter we will be mostly concerned with in this book. Even though providing a principled account of the relationships between a language's words has been a major goal of modern linguistic theory since at least Lakoff 1970, we will see in this chapter that previous models of the lexicon have not been entirely successful. They often miss one of the three intuitive properties of lexical knowledge I mentioned in the introduction— productivity, idiosyncrasies, and medium-size generalizations. At the heart of this book is the idea that an adequate theory of the relations between words reduces to a model of lexical categories, the set of cross-cutting classes into which speakers group their languages' words. In this chapter I introduce the kinds of relations between words which an adequate theoretical model of lexical knowledge must capture and discuss briefly why previous theories have failed. I do not discuss most of them in detail, since this would lead us too far afield and other published work has extensively discussed the issue. Rather, I take as my starting point a model particularly apt at capturing medium-size generalizations— the Hierarchical Lexicon (hereafter HL)— and explain in detail why it too cannot adequately account for the productive aspects of lexical knowledge. In chapters 3 through 5 I revise the HL. The revised architecture retains its ability to account for medium-size generalizations, but does not falter on productivity.

Let me start with an informal discussion of the kinds of relations among words which a lexical theory needs to capture. Intuitively, words can be related in two ways. They can belong to groups of words with similar properties. 'Bird' and 'tree', for example, are related through

---

This chapter is partly based on work done in collaboration with Dan Jurafsky and reported in Koenig and Jurafsky 1994.

their common membership in the class of nouns. I call these kinds of relations between words *classificatory*, since words are related through their common membership in a class. Such relationships among words are implicitly at the root of the notion of categories like *noun* or *verb*. More recently, classificatory relations have figured prominently in the notion of word class used in the work of Pinker 1989 or Levin 1993 or in work in HPSG on the structure of the lexicon (see Flickinger 1987, Pollard and Sag 1987). But words can also be related through their shared phonological material and morphosyntactic or semantic similarities. 'Bird' and 'birds', for example, share 'bird' as a part and have similar meanings; they are related through this common substring. I call such relations *morphological*, since words in this case are (typically) related through a morphophonological process (e.g. the addition of /s/ in the case of 'bird' and 'birds').

Both kinds of relations have figured in the study of lexical structure, although to a different degree. Classificatory relations among words are implicit in the definition of syntactic categories, but few frameworks provide for an explicit, theoretical foundation to the notion of word class— a notable exception being Hierarchical Lexicons and models of lexical knowledge built around the idea of structured inheritance networks. By contrast, morphological relations have been central to models of lexical knowledge since the early days of modern theoretical linguistics. Of course, these two kinds of relationships are not orthogonal. English nouns, for example, share a cluster of properties, which includes a certain semantic type (or prototype) and certain morphosyntactic potentialities— they can typically occur with or without the plural suffix (typically /-s/), they are typically preceded by determiners, etc. Conversely, 'bird' and 'birds' share not only phonological properties, but also semantic and syntactic properties. A major claim of this book is that the two kinds of relations can be modeled through the same simple device: (a refined form of) class abstraction. More precisely, morphological relations are argued to be a subclass of classificatory relations. Since I propose ultimately to reduce morphological relations to a (subclass of) classificatory relations, I begin this chapter with the model of classificatory relations I borrow from current HPSG. I then show its present inability to adequately account for morphological relations. In chapters 3 through 5 I outline a revised model that eschews the pitfalls discussed in the remainder of this chapter.

2.1 Classificatory Relations in a Hierarchical Lexicon

2.1.1 The Hierarchical Lexicon

The account of *classificatory relations* I adopt in this book is rooted in HPSG's Hierarchical Lexicon (herafter HL). Conceptually, the HL architecture embodies the idea that word classes are part of people's word knowledge. But HLs do not simply allow the expression of word classes. Because of their support for taxonomic classifications, they provide tools for an optimal encoding of lexical knowledge. Properties of individual lexical items can be factored out into various general classes, each defined by the common attributes of its members. We then reap the benefits of a distributed representation in the description of the properties of lexemes. Linguistic generalizations are captured by grouping the relevant entries under a single class (or type); information characteristic of all members is associated with the class as a whole and is automatically passed down to individual members. In technical terms, the information of the class is *inherited* by its members. For example, all English verbs require subjects (although they may sometimes be left unexpressed), all Latin nouns are marked for case. To capture these facts about the English or Latin lexicons, we can posit two word classes, say *verb-class* and *noun-class*, each with this information specified in it. Particular verbs or nouns, such as English 'meet' or Latin 'arbor' are then stipulated to be members of these classes (technically subtypes of the *verb-class* and *noun-class* types respectively) and inherit this information. In defining an individual lexical entry, any information that can be inferred from the lexeme classes to which it belongs need not be specified again for that entry. The hierarchy of word classes thus serves to minimize redundancy and express classificatory relations among a language's words.

But the power of this hierarchical view of grammatical and lexical information goes further. Linguistic objects, and words in particular, typically belong to several cross-cutting classes at once. In the same way we can classify animals along genetic lines, as well as preferred food, habitats, and so forth, we can classify words in terms of their part-of-speech (is a particular word a verb or an adjective?), as well as in terms of their complementation structure (is the word transitive or intransitive?). To model the pervasive cross-classificatory nature of linguistic information, Hierarchical Lexicons allow verbs such as 'meet' to be classified along multiple dimensions, a classificatory scheme often referred to as multiple inheritance (see Sag 1997). The properties of 'meet' as used in (1), for example, stem from its membership in several classes: *verb-class* for part of speech information, *transitive* for subcategorization information, and so forth. All properties of 'meet' shared with verbs are abstracted into the *verb-class*; all properties shared with transitive words are abstracted into the *transitive* class, as diagramed informally in figure 1.

(1)   Harry met Sally.

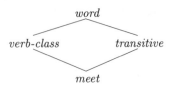

FIGURE 1 A simple example of multiple inheritance

Through multiple inheritance, word classes are arranged in a complex network of categories, with more specific classes inheriting information from more general ones. Each class embodies generalizations about sets of lexical entries that share a certain amount of information, whether relating to subcategorization, semantics, morphology, or phonology.

What makes this representational scheme particularly apt at modeling classificatory relations among words is the multidimensional nature of the classifications and the definition of an inheritance relation over these hierarchies. Researchers in Knowledge Representation Languages (henceforth KRL) have for a long time recognized the usefulness of representing knowledge in terms of a structured, hierarchical network of concepts (see Quillian 1968, Bobrow and Webber 1980, and Brachman and Schmolze 1985 for early and classic presentations of structured inheritance networks). They allow the knowledge engineer (or the cognitive scientist) to represent the knowledge of a particular domain in a compact, flexible, and intuitive manner as well as efficiently characterize inferences over the objects in the domain. If grammatical knowledge, whatever its nature, is part of human knowledge, we expect its organization to likewise consist in a hierarchically organized network of objects, assuming researchers in KRL are correct. But, whereas the nodes of the networks in KRL systems correspond to semantic concepts, in HPSG or CG, the (primary) nodes are signs or constructions, that is, associations of syntactic, semantic, and phonological information. Having briefly introduced the conceptual basis of Hierarchical Lexicons, let me now turn to some of the technical details of the formalism which underlies them (particularly, its HPSG II incarnation).[1]

---

[1]Following standard practice, I call HPSG I the grammatical theory presented in Pollard and Sag 1987 and HPSG II that of Pollard and Sag 1994.

2.1.2   The formalism

The representational scheme used by HPSG to develop a theory that incorporates the idea of a hierarchically organized representation of linguistic knowledge is a variant of Typed Feature Structures, as presented in Pollard 1991 and Carpenter 1992 (henceforth TFS). Although it is by no means the only possible scheme to develop the four leading ideas mentioned in the introduction, it possesses all of the crucial properties necessary to flesh them out. Moreover, its logical properties are well-understood and it underlies several currently available computer implementations. The TFS formalism enables us to express the following kinds of grammatical statements:

(2)   a. A taxonomic characterization of linguistic objects: all linguistic objects are classified according to several criteria (such as part-of-speech, subcategorization properties, and so forth).
      Example statement: 'All lexemes either belong to the class of *roots* or to the class of *complex-lexemes*'.

   b. A partonomic characterization of linguistic objects in terms of their properties.
      Example statement: 'All nominals bear case'.

   c. A recursive characterization of linguistic objects: (non-atomic) properties of linguistic objects are themselves linguistic objects which participate in a taxonomic and partonomic structuring of linguistic information.

   d. The binding (structure-sharing) and counter-binding of two substructures— i.e. the identification (or differentiation) of two properties of a linguistic object.
      Example statement: 'The case of an attributive adjective is the same as that of the nominal it modifies'.

It should be clear to the reader that such tools are not the unique province of the TFS formalism. Most frame-based languages or semantic networks in Artificial Intelligence have similar expressive power. Cognitive psychologists who make use of frames to model concepts and categories postulate the functional equivalent of these four kinds of statement (see Barsalou 1993). Finally, other linguistic frameworks base their linguistic analyses on similar kinds of descriptions. The TFS formalism constitutes a subset of the tools used in Langacker's Cognitive Grammar or Lakoff's Construction Grammar. To take but a few examples from Langacker's work: the taxonomic characterization of linguistic objects corresponds to Langacker's notion of schematicity; the partonomic characterization of linguistic objects corresponds to the (implicit) practice within Cognitive Grammar of naming (sub)parts of a linguistic object with particular names, as when the two major participants of a (dyadic) conceptual relation are named trajector and landmark respectively. Finally, the binding of two substructures corresponds to the idea of integration lines in Langacker's diagrams. Both devices encode the notion that two pieces of structure are in fact one and the same. Such parallels between the TFS formalism and Cognitive Grammar simply reflect the fact that both are category- and inheritance-based grammars. Of course, significant differences exist between the two approaches, both in style and substance. But this brief cross-theoretical translation table suggests that one should not tie the analyses to follow to the TFS formalism. They can be captured in most frameworks which espouse the leading ideas discussed in the introduction, provided they incorporate a formalism expressive enough to allow statements of the form in (2).

Technically, the TFS formalism models linguistic objects through two mechanisms:

- Features whose values can be complex categories and be equated.
- A multidimensional classification of linguistic objects in terms of classes.

The former is used to describe the organization of properties associated with linguistic objects, with equality representing identity between two objects or properties. The latter is used to model the organization of linguistic objects into categories. Given the interpretation of the relevant attribute labels presented in Pollard and Sag 1994 and summarized in appendix A, the Attribute-Value Matrix (hereafter AVM) in figure 2, for example, represents the head properties characteristic of non-auxiliary, non-inverted, finite verbs (or verb phrases). Labels in italics at the top left of AVM diagrams represent the category to which the linguistic objects they describe belong; names of attributes or properties are written in small caps. The label *verb* in figure 2, for example, indicates that the AVM characterizes a class of verbal head properties.

$$
\begin{bmatrix}
verb & \\
\text{VFORM} & finite \\
\text{AUX} & - \\
\text{INV} & -
\end{bmatrix}
$$

FIGURE 2 The verbal head properties type

Similarly, the AVM in figure 3 represents the syntactic information characteristic of non-auxiliary, non-inverted finite verbs which subcategorize for one argument and are the heads of phrases not preceded by markers such as *to* or *that*— the syntactic category of finite VP's, for example.[2]

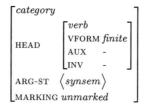

FIGURE 3 An example of a syntactic AVM category

Finally, the AVM in figure 4 represents the meaning of the noun 'book'. Its meaning is of type *npro*, an R-expression in Chomsky 1981's terms. The INDEX attribute specifies that its denotatum is a third person, singular, neuter discourse referent. Its RESTRICTION attribute indicates that the model-theoretic interpretation of this discourse referent is restricted to entities that are books (to entities that can participate in the state-of-affairs of 'being a book'). The necessary identity of the discourse referent's interpretation and the object classified as a book is insured through the tag ① in figure 4. The tag thus indicates that the discourse referent's index and the object categorized as a book are one and the same. In technical terms, the tag encodes token-identity between the values of the two attributes INDEX and INSTANCE.

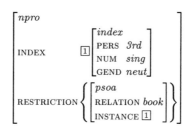

FIGURE 4 The meaning of the noun 'book'

Aside from the HPSG-specific assumptions concerning grammatical information embodied in the feature geometry and category labels, AVM's contain three kinds of information:

---

[2] Angle brackets in the figures denote lists. Thus, <*synsem*> describes a list that contains one *synsem* member.

1. A (recursive) characterization of properties of objects in the domain through attribute value pairs— where values can themselves be attribute value pairs;

2. The identification of substructures through numbered tags. The tag ⑴ in figure 4, for example, indicates that the discourse referent introduced by the noun 'book' and the semantic argument of its restriction are identical (roughly, co-numbered tags correspond to identical variables in a first-order predicate calculus formula);

3. The kind of linguistic objects described by an AVM. The label *category* at the top left of figure 3, for example, indicates that the AVM describes the class of syntactic categories. Category labels in general name linguistic classes to which the objects described by the AVM belong— or, to use a more technical word, they denote their *sorts*.[3] It is these sorts which are organized in a multiple inheritance hierarchy.

The class of (morphosyntactic) head properties (the values of the HEAD attribute, which was introduced in figure 3) provides a simple illustration of the use of inheritance networks to represent linguistic classifications. The relevant classification of head properties is represented in figure 5. Each node in the tree denotes a class of morphosyntactic head features borne by lexemes and phrases. The properties characteristic of the class of (English) *verb* head features is described in figure 6.[4]

$$
\begin{array}{cccc}
noun & verb & adjective & preposition
\end{array}
$$

FIGURE 5   The hierarchy of *substantive* head properties

$$
\begin{bmatrix}
verb & \\
\text{VFORM} & vform \\
\text{AUX} & boolean \\
\text{INV} & boolean
\end{bmatrix}
$$

FIGURE 6   The verbal head properties

---

[3]Throughout this book, I use the technical terms 'type' and 'sort' interchangeably. I also use the more informal terms 'class' or 'category'. Names of types always appear in italics in the text; names of words always appear within single quotes.

[4]The sorts *verb* and *noun* do not refer to classes of words; they refer to a class of syntactic (head) properties.

The AVM in figure 6 represents the head properties common to all verbal constituents (be they lexical or phrasal). They have a verb form, can be auxiliaries, and can be inverted. Since it is common to all verboids, this information is per force underspecified. We only know that the head properties of all verbs will be drawn from the class of verb forms (say, *finite*, *infinitive*, etc.) all of which are subsorts of the sort *verbform* and the class of +, - values, which are subsorts of the sort *boolean*. All verbs inherit those general properties, since their head features are of type *verb*. Particular verbs specify further whether they are finite or infinitive, auxiliary or not, and inverted or not. But by simply knowing that 'met' is a verb, we already know what *kind* of head properties it bears. It is this implicit general knowledge of the class of verbal head properties as a whole which is represented in figure 6.

$$\begin{bmatrix} noun \\ \text{CASE } case \end{bmatrix}$$

FIGURE 7 The nominal head properties

Similarly, the AVM in figure 7 describes the head properties of all nominals. It indicates that they carry some case attribute (indicated by the name of the class of case values, *case*). From knowing that Latin 'arbor' is a noun, we can expect it to bear case, although we might not know which one yet. Now, *verb* and *noun* share some properties, those common to all substantive (or major) categories. In HPSG, there are two such properties, whether or not the category is in predicative position and whether or not it is a modifier. These properties are represented in the AVM in figure 8.

$$\begin{bmatrix} substantive \\ \text{PRD } boolean \\ \text{MOD } mod\text{-}synsem \end{bmatrix}$$

FIGURE 8 The substantive head properties

Crucially, we do not need to specify that all nominal and verbal head features are also marked for the attributes PRD and MOD. This information is inferable from the definition of *substantive* and the information that the classes of *noun* and *verb* head properties are subclasses of *substantive*. More generally, only those properties specific to a class of objects needs to be stipulated for that class. All properties associated with superclasses can be inferred to hold of its subclasses. It is this built-in inference mechanism which is commonly referred to as inheritance. Technically, the redundancy of the PRD attribute on verbal and nominal head features is enforced by the requirement that properties of classes be declared for the most general class which bears them. The PRD property must therefore be part of the definition of the *substantive* class, not the *verb* or *noun* classes, since the former is the most general class of head properties for which it is relevant.

The previous example applies to simple cases in which linguistic objects are classified in only one way. But, as mentioned before, linguistic objects are often classified along several cross-cutting hierarchies. The simple hierarchy in figure 9 represents, for example, an hypothetical language in which all words are either verbs or adjectives and either transitive or intransitive. In other words, it divides the class of words into two orthogonal subgroupings. These two classificatory dimensions are indicated in figure 9 by boxes that surround their names, as shown between the type *word*, and *part-of-speech* and *valence*. Such branching is to be interpreted conjunctively: any word is classified both along a part of speech and a valence dimension or is both a certain kind of part of speech and has a certain kind of complementation structure.[5] Other branches, like the branches between *part-of-speech* and *vb* and *adj* are interpreted in the same way as branches in the case of uni-dimensional hierarchies such as figure 5, i.e. as partitioning their supertypes. In the case at hand, it means that every word is either a verb or an adjective and is either transitive or intransitive. Multi-dimensional classifications like the one represented in figure 9 are thus similar to AND/OR trees in Computer Science.[6]

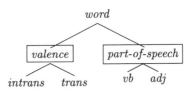

FIGURE 9 A simple AND/OR tree for word categories

If each non-boxed label in figure 9 denotes a linguistic category, what are the possible linguistic categories corresponding to this AND/OR net? This set— the set of categories subsumed by the category at the root of

---

[5]The names inside the boxes do not correspond to sorts or names of classes of objects, but are merely used as mnemonics for the dimensions.

[6]Since at times a single node can be the daughter of more than one parent, I use the expression AND/OR nets to refer to classifications like that in figure 9.

the net— is easy to determine, as shown in Carpenter and Pollard 1991 and Carpenter 1992. Consider again figure 9. Nine categories accord with the classification: words, intransitive and transitive words, verbs, adjectives, intransitive and transitive verbs, and intransitive and transitive adjectives. If we call *word, intrans, trans, vb,* and *adj* basic types, possible linguistic categories constitute a subet of the powerset of the set of basic types. In such a set-theoretic presentation, complex categories are represented as *sets* of basic types: the category of transitive verbs or intransitive adjectives would be described by the set {*trans, verb*} and {*intrans, adj*} respectively. More technically, given an AND/OR net, we can (constructively) define the set of corresponding linguistic categories as follows:

(3) *Conjunctive Type Construction*
The set of all possible types for an AND/OR net N is the (greatest) subset S of the power-set of the set of its basic types B[7] that satisfy the following constraints (expressed in N):

- No member τ of S contains redundant information: if τ contains a basic type a and a is a subtype of b, then, τ does not contain b (that τ is also of type b can be inferred).
- No member τ of S contains inconsistent information: if τ contains a basic type a and a is-not-a b, then τ does not contain b (otherwise τ would be inconsistent).

The subtype/supertype relation on members of S is defined as follows: a complex-type σ is a subtype of a complex type τ if and only if, for each member a of σ, there is a member b of τ such that a is-a b.

Intuitively, the set of complex types is the subset of members of the power set of basic types which respect the consistency and redundancy constraints imposed by the AND/OR net. The sets of basic and complex types corresponding to the AND/OR net in figure 9, are given in (4) and (5) respectively.[8]

(4) $\mathcal{B} = $ {*word, trans, intrans, vb, adj*}

(5) $\mathcal{C} = $ {*word, trans, intrans, vb, adj, trans* $\land$ *vb, intrans* $\land$ *vb, trans* $\land$ *adj, intrans* $\land$ *adj* }

---

[7]Basic types are all the types represented in the AND/OR net— i.e. all node labels in the tree minus the names of the dimensions. In the present set-theoretic presentation of type construction, basic types correspond to singleton sets, complex types are unions of basic types.

[8]Complex types are notated here by the addition of a conjunction symbol between the names of the basic types.

A representation of the conjunctively-built type hierarchy based on the AND/OR net of figure 9 is represented in figure 10. *Word* is the most general category and is represented at the top of the diagram. Below are represented four basic subtypes of *word*. Below those are represented conjunctively-built complex types. Each is the intersection of two categories. More technically, the hierarchy of word types is said to form a join semi-lattice, where the *join* operation corresponds to type conjunction.

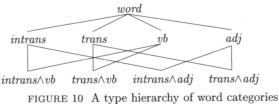

FIGURE 10 A type hierarchy of word categories

Now, the information defining each complex category is the conjunction of the information characterizing the basic types of which it consists. Consider the category of transitive verbs (the *trans* ∧ *vb* category). Its properties are those of transitive and verbal signs. If the former is defined as those signs which subcategorize for two NPs, one of which is the subject (see figure 11; see appendix A for a definition of some of the attributes involved in the figure and the definition of the NP abbreviation) and the latter is defined by the sign's head properties (see figure 12), the properties of their intersection is as shown in figure 13, page 23.[9]

As readers can readily see, combining two types amounts to (recursively) combining the information that defines them. The type of the resulting category is the join of the two categories and the properties characterizing this join is the conjunction of their properties. For example the *trans* category is characterized by its valence properties; it

---

[9] All figures in this book omit the two attributes SYNSEM and LOCAL for clarity. The following AVM on the left thus abbreviates the one on the right.

$$\begin{bmatrix} \text{CONT} & content \\ \text{CAT} & category \end{bmatrix} \qquad \begin{bmatrix} \text{SYNSEM} \begin{bmatrix} \text{LOCAL} \begin{bmatrix} \text{CONT} & content \\ \text{CAT} & category \end{bmatrix} \end{bmatrix} \end{bmatrix}$$

Figures 11-13 also use a *path* abbrevatory convention I employ throughout:

$$\begin{bmatrix} \text{CATEGORY} \,|\, \text{HEAD} \; verb \end{bmatrix}$$

abbreviates the expanded:

$$\begin{bmatrix} \text{CATEGORY} \begin{bmatrix} \text{HEAD} \; verb \end{bmatrix} \end{bmatrix}$$

$$\begin{bmatrix} trans \\ \text{CAT} \mid \text{VAL} \begin{bmatrix} \text{SUBJ} & \langle \text{NP} \rangle \\ \text{COMPS} \langle \text{NP} \dots \rangle \end{bmatrix} \end{bmatrix}$$

FIGURE 11 The transitive sign category

$$\begin{bmatrix} vb \\ \text{CAT} \mid \text{HEAD } verb \end{bmatrix}$$

FIGURE 12 The verb category

subcategorizes for a subject NP (recorded as the sole member of the list value of the SUBJ attribute) and an object NP (recorded as the first member of the list value of the COMPS attribute). The vb category is characterized by its head properties; they must be of type $verb$ (see figure 6 for a definition of this type). The resulting complex category $trans \wedge vb$ includes both kinds of properties. Following a long-standing tradition, I will speak of the unification of the information characterizing each category in such cases (see Shieber 1986 for a simple introduction to unification).[10]

$$\begin{bmatrix} trans \wedge vb \\ \text{CAT} \begin{bmatrix} \text{HEAD } verb \\ \text{VAL} \begin{bmatrix} \text{SUBJ} & \langle \text{NP} \rangle \\ \text{COMPS} \langle \text{NP} \dots \rangle \end{bmatrix} \end{bmatrix} \end{bmatrix}$$

FIGURE 13 The transitive verb category

We have now seen how to build complex linguistic categories from a set of basic categories and an AND/OR net. Do all members of a set of complex categories correspond to possible linguistic objects? More generally, what is the relationship between the set of complex types and the set of well-formed and interpretable linguistic objects? HPSG typically assumes that only a subset of those types are possible models of linguistic objects or correspond to linguistic constructs: intuitively speaking, those which are maximally specific. In the type hierarchy represented in figure 10, the maximal types are the leaves of the hierarchy— $trans \wedge$

---

[10]The formalization of grammatical analyses that use Typed Feature Structures or any equivalent do not need to rely on unification, as emphasized by King 1989 and King 1994. Since such issues are irrelevant to this book and the concept of unification is easy to grasp, I will nonetheless continue to talk of unification of information whenever two categories are intersected.

vb, intrans ∧ *vb, trans* ∧ *adj, intrans* ∧ *adj*. They are listed in (6). Figure 10, then, records the fact that any linguistically well-formed word must be a member of one (and one only) of these four categories or types. I call members of $\mathcal{S}$ (and maximally specific types in general) M-subtypes or M-subcategories. I call M-subcategories of the category *lexeme* L-categories.[11] Both are defined in (7):

(6) $\mathcal{S} = \{trans \wedge vb, intrans \wedge vb, trans \wedge adj, intrans \wedge adj\}$

(7) *Definition of* M-*subcategories and* L-*categories:*
     A type or category *s* is an M-subcategory of type *t* iff *s* is a maximally specific subtype of *t*.
     A type or category *s* is an L-category iff it is an M-subcategory of the type *lexeme*.

M-subcategories represent the collection of completely specified categories to which linguistic objects can belong; L-categories represent the collection of completely specified categories to which lexemes can belong. Each token word used in an utterance thus belongs to one and only one L-category. Interpreting an utterance partly consists in the retrieval of the L-categories of the words it contains.

2.2   Morphological relations

The last section outlined the model of classificatory relations I take for granted throughout the book as well as briefly presented the formalism through which it is realized. I will not justify this model further, since much work in HPSG has been devoted to this issue (see Flickinger 1987, Pollard and Sag 1987, and Pollard and Sag 1994 among many others). Suffice it to say that through its use of multidimensional classifications, the Hierarchical Lexicon provides an adequate model of classificatory relations *as long as* morphological relations are not considered. The central question that occupies me in the rest of this chapter is how well it captures morphological relations or how easy it is to integrate morphological relations within its architecture. Unfortunately, two well-known properties of lexical processes have rendered a principled account of morphological relations elusive. Firstly, as Lakoff 1970 observes, lexically governed processes are only partly regular and typically subject to exceptions. Secondly, many lexical regularities are not productive, even though they can serve as the basis of novel forms, as pointed out by morphologists such as Aronoff 1976, Bybee 1985, and others. Being able to adequately model those well-known aspects of lexical processes is even more important in modern frameworks where more and

---

[11]To reiterate what I said in chapter 1, I use the word 'lexeme' throughout this book to refer to the combined class of roots, stems, and words.

more burden is shifted from the phrase structural component to the lexicon. Traditional methods of representing lexical regularities— including
the Hierarchical Lexicon, as we will shortly see— can adequately handle either productive or unproductive morphological relations, but not
both. Since these shortcomings have been abundantly documented (see
Bochner 1993 among others), I simply mention them here for future
reference.

Traditional morpheme-based models of lexical regularities cover the
"generative" aspect of lexical processes, but can only represent in an *ad
hoc* manner, if at all, their idiosyncrasies, a point argued convincingly
by Bochner 1993, pp.31-39. Conversely, Jackendoff 1975's redundancy
rule approach to lexical regularities or Langacker's usage-based grammar easily account for non-productive lexical processes, but falter on
productivity.

Traditional morpheme-based morphology consists of a list of general
rules of morpheme combinations (typically some set of $\bar{\text{x}}$ constituent
structure rules since Lieber 1980 and Selkirk 1982) and a lexicon of
language-specific morphemes. Any property of output words which
cannot be traced back to their component morphemes or the grammar
rules— what I call morphological "non-compositionality"— is left unexplained. I briefly mention two well-known such cases. Firstly, the input
to a morphological process is sometimes non-existent. To represent the
fact that the word 'aggressive' contains the '-ive' suffix and shares the
properties of the class of *-ive* adjectives, for example, one must presume
that 'aggressive' is derived from the morphemes 'aggress' and the suffix
'-ive' through a general morphological constituent structure rule. But
we cannot then explain that '*aggress' is not an English verb (at least
for many speakers). Secondly, the output of a morphological process often contains information which is in neither its component morphemes
nor the constituent structure rule through which they are combined. To
represent the fact that the word 'transmission' is related to the verb
'transmit', one must assume that it results from the combination of the
morphemes 'transmit' and the suffix '-tion'. We are then at a loss to
explain its idiosyncratic semantics.

Various proposals have been made to remedy this situation, starting
with rule exception features of Lakoff 1970. Reviewing such proposals
would lead us too far afield (see Bochner 1993 for details). Suffice it
to say that none of them are entirely satisfactory. They all require
the introduction of *ad hoc* features or mechanisms. In other words,
the (partial) non-compositionality of morphology, an obvious property
of words cross-linguistically, is not adequately modeled by morpheme-
based approaches to word-structure.

Conversely, Jackendoff's redundancy rules do not falter on unproductive Word Formation Rules, but they do not account for truly productive lexical processes. Jackendoff proposes to handle lexical relations between words such as 'decide' and 'decision' or 'aggressor' and 'aggressive' through redundancy rules that measure the extent to which the information contained in an entry is redundant given other entries in a language's lexicon. But redundancy rules are not used to productively generate entries from other entries. They merely serve to evaluate non-redundant information in a set of independently listed words. Such a theory can easily account for non-productive processes or bound roots such as '*aggress', since redundancy is computed only over attested words. But it cannot directly model productive lexical processes such as '-er' suffixation in English. Lakoff introduced exception features to account for the non-productive or morphologically non-compositional aspects of word formation within a rule-governed generative grammar. Jackendoff's innovation was to by-pass the problem through the introduction of non-generative rules to relate lexical entries. These rules only measured the "simplicity" of a language's lexicon. The resulting model thus avoided the problem of nonexistent inputs, since the information common to 'aggression' and 'aggressive' was measured without having to derive either from '*aggress'. But the counterpart to redundancy rules' success in modeling morphological non-compositionality is their inability to model productivity. They are unable to create new morphological forms; what is needed in this case is truly generative rules.[12]

The same difficulty in modeling truly productive lexical processes is inherent in strictly usage-based models of grammatical knowledge, such as those presented in Bybee 1985 or Langacker 1987, where generalizations are simply abstractions over a list of encountered entries. In such models, the creation of a novel expression is essentially analogical in nature (see Langacker 1987, p.445 *et seq.*) The difference native speakers perceive between putative nonce forms such as '*hecticity' and grammatical, although as of yet unheard forms, such as 'xeroxer', is left unexplained. All previously unheard forms involve the analogical extension of a schema. The attested difference in grammaticality judgments between '*hecticity' and 'xeroxer' remains mysterious. More generally, the numerous contrasts in behavior of truly productive lexical processes and subregularities (see Pinker and Prince 1991, Marcus et al. 1995, among others) are left unexplained.

---

[12]More recent models of lexical relatedness which are inspired by Jackendoff's notion of redundancy rules try to avoid such pitfalls. See section 2.2.2 for arguments that they are unsuccessful.

2.2.1 Morphological relations in Type Hierarchies

Does HPSG's Hierarchical Lexicon improve on previous models of morphological relations? Unfortunately, not as is, even when supplemented with lexical rules *à la* Jackendoff 1975 or Bresnan and Kaplan 1982. One important aspect of typed feature structures as defined formally in Carpenter and Pollard 1991 and Carpenter 1992 is that the type hierarchy is compiled out. It is entirely constructed and stored in the grammar prior to producing or interpreting a sentence. In the absence of on-line lexical rules (see section 2.2.2) this means that the entire set of possible M-subcategories of lexemes (or L-categories) is defined in advance, prior to interpretation or production, as illustrated in figure 14,.[13]

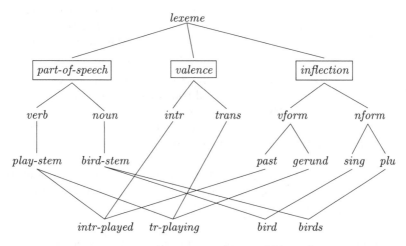

FIGURE 14 A more complex word hierarchy

In other words, if no lexical rules that can create new types on the fly are added, the hierarchy must include types for all of a word's forms, even for regularly inflected words, like 'played' and 'playing', 'bird' and 'birds', and so forth. Listing of all inflected forms is made necessary by the assumption that the entire hierarchy is compiled out or stored. Word forms such as 'played' and 'playing' belong to incompatible classes, *past* and *gerund* in this case. The complex types corresponding to fully

[13]The types *intr-played* and *tr-playing* in figure 14 describe the classes of intransitive and transitive uses of the strings 'played' and 'playing' respectively. The figure uses a hybrid representation between an AND/OR net and a representation of the lattice of types for perspicuity. As in all figures presented in this book, it is assumed that there are no unary branching in type hierarchies, even when only one branch is shown.

specified entries for these two words are therefore different. If all complex types are stored in the grammar (i.e. if the hierarchy is compiled out), two different (complex) types must correspond to both verb forms in the (stored) hierarchy. The same is true of singular and plural forms of nouns, and so forth.

Interpreted in such a fashion, a lexical type hierarchy is a refined version of Jackendoff's redundancy rules. It is a way of capturing generalizations among sets of occurring forms. It classifies existing word forms into classes of objects which share properties. Despite its usefulness in capturing lexical subregularities, such a compiled out lexical hierarchy cannot by itself model instances of lexical productivity, that is, cases where words are created while interpreting or producing an utterance. It can tell us what kinds of words English has, but does not tell us anything about how native speakers create new words or word forms. Put differently, it does not account for the creative aspects of word production/interpretation, some of which are listed below:

- Productive applications of inflectional processes or valence alternations (e.g. passivization or ditransitive formation). As shown in Gropen et al. 1989 and others, children and adults can extend the application of valence alternations to new verbs that fit the relevant conditions, as in recently introduced verbs such as 'e-mail'.[14]

- The morphology of morphologically recursive languages. Full listing of all possible lexical entries is not possible for such languages, as Hankamer 1989 argues for Turkish. We must allow for the on-line creation of words.
- The application of regular morphology to lexical borrowings and nonce words.

How can we keep the benefits of types in handling subregularities and classificatory relations while accounting for productive lexical processes? In Pollard and Sag 1987, it is suggested that a compiled out type system be supplemented by lexical rules to derive new types from the base types of words. Pollard and Sag 1994 makes even heavier use of lexical rules. Despite its apparent successes, such a system encounters many difficulties and does not constitute an optimal theory of the productive application of lexical processes, as the next section demonstrates.

---

[14]Gropen et al. 1989 also show that speakers can use a verb in the ditransitive subcategorization frame when presented with a nonce verb in the bare infinitive ('moop' in their experiment).

2.2.2 Why on-line application of lexical rules is not the optimal solution

HPSG I and II provide two ways of relating words that share some properties: through lexical rules, which can create new words on the fly and are the locus of morphological relations and lexical productivity, and through the type hierarchy, which is used to capture static regularities among words, what I call classificatory relations.[15] For example, the fact that the verb 'eat' has both transitive and passive realizations as in (8a) and (8c) might be captured with a valence affecting lexical rule, while the morphological relation between 'ate' and 'eats' in (8a) and (8b) might be captured with an inflectional lexical rule.

(8)   a. John ate a sandwich.
      b. John eats a sandwich every day.
      c. The sandwich was eaten.

Figure 15 represents a simplified version of a lexical rule mapping active verbs into (short) passives. Its effect is basically to suppress the subject requirement and make an intransitive verb out of a transitive verb. The ARG-ST list represents a verb's arguments. The coindexing of the first member of that list with the NP on the SUBJ list of the *trans-verb* verb class indicates that this argument must be realized as a subject. The coindexing of its second element with the NP on the COMPS list means that this argument must be realized as an object. This same element is coindexed with an NP on the SUBJ list in the definition of the *pass-verb* class output, thereby indicating that the verb's logical object is realized as a surface subject.

Verbs such as 'eat' and 'love', on the other hand, are related via their common membership in the class of verbs, i.e. through their relative position in a hierarchy of the kind in figure 14. To sum up, in classical HPSG, type hierarchies capture what is common to classes of words, while lexical rules capture the relationship between the various valences and morphological variants of a single word. The type hierarchy describes

---

[15]From this point on, I will call lexical rules that can create new entries on the fly "on-line lexical rules." By "on-line lexical rules," I thus mean that they apply while interpreting or producing a sentence to create new lexical entries (L-categories) from a single, stored, base entry (L-category). These new entries are then used while parsing or producing the utterance (see Copestake and Briscoe 1995 and Meurers and Minnen 1997 for details on how lexical rules might be represented in a TFS system). Lexical rules in HPSG differ from the usual lexical redundancy rules common since Jackendoff 1975. Goldberg 1991 presents several arguments against the adequacy of the latter kind of rules in modeling valence alternations. But her arguments do not directly apply to the more refined notion of lexical rules used in HPSG.

$$\begin{bmatrix} trans\text{-}verb \\ \begin{bmatrix} CAT & \begin{bmatrix} VAL & \begin{bmatrix} SUBJ & \langle \boxed{1}\ NP \rangle \\ COMPS & \langle \boxed{2}\ NP \rangle \end{bmatrix} \end{bmatrix} \\ ARG\text{-}ST\ \langle \boxed{1},\ \boxed{2} \rangle \end{bmatrix} \end{bmatrix} \implies \begin{bmatrix} pass\text{-}verb \\ \begin{bmatrix} CAT & \begin{bmatrix} VAL & \begin{bmatrix} SUBJ & \langle \boxed{2}\ NP \rangle \\ COMPS & \langle \rangle \end{bmatrix} \end{bmatrix} \\ ARG\text{-}ST\ \langle \boxed{1},\ \boxed{2} \rangle \end{bmatrix} \end{bmatrix}$$

FIGURE 15 A (simplified) passive lexical rule

classificatory relations among distinct words while lexical rules describe morphological relations among variants of a single word.

The main point of this section is that lexical rules, even when applying on-line, are not an optimal solution to the question of morphological relatedness and lexical productivity.[16] In place of the classical HPSG model of lexical relations which consists of a type hierarchy and lexical rules, the model proposed in chapters 3 through 5 includes solely an *underspecified* AND/OR net.[17] My arguments against lexical rules fall into two main groups.

- Well-known properties of lexical processes require additional, *ad hoc* machinery when lexical productivity is modeled through lexical rules. Two cases arise:
  1. Some properties require the same information to be represented twice, suggesting a generalization is missed.
  2. Some of the mechanisms introduced duplicate the logic of AND/OR nets needed to describe classificatory relations.
- Lexical rules are subject to ordering paradoxes like their transformational ancestors.

Although the specifics of my arguments pertain to particular analyses and target lexical rules as they are used within HPSG, the substance of my arguments is theory independent. If the examples are HPSG-specific, the shortcomings are of a kind shared by any attempt to model productivity with on-line application of lexical rules (including that of Bochner 1993, to the extent his rules are intended to model lexical productivity). I therefore view the evidence of the next few subsections as compelling

---

[16]In this section, I assume the theory of lexical rules sketched in HPSG I, and still in use in HPSG II. Under this view, lexical rules are mappings between fully specified words. Recently, some HPSG scholars have amended the structure of lexical entries, and have made lexical rules partly dispensable. The view of the organization of lexical information presented in such work is much closer to the one advocated in this book (see Krieger and Nerbonne 1993 and Riehemann 1993, for example). I discuss these alternative approaches in chapter 5.

[17]This last statement should be qualified: the lexeme AND/OR net I propose also comprises a typed constituent structure-based morphology, which is absent in classical HPSG.

enough to look elsewhere for a theory of morphological relations. Before going into the details of the disadvantages of relying on lexical rules to account for lexical productivity, let me mention a more HPSG-specific reason to look for another model.[18]

As Krieger and Nerbonne 1993 note, the very use of lexical rules should be avoided *ceteris paribus* in feature-based grammars. The assumption underlying these frameworks is that all grammatical information can be represented using feature structures. Using a different mechanism to model lexical productivity undermines the most general claim embodied in their representational scheme: grammatical structures result from combining the information contained in feature structures. This is especially true, given the centrality of the lexicon in lexicalist theories such as HPSG.

More importantly, as already pointed out by Krieger and Nerbonne, the use of lexical rules to model morphological relations prevents interleaving lexical, morphological and syntactic processing, which constraint-based grammars are specifically designed to promote (see Sag 1991). I illustrate some of the obstacles to interleaving the on-line application of lexical rules and syntactic principles with an example—the analysis of NP extraction and clitic "movement" in French presented in Sag and Godard 1994.

Unexpected interactions between lexical rules and syntactic principles. Following chapter 9 of Pollard and Sag 1994, Sag and Godard propose that the bottom of long-distance dependencies such as WH-extraction is the result of a Complement Extraction Lexical Rule (hereafter CELR). Informally and simplifying somewhat, this lexical rule takes as input an entry like $aime_1$ in (9) which subcategorizes for an (object) NP_1 and outputs a new lexical entry $aime_2$ which does not subcategorize for NP_1, but has a corresponding element on its slash set— the set which keeps track of (unrealized) long-distance dependencies. This slash set is then percolated up the tree by a general Lexical Amalgamation and Slash Inheritance Principle (see Sag 1997 and Appendix A for

---

[18]Carpenter 1991 presents one other possible motivation for rejecting the use of lexical rules to model lexical productivity. Carpenter proves that the use of unrestricted lexical rules bestows on HPSG or Categorial Grammar the computational power of an arbitrary Turing machine. Intuitively, this is true since lexical rules are the lexicalist equivalent of Generalized Phrase Structure Grammar metarules, which are known, when unrestricted, to bestow the same power as transformations. Whether such a fact constitutes a proper linguistic objection to the use of lexical rules remains to be determined, though. Firstly, we can always appropriately restrict lexical rules. Secondly, I know of no independent evidence which suggests that the human language capacity does not have in the limit the power of an arbitrary Turing machine.

a definition of the principles) until NP_1 is finally realized as the filler of a Filler-Head constituent-structure schema— 'qui' in (10).

(9) Marie aime   Jacques.
     Marie love-PR Jacques
     'Marie loves Jacques.'

(10) Qui crois-tu   qu' elle aime?
     Who believe-PR-you that she love-PR
     'Who do you think she loves?'

$$\begin{bmatrix} aime_1 \\ \text{COMPS} \left\langle \left[\text{LOCAL} \boxed{1} \right] \right\rangle \\ \text{SLASH } \{\} \end{bmatrix}$$

FIGURE 16 The complement structure of $aime_1$

$$\begin{bmatrix} aime_2 \\ \text{COMPS} \left\langle \right\rangle \\ \text{SLASH } \left\{ \boxed{1} \right\} \end{bmatrix}$$

FIGURE 17 The complement structure of $aime_2$

An informal sketch of the base entry for 'aime' as used in (9) is represented in the AVM in figure 16. The entry derived via the CELR which serves as the bottom of the unbounded dependency is represented in the AVM in figure 17. $Aime_2$ does not subcategorize for an object anymore, but has an argument missing. The (local) information of the (now missing) subcategorized object of $aime_1$ is in the SLASH set of $aime_2$. It is this derived $aime_2$ entry which serves as the embedded verb in the informal tree for sentence (10) in figure 18.

The information that $aime_2$ is missing an argument which is recorded on its SLASH attribute is "transmitted" from daughter to mother (see the identical $\boxed{1}$ tags in the tree) until the dependency is bound off by the interrogative pronoun 'qui'.

Sag and Godard also propose a Complement Clitic Lexical Rule (hereafter CCLR) whose effects are illustrated in sentence (11).

(11) Elle l'   aime.
     She   him/her   love.PR
     'She loves him/her.'

The CCLR passes elements from the slash set to a clitic set whose members are then realized through inflectional rules as verbal prefixes.

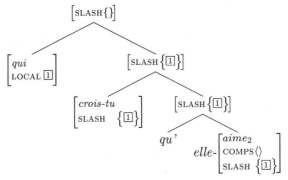

FIGURE 18   A tree-structure for (10)

The lexical entry for 'aime' as used in (11) thus results from the application of three lexical rules:

1. the CELR which passes the object subcategorization requirement of the basic entry for 'aime' from its list of subcategorized complements to its slash set;

2. the CCLR which passes the same element from the slash set to the clitic set;

3. a final rule which realizes this member of the clitic set as the prefix 'le'.[19]

Now, crucially, if lexical rule application is interleaved with syntactic processing, the combination of the CELR and CCLR wrongly licenses long-distance cliticization, as illustrated in the ungrammatical (12). The offending derivation of the lexical entry for 'le crois' used in (12) runs as in (13).

(12) *Tu   le   crois   qu'   elle   aime.
     You him   believe-PR   that   she   love-PR
     'You believe that she loves him.' (intended meaning)

(13)   1. The CELR applies to *aime*, and passes its object subcategorization requirement onto the slash set.

       2. The slash set of *aime* is transmitted to the slash set of *crois* through the application of the Slash Amalgamation constraint and the Slash Inheritance Principle.

---

[19]Sag and Godard hypothesize with Miller 1991 that so-called French object clitics are in fact prefixes. They still name the set which registers their presence the "clitic set" for ease of exposition. I follow their practice throughout this book. I furthermore interchangeably use the words "clitics", "affixes", or "prefixes" to refer to these object prefixes.

3. The CCLR applies to the "slashed" valence requirement transmitted to *crois* and introduces it on the clitic set of *crois*.

4. This member of the clitic set of *crois* is realized morphophonologically as the prefix 'le'.

Note that tbe derivation crucially depends on interleaving lexical processing (steps 1, 3, and 4) and syntactic processing (step 2). To avoid incorrectly generating (12), we therefore only need bar such interleaving. We can, for example, stipulate that lexical rules form an independent module which applies to members of the lexical hierarchy, not to instantiated entries as they occur in a particular sentence. Unfortunately, such modular separation of the lexical and syntactic components seems difficult to reconcile with the need to apply lexical rules on-line for productive lexical processes.

Let's assume that a speaker learns a currently non-existent French verb, say 'édire' ('to falsely tell'), and that this speaker has only heard the word used with full NP complements. We expect such a speaker to be able to correctly interpret sentences in which the complements of 'édire' are realized as clitics. We thus expect this speaker to understand (14a). For this to be possible, she must be able to apply in reverse, so to speak, the CCLR, and put on the verb's slash set the information corresponding to its clitic affixes. But it is then hard to see how (14b) would not be understood and deemed grammatical by such a speaker. The crucial steps in this hypothetical speaker's reasoning are represented in (15):

(14) a. Marc leur   édit   qu' elle l'   aime.
        Marc to.them falsely.say-PR that she him love-PR
        'Marc falsely told them that she loves him.'

     b.*Marc le   leur   édit   qu' elle aime.
        Marc him to.them falsely.say-PR that she love-PR
        'Marc falsely told them that she loves him.'

     c. Qui Marc leur   dit-il   qu' elle aime?
        Who Marc to.them say-PR-he that she love-PR
        'Who did Marc tell them that she loves?'

(15) 1. The entry $\acute{e}dit_1$ for 'édit' as used in (14b) derives from an entry $\acute{e}dit_2$ whose clitic set contains two members corresponding to 'le' and 'leur', respectively (reverse application of the morphological clitic affixation rule).

      2. $\acute{e}dit_2$ derives from an entry $\acute{e}dit_3$ in which the two elements on the clitic set are on the slash set (reverse application of the CCLR).

3. $\acute{e}dit_3$ derives from an entry $\acute{e}dit_4$ in which the member of the slash set bearing the dative case is on the COMPS list (reverse application of the CELR).

4. The remaining member of the slash set of $\acute{e}dit_4$ is token-identical to the member of the slash set of its sentential complement (Slash Amalgamation and Slash Inheritance Principle).

5. The head of the sentential complement of $\acute{e}dit_4$, $aime_2$, which has an element in its slash set through the Slash Inheritance Principle, derives from an entry $aime_1$ in which the said member of the slash set is on the COMPS list (reverse application of the CELR).

On-line application of the CELR and CCLR models speakers' ability to go beyond variants of words they have seen in the input and recognize 'leur édit' in (14a) at the cost of licensing (14b). We cannot try to escape the difficulty by a general requirement that all members of an entry slash set be targeted together by an application of the CELR to bar step 3 in (15), if lexical rules are ever able to apply on-line. Take the grammatical (14c), for example. The entry for 'dit' as used in (14c) contains one slashed element corresponding to the extracted WH-phrase 'qui'. But, since 'dit' also bears the clitic 'leur', the on-line reverse application of the CCLR will yield an entry for 'dit' which contains two members, one corresponding to its addressee argument, one to the loved argument of 'aime', via slash percolation. Clearly, the two members of the SLASH set of 'dit' are not the result of a single application of CELR: one member results from the application of the CELR to 'dit', one from the application of the CELR to 'aime'. There is no escaping: if the CCLR is to apply on-line to mirror the ability of our hypothetical speaker to understand sentence (14a) without prior exposure to a use of 'édire' with clitics, the same speaker must be able to (wrongly) rule sentence (14b) grammatical.

The moral of this example is clear: once lexical rules are allowed to apply on-line, we cannot insure that inputs to lexical rules contain only lexical information. They may also include information acquired through the application of various syntactic, feature percolation principles. Consequently, when the CCLR applies to 'édire' in (14b), it can target all members of its clitic set, including the member corresponding to the extracted object of 'aime', leading to the incorrect derivation outlined in (15). Importantly, this is true, even though within the lexicon proper one cannot generate an entry corresponding to 'édit' as used in (14b). Given a base entry for 'édire', no element can be introduced on its slash set via the CELR which does not correspond to one of its subcategorization requirements. Since the extracted object of 'aime' is not a subcategorization requirement of 'édire', it cannot be introduced onto the slash set of 'édire' to be subsequently introduced on its clitic set and realized as 'le'. Thus, no application of one or more lexical rules to the base, stored entry for 'édire' can lead to the offending entry used in (14b). But once the application of lexical rules and syntactic principles are interleaved, a sequence of lexical rule applications is not bound to start on a word's base, stored entry. A rule's input can also include information which results from the application of syntactic constraints. We can then find on the slash set of verbs which serve as input to the CCLR elements that do not correspond to subcategorization requirements of their base entry. In the example at hand, we only need apply the CELR, the Slash Amalgamation constraint, the Slash Inheritance Principle, and the CCLR in that order.

Of course, this infelicitous interaction of on-line application of lexical rules and syntactic processing might simply be a symptom of a faulty analysis of Romance clitics or of mistaken formulations of the principles which percolate (unresolved) unbounded dependency information. We can, for example, easily remedy the difficulty by letting the CCLR not target members of an entry's SLASH set. But this example is illustrative of a more general problem— how difficult it is to foresee the interaction of on-line lexical rules and syntactic principles. Lexical and syntactic analyses which are adequate by themselves can unexpectedly license ungrammatical sentences once the two modules are allowed to interact. Turning redundancy lexical rules into a generative mechanism which creates new entries on the fly requires more changes in the rest of the grammar than was anticipated.

Added machinery. Even if the obstacles to interleaving processing of lexical rules and syntactic principles can be overcome, more compelling arguments exist against the use of lexical rules to model morphological relations and lexical creativity. The first drawback of a lexical rule approach to lexical productivity is that it requires the addition of other devices to the apparatus provided by the TFS formalism presented in section 2.1.2. As we will see in chapters 3 and 4, none of these extra mechanisms are needed in the Type Underspecified Hierarchical Lexicon architecture I advocate. A lexical rule approach to lexical productivity should therefore be rejected on Occamian grounds.

Exception features. An on-line lexical rule approach requires the use of exception features. It is well-known that lexically-governed processes are subject to exceptions (see Lakoff 1970). Theories of lexical processes since Lakoff have generally distinguished positive and negative exceptions. Positive exceptions are cases in which the putative output of some rule is present, but not the input. Negative exceptions are cases in which the putative input to a rule is present, but not the output. Lexical rules need to posit extra machinery to handle both kinds of exceptions— if they are assumed to apply symmetrically (as in Flickinger and Nerbonne 1992)— or to handle just negative exceptions, if they are assumed to apply asymmetrically.

In an asymmetric interpretation, lexical rules are functions mapping unidirectionally from a lexical input (for example an active verb) to a lexical output (for example a passive verb). In the symmetric approach, they are relations bidirectionally relating two forms (active and passive for example). Symmetric lexical rules do not distinguish between negative and positive exceptions, since what is a negative exception, if the rule runs in one direction, is a positive exception, if the rule runs in the other direction.

Symmetric lexical rules are troubled by a large number of exceptions. These exceptions are typically modeled by marking the offending lexical item with rule-specific exception features. A lexical rule does not apply to any lexical item which is marked with its exception feature. Consider the verb 'rumored' exemplified in sentences (16):

(16)   a. It was rumored that the meeting would not be held.

　　　b.*People rumored that the meeting would not be held.

Since 'rumored' is an obligatory passive (there is no active form '*rumor'), we must specify in the entry for 'rumored' that the passive-lexical rule, which relates passive and active variants of a lexeme, cannot apply by including in its entry an attribute/value pair [PASSIVE-RULE -]. But in addition to marking the entry with this feature, a lexical rule system must still mark 'rumored' as an instance of the passive category, because it acts morphosyntactically like other passive forms. Thus the entry must be marked twice. It must be declared a passive verb, to capture its similarity to all other passive verbs. But it must also be declared an exception to the passive lexical rule, to prevent the derivation of the non-existent '*rumor'. By contrast, the on-line type construction approach I propose in the next chapter needs only *pre-type* the relevant entry to the passive template or lexeme class to model exceptions to productive processes.

Under an asymmetric interpretation of lexical rules, the passive rule applies unidirectionally from actives to passives. Words like 'rumored' do not present difficulties for such systems, since for them 'rumored' acts as a positive exception and can merely be listed as a subtype of the class of passive verbs. It is not an exception to the passive lexical rule, because the rule only applies to well-formed active entries. But asymmetric lexical rules are subject to other problems. Firstly, there is no independent evidence for asymmetric lexical rules. In particular, there is often no psycholinguistic evidence for asymmetry. Gropen et al. 1989 and Goldberg 1992, for example, argue that the ditransitive and the prepositional variants of verbs such as 'give' and 'bring' in English appear at the same time in children, and that there is no evidence that one variant is the base and the other derived from it. To account for verbs like 'deny' which only occur with a ditransitive valence, as illustrated in (17), an asymmetric interpretation of lexical rules would need to arbitrarily stipulate that the prepositional valence of ditransitive verbs is the base form.

(17)   a. Julia denied him a raise.
        b.*Julia denied a raise to him.

Secondly, asymmetric lexical rules still require exception features for those cases where the input exists, but not the output. Such cases are more difficult to find; indeed Pinker 1989 claims that no negative exceptions beset lexical rules once they are properly restricted in their domain of application. Even with such restrictions, we can, however, find examples which seem to be best treated as negative exceptions. One such example is the absence of a passive form for 'have' as exemplified in (18) below:

(18)   a.*The house was had by many people.
        b. This house was owned by many people.

Despite Pinker's claim to the contrary, no semantic difference seems to exist between the two verbs which their difference in passivizability can be said to depend on. Abeillé 1990, after Gross 1975, points out other examples of negative exceptions from French; one is the verb 'regarder' (see (19)). In its sense of 'to concern', 'regarder' cannot be passivized (see (19b)). Yet its synonym 'concerner' can be (see (20)). This argues that semantic constraints do not cause 'regarder' to be marked, simple lexical listing does; 'regarder' is a true negative exception.

(19)   a. Cette affaire regarde   Jean.
           This   matter watch-PR   Jean
           'This matter concerns Jean.'
        b.*Jean est   regardé   par cette affaire.
           Jean be-PR watch-PASS by this   matter
           'Jean is concerned by this matter.'

(20) a. Cette affaire concerne   Jean.
        This   matter concern-PR Jean
        'This matter concerns Jean.'

     b. Jean est   concerné   par cette affaire.
        Jean be-PR concern-PASS by this   matter
        'Jean is concerned by this matter.'

Citing examples from derivational morphology, such as 'un-' prefixation in English, Bowermann 1987 expresses the same doubts concerning Pinker's denial of the existence of negative exceptions. Numerous examples of negative exceptions in inflectional morphology can also be added. It is common for certain verbs to occur only in a restricted set of forms. Take a verb like 'clore' ('to close') in French, which has no past form, but has regular sets of present and future forms. To derive its forms productively, we must assume that there is a base form (or stem) from which future forms are derived. But since no past forms exist, 'clore' is a negative exception to the productive imperfective past word formation rule. Such facts cast further doubt on the absence of negative exceptions to valence alternations. Why would valence alternations behave differently from other lexical rules?

There is some irony in the observation that on-line application of lexical rules requires exception features. Jackendoff's original motivation for the introduction of lexical rules in generative linguistics was the desire to avoid the need to appeal to Lakoff-style exception features. And, when scholars such as Bresnan noticed later on that a large set of so-called bounded transformations are subject to exceptions, they found in Jackendoff's redundancy rules the perfect tool to answer the problem posed by these exceptions: passive and other bounded rules are not transformations, but lexical rules relating alternate, stored entries of the same verb. To a significant extent, the initial appeal of lexicalist frameworks such as LFG depended on the exception-safe theory of lexical rules presentend in Jackendoff 1975. But by increasing their load to a point where it is desirable to have them apply on-line, HPSG and other scholars that use lexical rules to model lexical productivity involuntarily reopened Pandora's box.

Lexical rule chains in inflectional morphology. The use of lexical rules to model morphology also requires additional machinery for inflectional systems of any complexity. Take the Latin verbal system. The morphological structure of a Latin verb is given in (21) below:

(21) a. stem+(aspect)+mood/tense+subj-agr/voice

b. ama-v-isse-m
love-PERF-PST.SUBJ-1ST.SG.ACT
'[I wish] I have loved (someone)'

The three Latin verbal affix-classes are productive and would therefore be modeled through on-line application of lexical rules in a lexical rule system. But note that the application of a single rule is not enough to produce a grammatical form for these cases. The application of the lexical rule which (optionally) concatenates the first aspectual affix must be followed by the application of a second lexical rule which concatenates the second tense/mood affix, which itself must be followed by the application of a third lexical rule that concatenates the third subject agreement/voice affix. Only after the third lexical rule has applied, is the output a well-formed Latin verb. I refer to this circumstance as a lexical rule chain.

In such cases, it is the entire lexical rule chain which maps well-formed words onto well-formed words. Single members of the chain do not generate well-formed words. Furthermore, there are several possible values for affixes 2 and 3 (mood/tense and person endings). This means that capturing Latin verbal morphology with lexical rules requires chains of sets of lexical rules, where a particular well-formed verbal form is derived from the base form by applying in sequence one member of each set of rules. As I show in the next three chapters, in a TUHL architecture, such chains are not necessary. The effect of the new formal apparatus of lexical rule chains is achieved through the independently motivated logic of AND/OR nets which is at the core of TFS-based grammars. This logic is enough to describe Latin verbal morphology and, more generally, the notions of conjunctively *vs.* disjunctively ordered rule blocks proposed in Anderson 1992. Assuming the validity of the overall claim that the logic of AND/OR nets captures a crucial aspect of linguistic categorization, the introduction of new, stipulated apparatus specific to morphology to mimic its effect should be viewed with skepticism.

Stem selection algorithm for suppletive stems. The third piece of added machinery required by a lexical rule approach is a stem selection algorithm. Consider the French lexeme 'aller', exemplified in (22).

(22) a. Marc est   allé   à   Paris.
         Marc be-PR go-PPT to Paris
         'Marc went to Paris.'

      b. Marc s'   en   ira.
         Marc 3.REFL of.it go-FUT
         'Marc will leave.'

c. Ce   costume te   va   bien.
   This suit   you   go-PR well
   'This suit becomes you.' (lit. goes well to you)

d. Il faut que j' y   aille.
   It must that I   to.there go-SUBJ.PR
   'I must go there.'

Its various forms are based on four different suppletive stems: 'all-' (1st and 2nd person plural of the indicative and imperative present, infinitive, past participle, and imperfective past), 'i-' (future and conditional), 'v-' (1st-3rd person singular and 3rd person plural of the indicative present), and 'aill-' (subjunctive present). These four suppletive stems are shared by all entries of the lexeme 'aller', the one which means 'to fit' as well as the one which means 'to leave', as shown in (22). In Aronoff 1976's terms, more than one word corresponds to the single morpheme 'aller'.

The endings which attach to these stems (with the exception of some of the forms based on the 'v-' stem) are regular. They are the same productive inflectional rules used for regular verbs. But, in this case, the rules must choose the proper stem to which to attach the endings. To insure the proper contextual selection of stem, the lexical rules responsible for tense and person-endings must be able to determine which of the four stems is appropriate in the sentence's morphosyntactic environment. The lexical rule adding the suffix marking the third person singular future of the indicative in (22b), for example, must select the stem-form /i/ before concatenating /ra/ to the stem phonology.

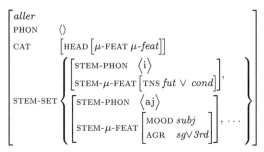

FIGURE 19 An hypothetical AVM for *aller*

How could a lexical rule approach effect such a stem selection? Since the alternating stems are shared among the various entries for 'aller', we need to include the information concerning the stems and the morphosyntactic environments in which they can appear in an abstract *aller* entry shared by all the more specific entries exemplified in (22). We could posit a special stem-set attribute within each entry to indicate its possible stem forms and the morphosyntactic environments in which each is used, as represented in figure 19.[20] This AVM stipulates that the lexical entry *aller* has four stem forms. Each is characterized by its phonology (which the STEM-PHON attribute records) and the morphosyntactic contexts to which it is restricted (which the STEM-μ-FEAT records). Two of them are the stems /i/ and /aj/, which are restricted to conditional or future and singular or third plural subjunctive forms respectively. Since this stem information is included in the abstract entry for 'aller', all particular 'aller' entries inherit it. Inflectional lexical rules can then map the base form of 'aller'— say its infinitive form— into other forms by concatenating the relevant tense-mood/person affixes to the stem-phonology of the member of the stem-set matching the morphosyntactic features of the rule's output. In the case of the lexical rule responsible for adding the third-singular person ending for the future of the indicative, it entails the following sequence of operations:

- Check the STEM-SET attribute of the lexeme's base entry and find the stem form whose morphosyntactic specification is compatible with the morphosyntactic features of the output (here the member of the STEM-SET which is restricted to future or conditional contexts).
- Take the value of the phonology attribute of this stem set (which is /i/), and suffix /ra/ to it.

Although observationally adequate, this solution is not optimal. To represent the fact that morphosyntactic feature information is a condition on stem selection, we are forced to duplicate in the value of the stem attribute information we need to specify elsewhere in the information-structure associated with any actual form. As shown in figure 19, morphosyntactic features must now appear twice in a word's entry, once as the morphosyntactic features of the actual word (see the topmost μ-FEAT in the diagram) and once as the conditioning environment for the use of one of the stems (see the value of the STEM-μ-FEAT attribute for each stem in the STEM-SET). Such systematic duplication of information is unmotivated and suggests a generalization is missed.

Furthermore, the effects of irregular stems on their possible contexts of occurrence are only indirectly modeled and must be stipulated as a unique property of the rules affixing mood, tense, or person endings.

---

[20]For ease of reading, I left out of figure 19 irrelevant information as well as two of the needed members of the STEM-SET, those for forms such as 'aller' and 'va'.

Each rule which targets an affix AFF that realizes a set of morphosyntactic features S now takes the following form:

(23)   'Concatenate AFF to the phonology of the member of the stem-set which matches (unifies with) S.'

By contrast, in the architecture proposed in the next three chapters, the required matching follows from the very nature of the process at the root of productive morphological relations, (on-line) type construction; no duplication of morphosyntactic information is necessary (see section 5.1.1 for details).

Note that the problem of stem selection, although quite dramatic in the case of French 'aller', is fairly general, and can appear under more mundane guises. Take the English third person singular forms of 'say' and 'do'. Although the person suffix is the ordinary /z/, the phonology of the stems to which it attaches is exceptional.[21] Their phonological values are /sɛ/ and /dʌ/ instead of the expected /seɪ/ and /du/. No productive English phonological rule is responsible for this stem alteration. We must again register in the morphophonology of English that the third person singular suffix idiosyncratically attaches to the strings /sɛ/ and /dʌ/. The same *ad hoc* technique of stem selection must be used here too.

An ordering paradox. The problems with lexical rules I mentioned in the previous subsections have been mainly related to elegance. The lexical rule approach can account for the data, but suffers in requiring excessive theoretical apparatus. Now, however, I turn to what is a deeper problem for lexical rule accounts of lexical productivity: the problem of ordering paradoxes.[22] Data from the French medio-passive reflexive and so-called inversion of indefinites valence constructions provide such a paradox. (24) illustrates the basic transitive use of the verb 'vendre' ('to sell'):

(24)   Jacques   vend   des   livres.
       Jacques   sell-PR   INDEF   books
       'Jacques sells books.'

(25)   a. A   la   dernière   foire   du   livre,
          At the   last   fair   of.the   book

---

[21]I owe this example to Bill Ladusaw (p.c.).

[22]That lexical rules bring back ordering effects unification-based grammars were built to avoid is well-known (see Shieber 1986, p.62, for example). Finding convincing examples of ordering paradoxes is not easy, though. In many cases, ordering paradoxes can be avoided by simply stipulating that the relevant rules apply to a more abstract type than originally assumed. They do exist, though, as this section shows.

tu t' es bien vendu.
you 2SG.REFL be-PR sell-PPT well
'At the last book fair, you sold well.'

b. A la dernière foire du livre,
At the last fair of.the book
nous nous sommes bien vendus.
we 1PL.REFL be-PR sell-PPT well
'At the last book fair, we sold well.'

(25a) illustrates the medio-passive reflexive use of the same verb ('se vendre').[23] The lexical rule approach would derive 'se vendre' (as in (25a)) from 'vendre' (as in (24)) via a medio-passive reflexive lexical rule which transforms an object requirement into a subject requirement and adds a reflexive marker agreeing with the subject (notice the difference between the (so-called) reflexive clitics 't'' and 'nous' in (25a) and (25b)). Figure 20 sketches such a rule: it removes the logical subject valence requirement of verbs to which it applies (see the tag $\boxed{1}$) and substitutes in its place the logical object, that is, the first NP on the list of subcategorized complements (see the tag $\boxed{2}$). Since a reflexive clitic prefixed to the verb always accompanies this valence alternation, an element is included in the set that keeps track of elements which must be realized morphophonologically as verbal prefixes. The CLI attribute encodes this information. Since the member of the clitic set and the subject requirement are (token) identical, so are their indices, as is (redundantly) indicated in the figure by the subscripted tag $\boxed{3}$.[24] This identity insures that the clitic's morphophonological realization co-varies with the subject's person and number.

Consider now (26), which illustrates the inversion of indefinites valence of 'se vendre'. The lexical rule approach would derive this valence of 'se vendre' via an inversion of indefinites lexical rule which transforms the subject requirement into an object requirement and adds an expletive subject requirement.

(26) Il se vend deux cent livres par an à Paris.
It 3.REFL sell-PR two hundred books by year to Paris
'Two hundred books are sold each year in Paris.'

[23] In examples involving first or second person pronouns, the pronoun refers literally to the author of the book being sold and metonymically to the book itself.

[24] Figure 20 adopts the following HPSG II conventions. Tags preceding a structure concern the entire structure they precede. Thus, the tag $\boxed{2}$ indicates that the entire syntactic and semantic information of the subject NP is token-identical to the first element of the ARG-ST as well as to the sole member of the CLI set. Subscripted tags following an NP, on the other hand, represent the value of the INDEX of the NP. $\boxed{3}$ in figure 20, for example, represents the index of the NP it follows.

$$
\begin{bmatrix} trans \\ \text{HEAD} \begin{bmatrix} \text{CLI}\{\} \end{bmatrix} \\ \text{CAT} \begin{bmatrix} \text{VAL} \begin{bmatrix} \text{SUBJ} \left\langle \boxed{1}\ \text{NP} \right\rangle \\ \text{COMPS} \left\langle \boxed{2}\ \text{NP} \right\rangle \end{bmatrix} \\ \text{ARG-ST} \left\langle \boxed{1},\ \boxed{2} \right\rangle \end{bmatrix} \end{bmatrix} \Longrightarrow \begin{bmatrix} intrans\text{-}refl \\ \text{HEAD} \begin{bmatrix} \text{CLI}\{\boxed{2}_{\boxed{3}}\} \end{bmatrix} \\ \text{CAT} \begin{bmatrix} \text{VAL} \begin{bmatrix} \text{SUBJ} \left\langle \boxed{2}\ \text{NP}_{\boxed{3}} \right\rangle \\ \text{COMPS} \left\langle \right\rangle \end{bmatrix} \\ \text{ARG-ST} \left\langle \boxed{1},\ \boxed{2} \right\rangle \end{bmatrix} \end{bmatrix}
$$

FIGURE 20 A (simplified) medio-passive reflexive lexical rule

Figure 21 sketches the inversion of indefinites rule. The NP preceded by the tag $\boxed{1}$ moves from the SUBJ list to the COMPS list, and an expletive NP$_{il}$ subject requirement is added. Note that this rule must apply after the medio-passive reflexive rule. The contrast between (27) and (28) shows that the inversion of indefinites construction only applies to intransitive verbs. In other words, only entries with no NP on the COMPS list can be input to the rule. It cannot apply directly to the transitive form of 'vendre', as shown in (29).

$$
\begin{bmatrix} intrans \\ \text{CAT} \begin{bmatrix} \text{VAL} \begin{bmatrix} \text{SUBJ} \left\langle \boxed{1}\ \text{NP} \right\rangle \\ \text{COMPS} \left\langle \right\rangle \end{bmatrix} \\ \text{ARG-ST} \left\langle \boxed{1} \right\rangle \end{bmatrix} \end{bmatrix} \Longrightarrow \begin{bmatrix} inv \\ \text{CAT} \begin{bmatrix} \text{VAL} \begin{bmatrix} \text{SUBJ} \left\langle \boxed{2}\ \text{NP}_{il} \right\rangle \\ \text{COMPS} \left\langle \boxed{1} \right\rangle \end{bmatrix} \\ \text{ARG-ST} \left\langle \boxed{2},\ \boxed{1} \right\rangle \end{bmatrix} \end{bmatrix}
$$

FIGURE 21 A (simplified) inversion of indefinites lexical rule

(27) Il est   arrivé   deux personnes.
      It be-PR arrive-PPT two   persons
      'There arrived two persons.'

(28) *Il mange des   champignons Jacques.
       It eats-PR INDEF mushrooms   Jacques
      'Jacques eats mushrooms.'

(29) *Il vend   des   livres Jacques.
       It sell-PR INDEF books Jacques
      'Jacques sells books.'

(29) is ungrammatical because we must first derive an intransitive valence by applying the medio-passive reflexive lexical rule. In other words, the medio-passive rule feeds the inversion of indefinites rule. The two possible orderings of the rules are sketched below:

(30)   Jacques a vendu un livre

$\overset{medio-pass}{\Longrightarrow}$ Un livre s'est vendu

$\overset{imp-inv}{\Longrightarrow}$ Il s'est vendu un livre

(31)   Jacques a vendu un livre

$\overset{imp-inv}{\Longrightarrow}$ *Il a vendu un livre Jacques

Other facts, however, show that the inversion of indefinites construction must apply before the medio-passive reflexive rule, causing an ordering paradox. I mentioned above that the reflexive clitic introduced by the medio-passive rule must agree with the subject. Note that in sentences where both lexical rules have applied ((32) and (33) below), the reflexive clitic agrees with the expletive subject introduced by the inversion of indefinites construction. Thus (32) is ungrammatical because the reflexive clitic 't'' agrees with the extraposed pronoun 'toi'.[25]

(32) *A   la   dernière   foire   du   livre   il
      At   the   last   fair   of.the   book   it

      ne   t'   est   bien   vendu que   toi.
      NEG   2SG.REFL   be-PR   sell-PPT   well   that   you
      'At the last book fair, only you sold well.'

(33) ?A   la   dernière   foire   du   livre,
      At   the   last   fair   of.the   book

      il   ne   s'   est   bien   vendu que   toi.
      it   NEG   3.REFL   be-PR   sell-PPT   well   that   you
      'At the last book fair, only you sold well.'

This means that the clitic agrees with the surface subject, not necessarily the subject requirement introduced by the medio-passive rule. Intuitively, the clitic must be introduced after the surface subject requirement is in place. Since in (33) the surface subject requirement is introduced by the inversion of indefinites rule, the medio-passive rule which introduces the clitic must follow the inversion rule. The medio-passive rule, on the other hand, must apply before the inversion of indefinites construction to create the appropriate intransitive environment for the application of the inversion rule— hence the ordering paradox.

The paradox does not depend on the details of my description of the medio-passive and inversion rules— for example, on the fact that the

---

[25]Sentence (33) is awkward pragmatically: inversion of indefinites sentences do not in general welcome definite NPs, particularly deictics. This pragmatically awkward sentence must be compared to the preceding truly ungrammatical one.

constraint on the presence of a reflexive marker is included in the output of the medio-passive reflexive rule. Even if the rule does not directly include this information in the output, but merely makes reference to a general template for reflexive verbs, the ordering paradox remains. Suppose, for example, that the output of the rule simply mentions that the verb must be a reflexive verb (i.e. of category *reflexive-verb*). The general category for reflexives must nevertheless specify that reflexive verbs take a reflexive clitic (or affix) which agrees with the subject. Since there are no restrictions on when inherited information can be cashed out, nothing prevents this inherited information from applying to the output of the medio-passive rule *before* the inversion rule applies. The ordering paradox therefore remains: (32) should be grammatical. As long as reflexive verbs form an independent lexical class, the paradox is in effect.

One possible way out is to shift the enforcement of the observed "agreement" of the reflexive clitic with the surface subject from the lexical to the syntactic component. If the "agreement" is not enforced lexically, the reflexive clitic can indeed "wait" until the surface subject is known, that is, until the inversion rule has applied. This is basically the strategy used by Godard and Sag 1995's response to Koenig and Jurafsky 1994. Since reflexive clitics seem to be reflexives (and therefore anaphors), they propose that the observed "agreement" follows from a (French-parametrized) condition A of binding theory: reflexives must be subject-bound.[26] Assuming as is customary that binding is a syntactic process, the satisfaction of condition A is not lexically enforced and cannot therefore interact with the application of lexical rules. The putative ordering paradox vanishes.

There are two difficulties with Godard and Sag's attempt to dissolve the paradox. Firstly, their solution requires the existence of a loop between lexical and syntactic processing. They assume, as argued in Miller 1991, that so-called French clitics are in fact person prefixes. Complement requirements corresponding to clitics must therefore be realized through a lexical rule. The problem is that in the case of reflexive clitics, which "clitic" to prefix to the verb cannot be determined lexically: only the syntactic application of condition A of the binding theory determines the antecedent of the reflexive affix, and thereby its person and number. Morphophonological operations must thus crucially wait until a point after the application of binding theory. Such an ordering of (lexical) morphophonological rules after syntactic processes is hard

---

[26]Their actual condition reads 'Reflexives must be a-subject bound', where a-subjects are defined as the first elements on a word's ARG-ST list.

to reconcile with the hypothesis that lexical rules apply entirely within the lexical module and do not have access to information resulting from the application of syntactic principles— an assumption at the root of Godard and Sag's answer to the putative ordering paradox. Moreover, as we saw earlier, insuring the proper interaction of lexical and syntactic processing in a TFS system endowed with on-line lexical rules is a non-trivial matter. From a descriptively adequate lexical theory (i.e. an adequate lexical hierarchy and set of lexical rules) and a descriptively adequate syntactic theory, we are not guaranteed an observationally adequate model, once lexical and syntactic processing are interleaved.

Secondly, and more importantly, analyzing the reflexive clitic as an anaphor contravenes HPSG binding conditions. In fact, evidence suggests that French reflexive clitics are agreement markers, not anaphors. As sentences (26) and (33) on pages 44 and 46 show, the reflexive clitic must sometimes be bound by an expletive subject. But HPSG condition A is defined in terms of O-command (obliqueness-command) which requires the commander to be referential. Analyzing the reflexive clitic as an anaphor is therefore incompatible with HPSG binding conditions which require antecedents to be referential. Furthermore, the reflexive clitic— contrary to the claim made by the medio-passive reflexive rule Godard and Sag posit— never corresponds to a semantic argument of the verb to which it attaches. In fact, it is never semantically potent. Consider sentences (34):

(34) a. Tu   t'   es   dénoncé.
         You 2SG.REFL be-PR denounce-PPT
         'You denounced yourself.'

      b.?Il ne   s'   est   dénoncé   que toi.
         It   NEG 3.REFL be-PR denounce-PPT that you
         'Only you denounced yourself.'

      c.*Il ne   t'   est   denoncé   que toi.
         It   neg 2SG.REFL be-PR denounce-PPT that you
         'Only you denounced yourself.'

Sentence (34a) exemplifies the co-referential use of the reflexive clitic. (34a) seems similar to its English counterpart— a subject-bound anaphor satisfying the patient argument of 'dénoncé'. But the apparent anaphoric nature of the reflexive clitic in (34a) is misleading. In fact, 't'' is not an anaphor semantically. Otherwise, when the inversion rule applies, the patient argument of 'dénoncé' should still be co-indexed with the inverted 'toi', since 'toi' is its alleged binder. But the ungrammaticality of (34c) shows this is not what happens. The reflexive clitic must agree with the expletive subject, not with the inverted 'toi', its alleged binder, as shown in (34b). Since the third person attribute of 'se' is incompatible with that of a second person patient, the reflexive clitic cannot satisfy the patient argument in (34b). Despite appearances to the contrary, so-called French reflexive clitics do not satisfy semantic arguments of predicators with which they combine. The binding of the index of the patient argument of 'dénoncé' in (34b) is independent of the co-indexing properties of the reflexive clitic. If French reflexive clitics are anaphors, as Godard and Sag claim, their properties are quite exceptional; they are the only examples of anaphors of which I am aware which can be bound by an expletive and can never correspond to a subcategorization requirement.

If, on the other hand, French "reflexive" clitics are analyzed as subject agreement markers, their properties are directly explained: agreement markers do not satisfy subcategorization requirements, they must be co-indexed with subjects (or objects) and they can be co-indexed with expletives. The traditional name "reflexive" clitic is somewhat of a misnomer in this respect. French reflexive clitics are not reflexive at all, although they are associated with a lexical construction which effects the semantic binding of one argument to an other. If my claim that French "reflexive" clitics are agreement markers is correct, Godard and Sag's attempt at dissipating the ordering paradox fails. Agreement constraints are imposed lexically in HPSG (see Pollard and Sag 1994). The reasoning I outlined applies, and the paradox still arises. I conclude that Godard and Sag's attempt at resolving the ordering paradox is unsatisfactory: it requires unmotivated changes to binding theory and misses the agreement-like behavior of French "reflexive" clitics. The import of the ordering paradox with which I started this section remains intact: lexical rules, like their transformational ancestors, do lead to ordering paradoxes.

2.3 Summary

This chapter discussed the two kinds of relations among words which theories of lexical knowledge must include: classificatory and morphological. Taking as my starting point the model of classificatory relations embodied in HPSG's Hierarchical Lexicon, I concentrated on the difficulties it faces when modeling morphological relations, particularly the drawbacks that plague its attempts to supplement lexical type hierarchies with on-line application of lexical rules. In brief, the latter require several additional theoretical mechanisms, they can lead to unforeseen and inappropriate interactions between syntactic and lexical processing, and are prone to ordering paradoxes. To ease the discussion, I exclusively considered HPSG-style lexical rules. But these shortcomings are not specific to this particular implementation of the notion of generative lexical rules. They are, I believe, inherent in the diversion of Jackendoff-style redundancy rules to model productive morphological relations. Once redundancy rules are used as generative devices, they are beset with many of the same difficulties as old-fashioned transformations— namely, exceptions, ordering paradoxes, unexpected interactions between different classes of rules, and so forth. In brief, to the extent they apply productively and on-line to create new words, lexical rules are no better than old-generative style transformations or morpheme-based approaches to morphology.

In the next two chapters, I present an alternative which abandons compiled out type hierarchies in favor of grammatically underspecified hierarchies and a syntax-like structure to multimorphemic words. The basic idea is to reduce all relations among lexemes to some form of categorization through the use of underspecification and 'boolean' operations on categories which are implicit in AND/OR nets. By contrast to theories that make use of lexical rules, this approach to morphological relations does not add to the theoretical apparatus presented in section 2.1. Both classificatory and morphological relations are handled through a single, independently motivated formal mechanism: the organization of lexemes into a multidimensional hierarchy of categories. We thus preserve the advantages of Hierarchical Lexicons while providing for a better model of morphological relations.

3

On-line Type Construction

3.1 Two kinds of lexical productivity

The previous chapter presented a lexical architecture particularly apt at modeling classificatory relations among a language's words. Unfortunately, this architecture does not fare better than others when it comes to morphological relations. Like others, it does not handle equally well two salient facets of morphological relations: productivity and partial idiosyncrasies. I briefly discussed some of the reasons other theories falter at the beginning of the last chapter. But why are productive morphological relations equally hard to model in Hierarchical Lexicons? Two reasons stand out. To understand the first one, we must consider again figure 14 from chapter 2, repeated below.

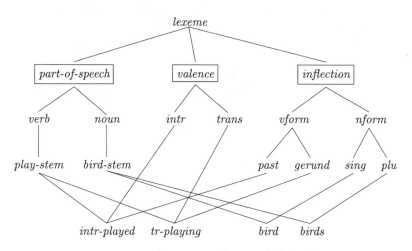

FIGURE 22 A more complex word hierarchy

A compiled out lexical hierarchy stores in the lexicon all possible M-subcategories of words (or L-categories), *intr-played, tr-playing, bird, birds*, etc. In other words, all subcategories that constitute the fully specified type of token words are listed prior to processing. By themselves, stored hierarchies do not therefore allow speakers to ever be linguistically creative and construct new L-categories for forms they have not yet encountered. Either the putative new form is an L-category already listed in their mental lexicon or it is not an L-category at all. Since all L-categories to which a language's tokens can belong are recorded in the hierarchy, speakers can only choose among already defined categories when interpreting or generating sentences. Such listing precludes the on-line construction of new L-categories. On-line application of lexical rules was intended to obviate the implausibility of this claim. But, as we saw, their use is theoretically costly.

A second reason that current linguistic theories which use a TFS formalism cannot (directly) model lexical productivity lies in the absence of structural "slots" in their definition of words. Compare lexical categories and phrase structural categories in HPSG. The definitions of M-subcategories of *phrase* in the hierarchy of phrase structural schemata presented in Pollard and Sag 1994 introduce phrase structural positions and constrain the general category to which their fillers must belong. A typical headed phrase structure construction, for example, states that it has a head-daughter which is of type *sign* (or *word*) and a list of complement daughters which are of type *phrase*, as shown in figure 23 and informally in more traditional tree-like form in figure 24 (see appendix A for details).

$$
\begin{bmatrix}
\text{CAT} & \begin{bmatrix} \text{VAL} & \begin{bmatrix} \text{COMPS}\,\langle\rangle \end{bmatrix} \end{bmatrix} \\
\text{DGHTRS} & \begin{bmatrix} \textit{head-comp-struc} \\ \text{HEAD-DGHTR} & \textit{word} \\ \text{COMP-DGHTRS} & \textit{list(phrase)} \end{bmatrix}
\end{bmatrix}
$$

FIGURE 23 The *Head-Complements* schema

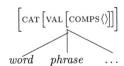

FIGURE 24 An informal representation of the *Head-Complements* schema

The definition of the *head-comp-struc* category does not indicate which particular word fills the head-daughter slot in the constructs it licenses. Nor does it indicate which particular phrases occupy the various complement-daughter slots (the members of the list of COMP-DGHTRS). Since they only constrain the general category of the fillers of phrase structural nodes, phrase structural constructions allow in those positions any member of the relevant class of words or phrases. Each M-subcategory of *phrase* thus describes a large class of possible feature structures: any word or phrase can act as filler of the category's structural positions provided it is informationally compatible with the constraints the phrase-structural schema imposes. Since the definitions describe the properties of fillers and does not list them individually— in other words is intensional— a single schema licenses an open-ended number of phrases. Syntactic productivity follows immediately. In the case of lexical categories, the situation is different. In HPSG II, lexical categories do not contain any structural "slot". Lexical productivity cannot therefore result from the various ways of filling structural positions.

Having elucidated its roots, the solution to the problem of lexical productivity is conceptually simple: allow the on-line creation of L-categories or introduce structural "slots" in the definition of lexemes— that is, include constituency information in the definition of the category *lexeme*. I will argue that both are ultimately needed. Consequently, the lexical architecture I propose— called the Type Underspecified Hierarchical Lexicon (hereafter TUHL)— consists of two parts: a typed, construction-based constituent structure morphology and an on-line approach to type construction. Chapter 4 introduces word-internal constituent structure schemata with structural positions that only partially specify the types of their fillers. Lexical categories of this kind model productivity in the same way phrase structural categories do. They contain structural positions whose slots can be occupied by any member of the relevant class of linguistic objects. I call this sort of productivity "structural productivity".

Concomitantly, I reject the idea underlying compiled out lexical hierarchies that all L-categories are stored in the lexicon. What is stored is a set of underspecified, basic categories (including underspecified roots) and constraints relating these categories (statements to the effect that a category is or is not a subclass of another). Complex categories are constructed on an as-needed basis when producing or interpreting utterances. Thus, fully type-specified entries— i.e. L-categories— arise only while processing sentences. Productivity follows here from the ability speakers have to create complex categories. I call this second sort of productivity "categorial productivity".

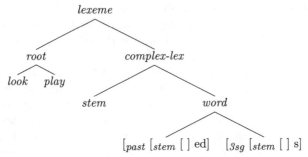

FIGURE 25 A simplified hierarchy of morphological types

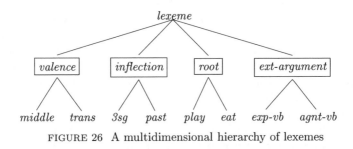

FIGURE 26 A multidimensional hierarchy of lexemes

These two complementary approaches to lexical productivity are illustrated in figures 25 and 26 respectively. The first diagram describes parts of the hierarchy devoted to a classification of morphological objects. The details of the hierarchy are not important. The intuitive idea is that, on a par with phrase structural constructions, there are inflectional morphological constructions that build up complex lexemes from roots so that a word like 'played' will be analyzed as [[play] ed], as indicated informally in the definition of the *past* category in figure 25. In other words, I assume a (variant of a) constituent structure approach to morphology as proposed by Lieber 1980, Selkirk 1982, Williams 1981, and others.[1] Productivity in this case is a consequence of the fact that an open-ended number of stems can fill the inner bracket.

The second diagram illustrates On-Line Type Construction (henceforth OLTC).[2] In this expository diagram, the class of lexemes is divided into subclasses along four dimensions: valence, inflectional morphology, root, and external-argument-mapping. In this hierarchy, only one type is stipulated for each root, whatever its valence structure or morphological form; only one *play* or *eat* root is included in the AND/OR net. Compare this diagram with the HPSG-II-style hierarchy in figure 22, where all forms of 'play' (i.e. 'playing', 'played', and so forth) had corresponding types in the hierarchy that gathers stored grammatical objects.[3]

The single abstract lexeme *play* in figure 26 is underspecified with respect to its type. It does not represent the full category of a token word; it is only a basic type. The set of fully type-specified entries or L-categories for this abstract lexeme are constructed by intersecting the category *play* with one other category along each of the three other dimensions. Because word classes along each dimension do not enumerate their members, they freely combine with any informationally compatible category. Productivity follows in this case from two facts:

1. Entries are stored as basic types rather than fully type-specified (they are type-underspecified);

---

[1] The constituent structure approach to morphology advocated in chapter 4 is not X̄-theoretic in nature. The notion of morphological constituent structure only refers to the abstract format of morphological constructions rather than a specific hypothesis regarding their nature. Note also that '-ed' is not a morphological daughter as indicated informally in the figure by the fact it is not enclosed in square brackets. See chapter 4 for details.

[2] As readers have probably noticed, the organization of the hierarchy presented in figure 25 does not match that of figure 26. The hierarchy in figure 26 is only used for the purposes of illustrating On-Line Type Construction. More adequate hierarchies are provided in chapter 4.

[3] This is not true if we assume on-line lexical rules. Only base forms need to be stored then.

2. Classes of words such as *trans* or *agnt-vb* do not enumerate extensionally their members, but merely intensionally constrain properties all their members share.

Since not all possible word categories are stored, speakers can create new forms on the fly. They need only intersect their stored categories. The mental lexicon specifies basic types— including underspecified roots— and constraints among types. Fully type-specified complex categories which constitute a language's set of possible lexemes— what I call its L-categories— are only constructed when producing or interpreting utterances. The lexicon gives us the basic classes from which to construct linguistically well-formed words; the processing component builds them. Speakers that have heard the word 'played' as used in (1), for example, and have abstracted from it the root *play*, but have not yet encountered its third singular present form, 'plays', can still interpret or produce sentence (2) by simply constructing on-line the L-category *agnt-vb* $\wedge$ *play* $\wedge$ *3sg* $\wedge$ *middle* from the set of basic types their lexicon contains.

(1)   Claudio played the sonata.

(2)   This sonata plays well on an organ.

The fact that the TUHL architecture models productive morphological relations in two ways (a constituent structure approach to morphology and type-underspecified lexical entries) raises an immediate question: do we need both mechanisms? The answer is yes. A constituent structure morphology is generally ill-suited to model valence alternations which are not mediated by morphophonological changes. Examples of such alternations are given in sentences (3)-(5).

(3)   a. That he will come before midnight is unlikely.
        b. It is unlikely that he will come before midnight.

(4)   a. Barbara imagined that he was taller.
        b. Barbara imagined him taller.

(5)   a. Deux personnes sont   arrivées.
           two   people   be.PR   arrive.PPT
           'Two people arrived.'

        b. Il   est   arrivé   deux   personnes.
           he   be.PR arrive.PPT   two   people
           'There arrived two people.'

Sentences (3a) and (3b) illustrate two entries for the adjective 'unlikely', one which subcategorizes for a sentential subject and one which subcategorizes for both an expletive subject and an extraposed sentential complement. Similarly, sentences (4a) and (4b) illustrate non-raising *vs.* raising entries for the verb 'imagine'. Finally, sentences (5a) and (5b) illustrate personal *vs.* inversion of indefinites entries of the French verb 'arriver' ('to arrive'). In all three cases, the relationship between the two entries is regular and productive within the relevant adjective or verb classes. In all three cases, the valence alternation is not accompanied by morphophonological changes.

A theory that only uses constituent structure schemata to model productive morphological relations is required to posit a constituent structure template to relate the two sets of valence alternates. Consider the two variants of 'imagined' in (4). The variant in (4b) belongs to the class of *raising* verbs, the variant in (4a) does not. The L-categories corresponding to these two variants are therefore different. How can we relate the two variants if we do not avail ourselves of on-line lexical rules? Since we excluded (underspecified) category intersection as a possible tool, we are left with constituent structure schemata. We could assume for example that the entry for 'imagined' exemplified in (4b) is derived from that in (4a) through the embedding of the latter in a morphological constituent structure tree, as indicated semi-informally in figure 27. The local tree's daughter subcategorizes for an NP and a sentence; the mother for two NPs and a VP. Furthermore, the second of the mother's two subcategorized NPs is token-identical to the VPs subject requirement. In other words, the daughter has the argument-structure of sentential complements verbs, whereas the mother has the argument-structure of so-called raising-to-object verbs.

$$
\begin{bmatrix} \textit{raising-verb} \\ \text{CAT} \mid \text{ARG-ST} \left\langle \text{NP}, \; \boxed{1}\text{NP}, \; \text{VP}[<\boxed{1} \text{ NP}>] \right\rangle \end{bmatrix}
$$
$$
\mid
$$
$$
\begin{bmatrix} \text{CAT} \mid \text{ARG-ST} \left\langle \text{NP}, \; \text{S} \right\rangle \end{bmatrix}
$$

FIGURE 27 A tree-based representation of raising alternations

Three arguments militate against this analysis. Firstly, no affixal material regulates the argument-structure alternation, and no other kind of evidence exists for the postulated constituent structure. Secondly, using constituent structure schemata would force us to choose a basic variant among the two alternates as the daughter of the morphological tree, which, as we have seen in section 2.2.2, is not always motivated. Finally, it would prevent us from predicting cyclicity effects from morphological constituent structure, following the approach of Orgun 1994. If we introduce morphological constituent structure embedding for any two valence alternates of a single word, many more local morphological trees will be built than required for morphophonological reasons. The isomorphism between a word's constituent structure and the phonological "cycles" it underwent then disappears. By contrast, the lexical underspecification approach developed in this chapter and the following does not need to posit *ad hoc* additional structural levels, since modeling some of the alternations through On-Line Type Construction relieves us from the need to introduce a morphological constituent structure tree each time we must relate two lexeme variants. We can thus preserve the correlation between phonological cyclicity and constituent structure.

Valence alternates in (3)-(5) demonstrate that categorial productivity is independent of morphophonological marking, thereby justifying OLTC. What about constituent structure schemata? Are they needed too, or can we make do solely with OLTC? I defer the justification of the independent need for morphological constituent structure schemata to the next chapter which presents in detail a typed constituent structure approach to morphology. I only briefly mention the major argument. Simply put, type underspecification cannot model morphological processes which alter the properties of lexemes to which they apply, be they category-changing or semantic-changing derivational processes. In all such cases, we need two layers of structure to monotonically describe the change in information structure caused by the morphological process.

3.2 How on-line typing works

Having briefly outlined how the TUHL models productive morphological relations, let me know present in detail its first component, On-line Type Construction. To explain what OLTC means, I first present how it works on a (simplified) example simultaneously involving verbal valence, linking, and morphology. I show how a type inference system presented with the sentences in (6)-(8) would build the L-categories (or fully type specified entries) of the various forms of the lexeme *play*. I assume that the inference system has the hierarchy in figure 26.[4]

(6)   Claudio played the sonata.

(7)   This sonata plays well on an organ.

(8)   Claudio plays the sonata well on her harpischord.

---

[4] As already mentioned above, figure 26 is simplified for purposes of exposition. In particular, it (*wrongly*) assumes that inflections should not be modeled through constituent structure schemata, but rather via the separation of a word's stem-phonology from its phonology *simpliciter*. The latter consists of the concatenation of the stem-phonology and inflectional affixes, as proposed in Krieger and Nerbonne 1993.

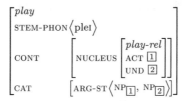

FIGURE 28 The underspecified entry for *play*

Consider example (6) which contains the verb form 'played'. Determining the entire set of categories to which this variant of *play* belongs requires on-line type construction. From the stored lexical hierarchy, we can only retrieve the entry for 'play' represented in figure 28 which contains a minimal amount of information. It only indicates its phonology and its semantics— the stem describes a playing event which relates two participants, an ACTOR and an UNDERGOER, each of which corresponds to the index of an argument on the ARG-ST list (see the tags $\boxed{1}$ and $\boxed{2}$). It does not specify the lexeme's inflectional form or its valence properties (determined by the transitivity of the verb and the semantic role of its external argument in the theory of linking assumed here), all of which constitute lexical information which is projected syntactically. Interpreting (6) therefore necessitates that the hearer decides which other categories this variant of *play* is a member of: does it belong to the category of transitive or middle verbs, does it belong to the category of third-singular present or past forms, and so forth? The type inference the hearer must draw resembles top-down parsing. Given the interpretation of AND/OR nets discussed in section 2.1.2, the parser/interpreter knows that any well-formed word must belong to a single class from each of the four dimensions involved in figure 26: she must create a type which is compatible with the string 'played' and which is specified along all four of the *root, ext-argument, inflection,* and *valence* dimensions.

Intuitively, this means choosing one type in each dimension and combining their information structure via unification. So, suppose that a parser/interpreter has determined that the form 'played' is of root type *play*. Since *play* has an actor argument (the player), it is compatible with the *agnt-vb* type in the *ext-argument* dimension represented in figure 29, and the two types can be combined into a more specific entry in which the external-argument or designated argument is specified as the actor of the playing event, as shown in figure 30. We can read the new feature structure as specifying a stem-phonology /pleɪ/, a semantic relation with two arguments, of which the ACTOR is the external or designated argument, and a set of two argument-structure elements that correspond to the player (an actor) and the music (an undergoer) respectively.

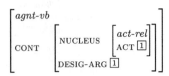

FIGURE 29 The category of agentive verbs

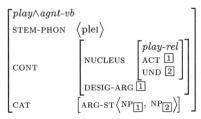

FIGURE 30 The result of combining the *play* and *agnt-vb* categories

Now we need to specify the form along the inflection dimension. In the case of (6), we cannot choose the *3sg* inflectional template, since some of the information specified in the template (that the suffix is /s/) is incompatible with the input string. The only inflectional construction compatible with the input is the *past* template described in figure 31. (⊕ in the diagram denotes the concatenation of two lists.) Figure 32 shows the new partially filled-out type. Note that I have added in morphological information from the *past* type.

FIGURE 31 The category of past verbs

Finally, we must choose a valence template. The only choice to be made in this simplified graph is between the middle and transitive valence templates. The result of combining each of these templates with the entry we have so far is shown in figures 33 and 34.

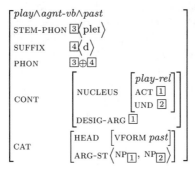

FIGURE 32 The intersection of the *play*, *agnt-vb*, and *past* categories

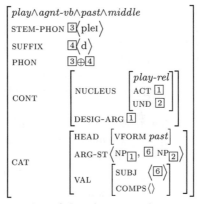

FIGURE 33 The intersection of the *play*, *agnt-vb*, *past*, and *middle* categories

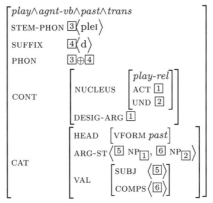

FIGURE 34 The intersection of the *play*, *agnt-vb*, *past*, and *trans* categories

In both cases, the grammatical functions of the two valence require-ments are specified. If the *middle* category is chosen, the undergoer argument of *play* (which corresponds to the second element on the ARG-ST list) is co-indexed with the subject valence requirement (the sole member of the SUBJ list, see tag ⑥) and the actor argument is not realized syntactically. If the *trans* category is chosen, the actor argu-ment of *play* is co-indexed with the subject valence requirement and its undergoer argument is co-indexed with an object requirement (the first member of the COMPS list), see tags ⑤ and ⑥ respectively. Both feature-structures represent fully type-specified entries compatible with the input form 'played'. Ultimately, of course, only the transitive type will prove compatible with the input sentence. The middle template specifies that the external or distinguished-argument is not syntactically expressed. It thus leaves a verb like 'played' with only one argument to be satisfied syntactically and is incompatible with a sentence such as (6) which contains both a subject and an object. In the end, only the combination of the categories *play*, *agnt-vb*, *past*, and *trans* proves com-patible with the input string. Sentences (7) and (8) would be analyzed similarly, although other choices would be made along the inflectional or valence dimensions.

The reader can gather from this example that the (constructive) definition of On-line Type Construction is quite simple. To infer the full type of a lexeme— i.e. the set of M-subcategories of *lexeme* or L-categories to which it might belong— the parser/interpreter must:

1. Successively choose a (maximally specific) class from each dimen-sion;
2. Successively combine (via unification) the information shared by all members of the class;
3. Disregard all combinations that fail.

All remaining categories are the possible L-categories of the lexeme under consideration. In our example, for the basic type *play*, there are two remaining possible L-categories *play* ∧ *agnt-vb* ∧ *past* ∧ *trans* and *play* ∧ *agnt-vb* ∧ *past* ∧ *middle*, only one of which matches the input.

It should be clear that this informal definition of OLTC closely par-allels Carpenter and Pollard's conjunctive type construction presented in section 2.1. In both cases, we build a word's full type from a set of basic types organized in an AND/OR net. In fact, the definition of OLTC requires only two simple changes in the mathematics of off-line type construction, allowing us to rely on the axiomatization presented in Carpenter 1992. To understand why, I must very briefly introduce one additional technical detail. In Carpenter's approach to Typed Feature

Structures, types are ordered according to their specificity; they form an information-theoretic lattice. Conjoining two types or intersecting two categories σ and ρ means taking their join in the lattice. Generalizing two types into their common supercategory means taking their meet in the lattice. Figure 35 illustrates. The conjunction of the two categories *verb-class* and *trans* is defined as their join, the *trans-verb* category. Conversely, the generalization of *verb-class* and *trans* into their common supercategory is defined as their meet, the *word* category.

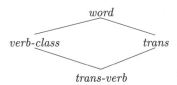

FIGURE 35 A simple example of a lattice of types

Now, type hierarchies are compiled out and stored prior to processing in Carpenter's system. This means conjunctive type construction is not used at parse-time. We can characterize the upshot of OLTC as letting conjunctive type construction apply at parse-time. Carpenter's compiled out type lattice can thus be viewed as *virtually* present in a TUHL, although the entire lattice is not actually constructed. Any time his axioms refer to a join in the lattice of types, where a compiled out type lattice merely looks up the join (via the least upper bound operation on lattices), the underspecified network must actually perform a complete unification at parse-time.

More generally, there are two differences between on-line conjunctive type construction and Carpenter's conjunctive type construction presented in chapter 2. Firstly, Carpenter's type hierarchy is constructed and stored in the grammar before any processing occurs. All possible categories of words (all L-categories) are stored. By contrast, in the architecture proposed in this section, grammars merely contain a representation of the AND/OR net, not a complete type hierarchy. Basic categories and subclass/superclass or disjointness relations among basic categories are stored; the type hierarchy itself is constructed only as required by interpretation or production. Secondly, types that are not declared to be incompatible can always be combined in Carpenter's system. To return to our example, in a compiled out hierarchy, if the types *play* and *exp-vb* are not stipulated to be incompatible, their combination is a possible category. In an OLTC system, we cannot make this assumption. Categorial productivity follows from the assumption that only basic subcategories of lexemes are stored and word classes can be defined intensionally— i.e. without enumerating their members. Specifying in advance the impossible category combinations for each lexeme amounts to listing all members of a word class. In the case of the *exp-vb* or *past* categories, it means listing all verbs which have an experiencer argument or are past verb forms. But if we know prior to processing what the possible members of the class of *past* verbs are, we cannot add new members to the class upon encountering new past forms. Categorial productivity is now impossible. We must therefore amend those parts of Carpenter's axiomatization that refer to the fail-type (the inconsistent category) and allow type combination to fail, not only when two types are explicitly declared to be incompatible, but also when their informational content conflicts. This is easy enough. Carpenter's type system relies on the following two axioms for type combination:

(9) $\sigma \wedge \tau \Leftrightarrow \rho$ (if $\sigma \sqcup \tau = \rho$)
      A feature structure of type σ and τ is also of type ρ (and conversely), if ρ is the join of σ and τ in the lattice of types.

(10) $\sigma \wedge \tau \Leftrightarrow \bot$ (if $\sigma \sqcup \tau$ does not exist)
      A feature structure of type σ and τ is also of type $\bot$ (fail) (and conversely) if the join of σ and ρ does not exist.

Informally speaking, 'played' is a member of the class of words formed on the root *play* and the class of *past* verbs, if and only if it belongs to their intersection. We can keep those two axioms, and therefore not change Carpenter's axiomatization of sorted feature logics. We only need change how the join of σ and τ is computed. In Carpenter's system computing the join means looking up whether there is such a join in the type hierarchy, since the entire hierarchy is stored. In the system I propose, computing the join means:

1. Performing the unification of the two (most general) feature structures corresponding to the two types.[5]

2. Defining the join of the two types as the result of this unification (which is $\bot$, the fail type, if unification fails).

This amounts to adding one clause to the definition of conjunctive type construction presented in section 2.1.2, as shown in (11):

---

[5]Since the unification of two feature structures of type σ and τ requires taking the join of their types, we must determine first if the two feature structures unify without considering the existence of a join in the lattice, and if this unification succeeds, unify the two types themselves by positing a join in the lattice which corresponds to their combination.

(11) *On-line Conjunctive type construction:*
The set of all possible types for an AND/OR net N is the (greatest) subset S of the power-set of the set of its basic types B that satisfy the following constraints (expressed in N):

- No member τ of S contains redundant information: if τ contains a basic type a and a is a subtype of b, then, τ does not contain b (that τ is also of type b can be inferred).
- No member τ of S contains inconsistent information:
    1. If τ contains a basic type a and a is explicitly declared not to be a b, then τ does not contain b (otherwise τ would be inconsistent).
    2. Any two members a and b of τ are informationally compatible (the component categories of τ must be mutually consistent). More technically, for any member τ of S, the unification of the (most general) feature structures of any pair of basic types a and b that τ contains exists.[6]

Despite its advantage, it should be noted that OLTC comes at a computational cost: the number of steps involved in inferring the full type of a lexeme is increased. The additional cost is due to the last clause of (11). In a (sort-resolved) compiled out system such as Carpenter's, the number of subtypes to which a lexeme can belong is merely the set of nodes immediately dominating the (fully type-specified) leaves of the hierarchy— that is, the set of predefined L-categories. To determine a lexeme's L-category we need only choose among the appropriate types in this set. But in on-line typing systems, not all possible L-categories are listed. The number of potential types to which a linguistic object can belong is the product of the intersection of the (type underspecified) leaves of each dimension. Since some intersections of categories might result in inconsistent types, only a subset of these potential categories corresponds to consistent (most specific) types of a compiled out hierarchy. Crucially, the determination of the consistent potential categories must be done at parse-time. To infer the L-category of a lexeme, we must first determine the consistent L-categories before choosing which one is instantiated by the lexeme under consideration. Note, though, that comparable additional computational steps are also incurred by on-line application of lexical rules, since not all lexemes will be possible inputs

---

[6]Fortunately, we do not have to check the existence of the unification for each pair. Since unification is a monotonic operation, if the unification of a set of feature structures $a_1...a_i$ exists ($\bigsqcup a_1...a_i \neq \bot$), so does the unification of any two structures a_j and a_k taken from that set. We can therefore successively combine types in any order; the ultimate result is always identical.

to all rules. Furthermore, the difference is not as big as it may seem. In on-line typing systems, leaves are underspecified entries or lexeme classes. Many of the stored L-categories in a compiled out type hierarchy therefore correspond to possible combinations of type-underspecified leaves in an on-line system. Only failed combinations which the OLTC approach is forced to check add to the task. The number of added computational steps is equal to the product of the number of leaves of each (sub)dimension *minus* the number of successful combinations.

3.3 Morphological relations within a TUHL

A major claim of this book is that all lexical relations reduce to some form of categorization. I have described in the preceding section the basic method by which we can reduce lexical productivity to category intersection. Let me now illustrate this method on a simple example and show how OLTC models (some) morphological relations and can get out of lexical rules. The adjective 'likely' in English either subcategorizes for a single sentential subject as shown in (12a), or for both an expletive 'it' and an extraposed sentential complement, as shown in (12b). The verb 'happens' displays the same alternation as illustrated in (13) and (14).

(12)   a. That they will miss the deadline is likely.
      b. It is likely that they will miss the deadline.

(13)   a. That he failed to do it happens to be true.
      b. It happens to be true that he failed.

(14)   a. That he failed to do it happened to be true.
      b. It happened to be true that he failed to do it.

$$\left[\text{CAT}\left[\begin{array}{l}\text{VAL}\left[\begin{array}{l}\text{SUBJ} \left\langle \boxed{1}\ \text{S}[\textit{fin}]\right\rangle \\ \text{COMPS}\left\langle\right\rangle\end{array}\right] \\ \text{ARG-ST}\left\langle\boxed{1}\right\rangle\end{array}\right]\right] \implies \left[\begin{array}{l}\textit{extr-verb} \\ \text{CAT}\left[\begin{array}{l}\text{VAL}\left[\begin{array}{l}\text{SUBJ} \left\langle\boxed{2}\right\rangle \\ \text{COMPS}\left\langle\ldots\boxed{1}\ldots\right\rangle\end{array}\right] \\ \text{ARG-ST}\left\langle\boxed{2}\ \text{NP}_{it},\boxed{1}\right\rangle\end{array}\right]\end{array}\right]$$

FIGURE 36   A (simplified) extraposition lexical rule

A simple Hierarchical Lexicon would handle the relationship between their two subcategorization frames through a lexical rule such as the one represented in figure 36. The rule adds an expletive NP requirement in front of the sentential subject requirement for which the base entry subcategorizes. (See appendix A for a definition of NP$_{it}$ and S[*fin*].) The relationship between the two contexts of occurrence in which 'likely' can be embedded is thus modeled by a general rule to the effect that:

'When the lexicon contains an entry which subcategorizes for a sentential subject, we can add an otherwise similar entry which subcategorizes for an expletive 'it' and a sentential complement'.

A Type Underspecified Lexicon analysis of the same data eliminates the need for the rule. We only posit an underspecified entry for 'likely' and the lexeme class defined in the output of the rule (on the right hand side of the arrow in figure 36).

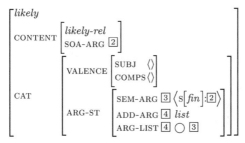

FIGURE 37 An underspecified entry for *likely*

The underspecified entry for 'likely' is represented in figure 37. It simply says that its argument-structure includes a sentential complement which expresses its situational argument. The latter is represented as the value of its SOA-ARG (state-of-affairs) argument in the figure. The identity between the semantics of the sentential subcategorization requirement and the situational argument is indicated by the tag ②. To keep track of which members of the ARG-ST list are semantically motivated arguments and which ones are added through extraposition or raising, I define the ARG-ST list— renamed the ARG-LIST— as the (sequence) union of the semantic arguments (members of the SEM-ARG list) and the added arguments (members of the ADD-ARG list). (Sequence union is denoted by the symbol ◯; see Reape 1994 and appendix A on the notion of sequence union.) Thus the added arguments list tagged ④ in figure 37 combines with the semantic argument list tagged ③. Nothing substantial hinges on this particular choice.

The *extr-verb* class is represented in figure 38. It specifies that its members contain, in addition to one sentential semantic argument (member of the SEM-ARG list), an expletive *it* argument (member of the ADD-ARG list). Because of the first constraint, the *extr-verb* class cannot encompass (minimal) entries which do not contain a sentential semantic

$$
\begin{bmatrix}
\textit{extr-verb} \\[4pt]
\text{CAT}
\begin{bmatrix}
\text{VALENCE}
\begin{bmatrix}
\text{SUBJ} & \langle\boxed{2}\rangle \\
\text{COMPS} & \langle\ldots\boxed{1}\ldots\rangle
\end{bmatrix} \\[10pt]
\text{ARG-ST}
\begin{bmatrix}
\text{ADD-ARG} & \langle\ldots\boxed{2}\ldots\rangle \\
\text{ARG-LIST} & \langle\ldots\boxed{2}\ \text{NP}_{it},\ \ldots\boxed{1}\ \text{s}[\textit{comp}]\rangle
\end{bmatrix}
\end{bmatrix}
\end{bmatrix}
$$

FIGURE 38 The *extraposition* category

argument. It cannot include 'touch', for example, whose entry is represented in figure 39. By contrast the adjective 'likely' or the verb 'happen'
contain a sentential argument and can freely combine with the *extr-verb*
category. Combining these two types— intersecting the two classes of
lexemes they describe— results in a category equivalent to the application of the extraposition lexical rule to *likely*, as the AVM in figure 40
attests. (modulo the renaming of the ARG-ST list as the ARG-LIST).

$$
\begin{bmatrix}
\textit{touch} \\[4pt]
\text{CONTENT}
\begin{bmatrix}
\textit{touch-rel} \\
\text{ACT} & \boxed{1} \\
\text{UND} & \boxed{2}
\end{bmatrix} \\[10pt]
\text{CAT}
\begin{bmatrix}
\text{ARG-ST} & [\text{SEM-ARG}\ \langle\text{NP}_{\boxed{1}},\ \text{NP}_{\boxed{2}}\rangle]
\end{bmatrix}
\end{bmatrix}
$$

FIGURE 39 An underspecified entry for *touch*

$$
\begin{bmatrix}
\textit{likely}\wedge\textit{extr-verb} \\[4pt]
\text{CONTENT}
\begin{bmatrix}
\textit{likely-rel} \\
\text{SOA-ARG} & \boxed{2}
\end{bmatrix} \\[10pt]
\text{CAT}
\begin{bmatrix}
\text{VALENCE}
\begin{bmatrix}
\text{SUBJ} & \langle\boxed{3}\rangle \\
\text{COMPS} & \langle\boxed{1}\rangle
\end{bmatrix} \\[14pt]
\text{ARG-ST}
\begin{bmatrix}
\text{SEM-ARG} & \langle\boxed{1}\ \text{s}[\textit{fin}]{:}\boxed{2}\rangle \\
\text{ADD-ARG} & \langle\boxed{3}\ \text{NP}_{it}\rangle \\
\text{ARG-LIST} & \langle\boxed{3},\ \boxed{1}\rangle
\end{bmatrix}
\end{bmatrix}
\end{bmatrix}
$$

FIGURE 40 The intersection of the *likely* and *extr-vb* categories

We can pursue this approach further. Whether a particular word
instantiates the extraposition pattern is orthogonal to its inflectional
properties. To model the inflectional potentialities of lexemes, we can
introduce an inflectional dimension (see the example hierarchy in fig-

ure 26). Consider the verb 'happen' again. Whereas the morphological relation between the base form 'happen' and the past form 'happened' is modeled via a lexical rule in HPSG II, the same morphological relation is modeled through their common sharing of an underspecified lexeme type in a TUHL. More generally, where a traditional Hierarchical Lexicon describes morphological relations through rules which apply to fully type-specified categories, the TUHL describes them through a shared, underspecified type. What the unextraposed versions of 'happen', 'happened', as well as their corresponding extraposed valence alternates have in common is the abstract lexeme *happen*. One way to think of this abstract *happen* lexeme category is that it represents what is common to all morphophonological and morphosyntactic variants of 'happen' one finds in English sentences. Before interpreting or producing a sentence, this common information is all we *need* to store. The full set of categories to which any token of 'happens' or 'happened' belongs is determined on-line when interpretation or production occurs. In other words, the L-category to which 'happens' belong in (13a) or (13b) is not known prior to processing this sentence. It results from intersecting the abstract *happen* category common to all variants of 'happen' with a certain number of categories, in the (simplified) case at hand, intersecting it with the informationally-compatible inflectional as well as valence categories.

3.4 The benefits of on-line type construction

I argued at length in the previous chapter that a lexical rule approach to lexical productivity is plagued by several shortcomings. Now that I have illustrated how (productive) morphological relations reduce to category intersection, let me demonstrate that indeed OLTC eschews many of these drawbacks. The remaining problems are tackled in the next two chapters.

3.4.1 Categorial productivity

A first theoretical advantage of the TUHL architecture is that (productive) morphological relations are described through the same mechanism used to model classificatory relations, namely class abstraction. The architecture is parsimonious in using the same logic of classes independently needed to model medium-size generalizations (see section 2.1). The key to this theoretical economy lies in the storage of lexemes stripped of all contextual information they bear in particular sentences. To such abstract entries correspond a set of fully specified lexemes, each of which is built through intersection with categories of the relevant AND/OR nets. In the simple hierarchy represented in figure 41, for example, the set of L-categories for the entry *happen* is the set $\mathcal{M}$ in (15)—

the product of the intersection of the root *happen* with each possible choice along the two other dimensions of lexeme classification.

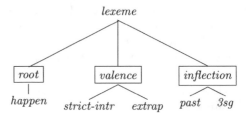

FIGURE 41 Determining the L-categories of *happen*

(15) $\mathcal{M} = \{$ *happen* $\wedge$ *strict-intr* $\wedge$ *past, happen* $\wedge$ *extrap* $\wedge$ *past,*
        happen $\wedge$ *strict-intr* $\wedge$ *3sg, happen* $\wedge$ *extrap* $\wedge$ *3sg}*

If *happen* is the name of a category and so is *past*, productively deriving the past form of *happen* (given this simplified type-hierarchy) consists in conjoining the information of the two categories as indicated in (11), page 65. Conversely, deciding which L-category is instantiated by 'happens' in (13a) means determining the categories to which it conjunctively belongs. To the notion of rule application we have thus substituted the notion of category intersection (or, more technically, type conjunction).

Another benefit of the OLTC account of lexical productivity is its exclusive reliance on order-independent category intersection and concomitant elimination of ordered rule application. Category intersection cannot *ex principio* lead to ordering paradoxes. The medio-passive reflexive and inversion of indefinites ordering quandaries I discussed in the previous chapter illustrate this point. For purposes of this discussion, I assume the simplified AND/OR net shown in figure 42, which represents a classification of lexemes along three dimensions:

1. Does the word only contain semantically potent arguments or does it contain additional expletives (no additional argument *vs.* extraposition of indefinites)?

2. Does the word "demote" the verb's external-argument or not (active *vs.* medio-passives)?

3. Is the verb transitive or intransitive?

To these three dimensions, one must, of course, add a list of underspecified individual lexemes (in the diagram, *vendre*). By following the method described in (11) except for the last clause, we obtain the set of complex categories in (16):

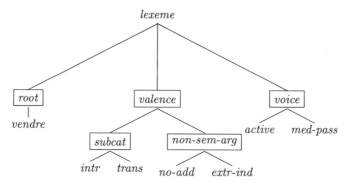

FIGURE 42 Determining the L-categories of *vendre*

(16) $\mathcal{M} =$ {*vendre* $\wedge$ *intr* $\wedge$ *no-add* $\wedge$ *active*,
                vendre $\wedge$ *trans* $\wedge$ *no-add,* $\wedge$ *active*
                vendre $\wedge$ *intr* $\wedge$ *no-add* $\wedge$ *med-pass*,
                vendre $\wedge$ *trans* $\wedge$ *no-add* $\wedge$ *med-pass*,
                vendre $\wedge$ *intr* $\wedge$ *extr-ind* $\wedge$ *active*,
                vendre $\wedge$ *trans* $\wedge$ *extr-ind* $\wedge$ *active*,
                vendre $\wedge$ *intr* $\wedge$ *extr-ind* $\wedge$ *med-pass*,
                vendre $\wedge$ *trans* $\wedge$ *extr-ind* $\wedge$ *med-pass*}

Many of these categories are inconsistent, since the conjoined types which describe them bear incompatible properties. To see why, I must anticipate what is introduced in detail in the next chapter, in particular, the idea that many lexemes have an internal morphological constituent structure.[7] This internal structure is represented by a μ-STRUC attribute in the AVM diagrams I introduce below (see next chapter for more details). To illustrate my claim that some type combinations are inconsistent, consider the category *vendre* $\wedge$ *intr* $\wedge$ *no-add* $\wedge$ *active*. Simplified representations of the information associated with each of these four categories is presented in figures 43-46. As usual, I omit from the definition of the various types information which is not characteristic of those categories and is inherited from their supertypes. (See appendix A for the relevant type declarations that contribute this additional information.)

The stem on which any form of 'vendre' is based, is represented in figure 43. It denotes a selling relation between two participants, that is a relation which belongs to the semantic category of *sell-rel*. Each of the arguments of this relation is co-indexed with the semantic content of

---

[7]The presentation of the internal constituency of words and the representation of roots, *vendre* in our example, is simplified and inaccurate for purposes of exposition. A more adequate representation must await the next chapter.

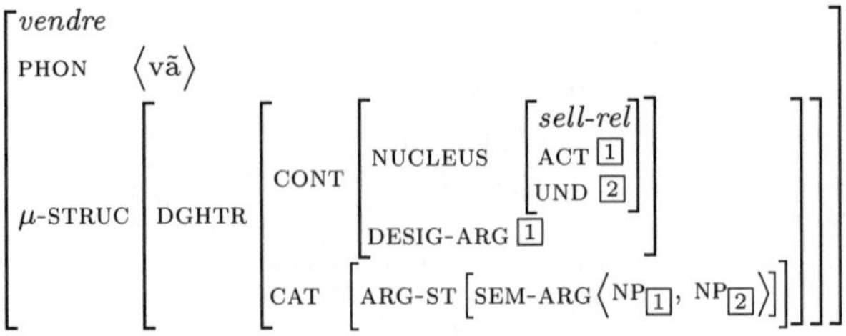

$$
\begin{bmatrix}
vendre \\
\text{PHON} \quad \langle \text{vã} \rangle \\
\mu\text{-STRUC} \begin{bmatrix} \text{DGHTR} \begin{bmatrix} \text{CONT} \begin{bmatrix} \text{NUCLEUS} \begin{bmatrix} sell\text{-}rel \\ \text{ACT} \boxed{1} \\ \text{UND} \boxed{2} \end{bmatrix} \\ \text{DESIG-ARG} \boxed{1} \end{bmatrix} \\ \text{CAT} \begin{bmatrix} \text{ARG-ST} \begin{bmatrix} \text{SEM-ARG} \langle \text{NP}_{\boxed{1}}, \text{NP}_{\boxed{2}} \rangle \end{bmatrix} \end{bmatrix} \end{bmatrix} \end{bmatrix}
\end{bmatrix}
$$

FIGURE 43 An underspecified entry for *vendre*

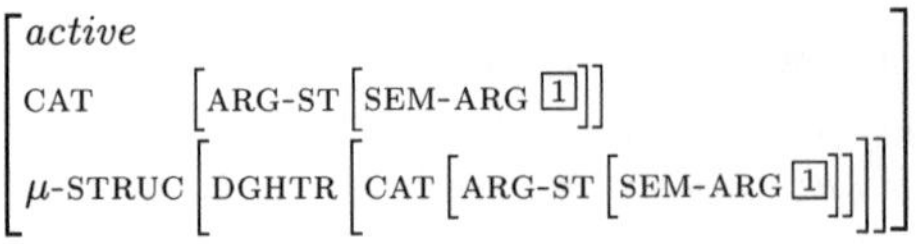

$$
\begin{bmatrix}
active \\
\text{CAT} \quad \begin{bmatrix} \text{ARG-ST} \begin{bmatrix} \text{SEM-ARG} \boxed{1} \end{bmatrix} \end{bmatrix} \\
\mu\text{-STRUC} \begin{bmatrix} \text{DGHTR} \begin{bmatrix} \text{CAT} \begin{bmatrix} \text{ARG-ST} \begin{bmatrix} \text{SEM-ARG} \boxed{1} \end{bmatrix} \end{bmatrix} \end{bmatrix} \end{bmatrix}
\end{bmatrix}
$$

FIGURE 44 The *active* category

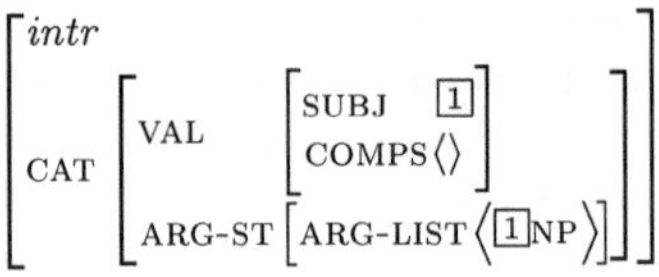

$$
\begin{bmatrix}
intr \\
\text{CAT} \begin{bmatrix} \text{VAL} \begin{bmatrix} \text{SUBJ} \quad \boxed{1} \\ \text{COMPS} \langle \rangle \end{bmatrix} \\ \text{ARG-ST} \begin{bmatrix} \text{ARG-LIST} \langle \boxed{1} \text{NP} \rangle \end{bmatrix} \end{bmatrix}
\end{bmatrix}
$$

FIGURE 45 The *intransitive* category

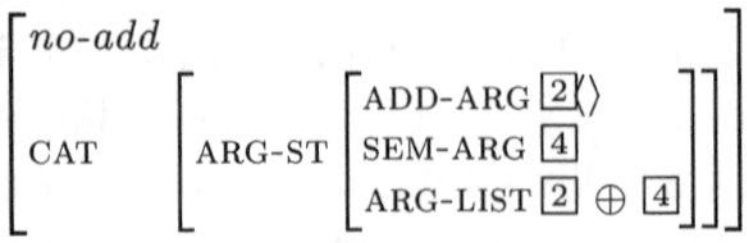

$$
\begin{bmatrix}
no\text{-}add \\
\text{CAT} \begin{bmatrix} \text{ARG-ST} \begin{bmatrix} \text{ADD-ARG} \boxed{2} \langle \rangle \\ \text{SEM-ARG} \boxed{4} \\ \text{ARG-LIST} \boxed{2} \oplus \boxed{4} \end{bmatrix} \end{bmatrix}
\end{bmatrix}
$$

FIGURE 46 The *no additional argument* category

two subcategorized arguments on the SEM-ARG list (see the tags [1] and [2]).[8] Active verbs (members of the *active* category) do not suppress elements from the list of subcategorized semantic arguments of the stem on which they are based. In the simplified lexicon we presently discuss, this means that the semantic arguments of active forms of 'vendre' are identical to those of their stem (see tag [1] in figure 44). Verbs that are both based on the stem *vendre* and members of the *active* category therefore have (at least) two members on their SEM-ARG list. And since a lexeme's ARG-LIST contains its semantic arguments, the ARG-LIST of *vendre* ∧ *active* must contain at least two members. Now, the type *intr* requires a word's ARG-LIST to contain only one member: intransitive verbs subcategorize for only one argument. Intersecting this category with the *vendre* ∧ *active* type thus results in a contradiction: the former subcategorizes for only one phrase, the latter at least two! No form of 'vendre' can satisfy the constraints imposed by all three categories. Their intersection is empty (technically, the unification of the three types is the fail type).

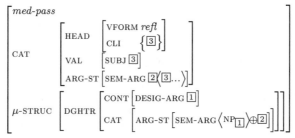

FIGURE 47   The *medio-passive* type

$$
\begin{bmatrix}
\textit{trans} \\
\text{CAT}
\begin{bmatrix}
\text{VAL}
\begin{bmatrix}
\text{SUBJ} \; \langle [1] \rangle \\
\text{COMPS} \; \langle [2] \rangle
\end{bmatrix} \\
\text{ARG-ST} \; \big[\text{ARG-LIST} \; \langle [1]\text{NP}, [2]\text{NP} \rangle \big]
\end{bmatrix}
\end{bmatrix}
$$

FIGURE 48   The *transitive* category

---

[8] For clarity, I have built in the minimal entry for 'vendre' the identity between its designated argument and its actor role. In a truly minimal entry for 'vendre', such information would be removed, since it results from its combination with the *agnt-vb* category defined in figure 29.

Similarly, attempts to combine *vendre* ∧ *med-pass* ∧ *no-add* ∧ *trans* fail to lead to an informationally consistent category. The *med-pass* type is represented in figure 47. It describes words whose lists of semantic arguments (recorded on the outermost SEM-ARG list in the figure) contain one less element than their stems' (recorded on the SEM-ARG list of their μ-STRUC|DGHTR).[9] Since the stem 'vendre' in figure 43 has two such elements, *vendre* ∧ *med-pass* only has one. The *no-add* category for its part describes words which only subcategorize for their semantic arguments— that is, have an empty list of ADD-ARG and therefore identical SEM-ARG and ARG-LIST lists. Intersecting it with the *vendre* ∧ *med-pass* category results in a verb which subcategorizes for only one argument. The resulting information contradicts what the *trans* category represented in figure 48 stipulates, namely that transitive verbs subcategorize for *two* NPs. Again, the conjunction is inconsistent. In fact, as the reader can check, only three complex categories are informationally coherent L-categories for the AND/OR net of figure 42. They are listed in (17).

(17) $\mathcal{M}$ = {*vend* ∧ *trans* ∧ *no-add* ∧ *active*,
        vend ∧ *intr* ∧ *no-add* ∧ *med-pass*,
        vend ∧ *trans* ∧ *extr-ind* ∧ *med-pass*}

Having illustrated the mechanics of category intersection for the AND/OR net of figure 42, let's now look at the complex category which trapped the lexical rule approach— namely, the variant of *vendre* which is both medio-passive and has its (indefinite) subject extraposed. It is illustrated in sentence (18) repeated from chapter 2. This use of 'vendre' instantiates the category *vendre* ∧ *trans* ∧ *med-pass* ∧ *extr-ind*. This last class is diagrammed in figure 49: its list of subcategorized arguments (members of the ARG-LIST) contains not only the lexeme's semantic arguments, but also an additional expletive 'il' subject NP.

(18) Il se   vend   deux cent   livres par an   à   Paris.
      It 3.REFL sell-PR two hundred books by   year to Paris
      'Two hundred books are sold each year in Paris.'

Since type conjunction is commutative and associative, intersecting categories in any order does not alter the properties of the final result. Varying the order of combination cannot lead to two different information structures. Furthermore, the single resulting category— *vend* ∧ *trans* ∧ *med-pass* ∧ *extr-ind*— displays the appropriate agreement between the "reflexive clitic" and the subject. The *med-pass* category

---

[9]The description of French medio-passive reflexives in figure 47 differs slightly from that presented in the previous chapter. All differences are irrelevant to the issue at hand.

$$\begin{bmatrix} extr\text{-}ind \\ \text{CAT} \begin{bmatrix} \text{ARG-ST} \begin{bmatrix} \text{ADD-ARG} \left\langle \boxed{1}\ \text{NP}_{il} \right\rangle \\ \text{SEM-ARG}\ \boxed{2} \\ \text{ARG-LIST}\ \boxed{1} \oplus \boxed{2} \end{bmatrix} \end{bmatrix} \end{bmatrix}$$

FIGURE 49 The *extraposition-of-indefinites* category

constrains "reflexive clitics" (recorded in the CLI set) to have identical syntactic and semantic information to that of the subject for which the verb subcategorizes (see the tag $\boxed{3}$ in figure 47). Whether the lexeme also belongs to the *extr-ind* class or not is orthogonal to the satisfaction of this constraint. If the word is a member of the *extr-ind* class, an expletive is added at the beginning of the ARG-LIST and it is this added expletive which will serve as the verb's subject; if not, the logical object is the initial member of the ARG-LIST and will serve as the subject of the *med-pass* form. In both cases, the initial element of the ARG-LIST becomes the surface subject through its token-identity with the SUBJ list member (see the definitions of the *intr* and *trans* categories in figures 45 and 48 respectively). Either way, the constraint on *med-pass* is satisfied: the "reflexive clitic" agrees with the word's subject, since it agrees with the first element on the ARG-LIST.[10] Note that the order-independence of the combination of lexeme categories is not tied to the particulars of my analysis. What allows the *med-pass* construction to "wait" until the surface subject requirement is assigned is the fact that the agreement constraint is not part of a rule which maps fully specified entries to fully specified entries. Because both inputs and outputs of a lexical rule are fully type-specified, the token-identity between the first element of the ARG-LIST and the (reflexive) member of the clitic set is locked in as soon as the passive-reflexive lexical rule applies. When its output serves as input to the inversion of indefinites rule, the correspondence between the reflexive clitic and the first ARG-LIST element is preserved, even though this element is "demoted" to second position on the ARG-LIST, thus leading to the offending agreement pattern. By contrast, intersecting the *med-pass* category with the underspecified *vendre* category does not result in a fully type-specified category; it merely imposes a constraint on the ultimate L-category of a particular use of *vendre*: its subject must agree with a "reflexive clitic". The determination of the verb's ac-

---

[10]I assume that the entire syntactic and semantic information of the "clitic" is identified with that of the subject to parallel Godard and Sag 1995's analysis discussed in chapter 2. But if my arguments that "reflexive clitics" are agreement markers are correct, only the relevant semantic indices should be identified. The distinction is inconsequential to the point I make in this section.

tual subject falls onto other lexeme categories. The necessary "waiting" follows from the underspecification of the intersected categories, *vendre* and *med-pass*, and the commutativity and associativity of category intersection. We are thus lead to a model of categorial productivity which does not run the risk of allowing ordering paradoxes back in. The major stumbling block of Hierarchical Lexicons discussed in the previous chapter is removed.

The benefits of substituting category intersection for rule application do not stop at the conceptual simplicity of the ensuing architecture or its ordering-paradox-free behavior. It also provides an economical method for encoding exceptions and partial productivity, as the next section demonstrates.

3.4.2 Intensionally *vs.* extensionally defined word classes: the problem of exceptions

A major characteristic of lexical processes is their propensity for exceptions. In fact, their presence is often a test of lexicality (see Wasow 1977). I mentioned the cases of 'rumored' and 'have' in section 2.2.2. But the situation is more general than these examples suggest: most lexical processes have positive exceptions. I mention three French constructions here. All can productively apply to an open-ended class of verbs, but must also apply to a closed list of other verbs.

Inchoative-reflexive construction

(19) La   police a   dispersé   la   foule.
      The   police have.PR   scatter.PPT the   crowd
      'The police scattered the crowd.'

(20) La   foule   s'   est   dispersée.
      The   crowd   3.REFL   be-PR   disperse-PPT
      'The crowd scattered.'

(21) *Jacques a   encanaillé   Eric.
      Jacques have.PR   make.vulgar.PPT Eric
      'Jacques made Eric become vulgar.' (intended meaning)

(22) Eric s'   est   encanaillé.
      Eric 3.REFL   be.PR   make.vulgar
      'Eric became vulgar.'

The French inchoative reflexive valence alternation illustrated in (19)-(20) applies productively to verbs which denote causal events that result in a final state. But it also *must* exceptionally apply to verbs such as 's'encanailler' (see (22)). 'S'encanailler' includes the causative prefix 'en-' and we predict the existence of a causative variant 'encanailler' along with the inchoative 's'encanailler'. In fact, 's'encanailler' cannot be used causatively, as the ungrammaticality of (21) demonstrates.

Similarly, the dative predication construction illustrated in (24) (see Ruwet 1982, Koenig 1993, and Koenig 1995) applies productively to verbs of thinking and saying. But it also *must* exceptionally apply to a small class of verbs such as 'prêter' which, metaphorically means '(people) say', as the contrast between (25) and (26) shows.

Dative predication construction

(23) Je croyais qu' il avait
     I believe-PST that he have-PST

     de la classe.
     of the class
     'I thought he had some class.'

(24) Je lui croyais de la classe.
     I to.he/she believe-PST of the class
     'I thought he/she had some class.'

(25) *On prête qu' il a de bons sentiments.
     People say.PR that he have.PR INDEF good feelings
     'People say that he has finer feelings.'

(26) On lui prête de bons sentiments.
     People to.he/she say.PR INDEF good feelings
     'People say that he/she has finer feelings.'

Finally, the extraposition construction applies productively to a few classes of adjectives and verbs, but again *must* apply to the verb 'falloir', as shown in (29)-(30). All three valence alternations are productive and define an open-ended intensionally defined class (illustrated in examples (19)-(20), (23)-(24), and (27)-(28)), but must also apply to a closed, extensionally defined verb class (illustrated in examples (21)-(22), (25)-(26), and (29)-(30)).

Extraposition construction

(27) Qu' il soit arrivé à l' heure
     that he be-SUBJ arrive-PPT to the hour

     est à peine croyable.
     be-PR to effort believable
     'That he arrived in time is hard to believe.'

(28) Il est à peine croyable qu' il
     It be-PR to effort believable that he

soit   arrivé   à   l'   heure.
be-SUBJ arrive.PPT to the hour
'It is hard to believe that he arrived in time.'

(29) *Qu' il   arrive   à   l'   heure faut.
That he arrive.PR to the hour must.PR
'That he arrives in time must.' (intended reading)

(30) Il faut   qu' il   arrive   à   l'   heure.
It must.PR that he arrive.PR to the hour
'It must (be the case) that he arrives in time.'

For the alternations illustrated in (19)-(30) we need to define an open-ended subcategory as well as a list of exceptions. The open-ended subcategory accounts for the process' productivity: any lexeme which satisfies its intensional characterization can combine with it. The subcategory whose characterization includes a list of members accounts for the process' positive exceptions. These lexemes are registered in the mental lexicon as members of the category and no on-line type construction can violate this constraint: their full type specification must always include the category to which the mental lexicon says they belong.

Alongside productive processes to which we must also register positive exceptions, there exist many lexical regularities which are not productive. One such process is the English *ity* noun class. Although all words conforming to the pattern share a set of properties, we cannot extend it to new adjectives. For these sheer regularities, the *entire* category must be both intensionally-defined to capture its members' common properties and extensionally-defined by enumerating the set of lexemes to which it applies. Since members of the category are explicitly listed, the category is closed: no new member can be added through OLTC.

Both unproductive processes and exceptions to productive processes receive a direct representation in an on-line typing system, either through the pre-typing of the relevant lexemes to the word classes of which they are members or through the pre-specification of some of the entry's attributes. Pre-typing of lexemes to word classes is illustrated in figure 50, where part of a (simplified) English word hierarchy is represented (the same caveats apply as for all AND/OR nets presented in this chapter).

The category *love* exemplifies a word to which the transitive/passive alternation applies regularly. Since 'love' can be either transitive or intransitive, *love* is not pretyped to either valence template. It is free to combine with each category. The category *rumored* represents a so-called positive exception. It is pre-typed to the passive template. It therefore obligatorily inherits the properties associated with passives and cannot combine with the transitive template since the two categories are

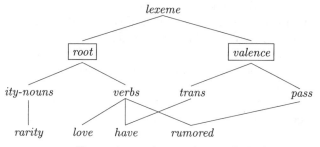

FIGURE 50 Pre-typing and exceptions to lexical processes

disjoint subcategories of the valence dimension. The lexeme *have* is an example of so-called negative exception and is pre-typed to the transitive template. It too obligatorily inherits the properties of the template to which it is pre-typed. Note that in an on-line typing system, so-called negative and positive exceptions receive the same analysis: pretyping of the lexeme to the relevant lexeme or word class. Finally, the noun *rarity* and other *ity* nouns (but see section 5.3 for more details) are listed as members of the *ity-nouns* category to reflect its unproductive character. Only stored instances are members of the category; speakers cannot freely create new instances of the category at will.

The difference between non-alternating words or unproductive and productive processes boils down to the difference between extensional and intensional definitions of categories, as already suggested in another context by Jurafsky 1991. In the case of productive processes, lexeme classes are defined by the properties their members share. In the case of unproductive processes, lexeme classes are defined by listing their members as well as their shared properties.[11]

Although I suggested that the exceptionality of both 'rumored' and 'have' arises from the fact that each is pretyped to the relevant valence category, we can model the difference between exceptional and regular lexemes in another way. Exceptionality can also result from the pre-specification of certain of the entry's properties, in case an attribute-value pair that is uniquely associated with a lexeme class can be independently motivated. Take the categories *rumored* and *have* again and let's assume there is independent motivation to include in the list of

---

[11] In the case of exceptions to otherwise productive processes, such as English 'have', there are in fact two subclasses. One subclass, the general transitive class is defined exclusively intensionally through the properties of its superclass, while the other, which consist of 'have' and other so-called negative exceptions, is defined via the properties of its superclass as well as a list of its members.

properties of English verbs a [VOICE *act/pass*] attribute such that the transitive template includes a [VOICE *act*] specification and the passive template a [VOICE *pass*] one. We can now account for the exceptionality of 'rumored' and 'have' by including [VOICE *pass*] and [VOICE *act*] in the definition of their respective minimal entries. The effect of prespecifying an entry's properties is equivalent to pre-typing it to categories bearing those properties. Pre-typing an entry to a category restricts its combinatorial potential through the second clause of (11): no object can belong to two classes explicitly declared to be disjoint. Pre-specification of properties restricts the combinatorial potential of exceptional entries through the last clause of (11): no object can belong to categories that have properties which contradict its own. If the entry for 'rumored' contains the feature pre-specification [VOICE *pass*], any of its fully type-specified variants must bear this property and be a member of the *pass* category, since its information-structure conflicts with that of the *trans* category. The same reasoning applies to 'have' and the *trans* class. We thus have two ways to model exceptions in an On-Line Type Construction system; each corresponds to one of the two ways of referring to a class of entities— by naming a category or by implicitly referring to an unnamed class of objects through a distinguishing property. Which solution is better depends on the specifics of the cases involved.

3.4.3 AND/OR nets and conjunctive *vs.* disjunctive application of rules

Section 2.2.2 argued that a lexical rule approach to morphological relations needs the extra mechanism of rule chains to model inflectional systems in which fully inflected words are derived via the concatenation of several affixes. I suggested at that time that the TUHL architecture directly models this class of phenomena through the logic of AND/OR nets. It is time to make good on this promissory note. Let's take our Latin example again, the form 'amavissem' ('[I wish] I had loved (somebody)'). I treat Latin morphology in more detail in chapter 4. I concentrate here on the benefits of OLTC and simplify the treatment by assuming that no constituent structure schemata are involved in inflectional morphology. The relevant portions of the Latin *lexeme* hierarchy are represented in figure 51.[12]

The details of the representation of the individual types are not important. Suffice it to say that the lexeme type *amare* specifies that the (root)phonology is /ama/, and each affix-type construction speci-

---

[12] The same logic of AND/OR nets I illustrate in this section is also all that is needed to model suppletive stem selection. To avoid unnecessary duplication, I delay discussion of suppletive stem selection until chapter 5.

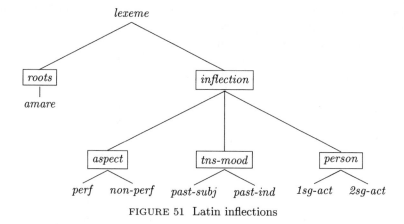

FIGURE 51 Latin inflections

fies both a set of morphosyntactic features and the phonology of the relevant affix. The *past-subj* category, for example, specifies the set of morphosyntactic features [[MOOD *subj*] [TNS *pst*]] and the phonology of the affix, i.e. /is/. The abstract type for words, which is not represented in the figure, also specifies that the phonological representation of words is the concatenation of the phonology of roots, and aspect, tense/mood, and agreement/voice affixes in that order.

All forms of the stored entry *amare* are constructed by choosing one type for each of the various inflectional templates' dimensions. In the case of our input form 'amavissem', the fully inflected form corresponds to the complex type *amare ∧ perf ∧ past-subj ∧ 1sg-act*. What required the introduction of otherwise unmotivated lexical rule chains in the rule-based approach discussed in the previous chapter follows here from the logic of ordinary AND/OR nets and the definition of OLTC. The fact that the complex category *amare ∧ perf ∧ past-subj ∧ 1sg-act* is a possible inflected verb, but *amare ∧ perf* ('*amav') is not can be deduced from the organization of lexical categories. Figure 51 stipulates that all Latin words are constructed by picking out one member of three sets of inflectional categories. Consequently, *amare ∧ perf* violates the constraints on Latin L-categories encoded in the net. The requirement that each Latin word be the intersection of three inflectional categories is clearly language and morphology specific. But the OLTC mechanism through which fully inflected words are constructed is not. It is a general procedure for productively building (linguistic) categories. It is neither restricted to Latin nor to morphology. By relying on category combination to model productivity, we avoid postulating operations which have no application outside of morphology.

More generally, as readers may have noticed, the combination of AND/OR logic and OLTC produces the effects of conjunctive *vs.* disjunctive morphophonological rule application in Anderson 1992's framework. AND branches in a portion of the graph correspond to conjunctive rule blocks, OR branches to disjunctive rule blocks. By contradistinction to Anderson's rule blocks approach, though, the AND/OR logic is not specific to morphological structure. It is amply motivated in other areas of grammars, particularly syntax and semantics (see Pollard and Sag 1994, Davis 1996, and others). It is used whenever a set of objects is classified along multiple dimensions. Moreover, it is purely declarative and does not require stipulated orderings of rule application for which, *pace* Anderson, there seems to be very little theory-independent evidence and which is theoretically dubious, as Pullum and Zwicky 1991 convincingly argue.

3.5 Summary

This chapter outlined a model of lexical knowledge which, unlike previous models, captures all of its productive, partially productive, and unproductive characteristics. This model is based on two ideas:

- The set of possible kinds of lexemes— a language's L-categories— is not listed in the lexicon, but constructed while processing words.
- Lexeme categories have internal structure akin to phrases.

This chapter concentrated on the first idea, what I call categorial productivity. Categorial productivity only requires minimal changes to the procedure for conjunctive type construction we discussed in chapter 2. By letting L-categories be determined only at parse-time— that is by shifting the construction of complex lexeme categories to the processing component— only category intersection is needed to account for speakers' ability to build new word forms. That they can interpret or produce word categories they have not previously heard follows from the fact that not all L-categories are listed within mental lexicons; some are created on the fly. Many more variants of words can be produced and interpreted than were encountered because underspecified lexemes and constraints on L-categories are included in mental lexicons, not their complete list.

Several well-known properties of lexical processes fall out of an architecture which lets productivity result from category intersection. I discussed exceptions to productive processes and unproductive lexical generalizations, as well as the organization of morphological processes in what Anderson 1992 calls disjunctively *vs.* conjunctively ordered rule blocks. Stem selection is tackled in chapter 5. But to explain stem selection, I must first introduce in more detail the second component of lexical productivity, structural productivity.

4

A typed constituent structure-based morphology

On-Line Type Construction contributes an important tool for modeling lexical productivity. We can let entries be type-underspecified in the mental lexicon and acquire their full information structure on an as-needed basis when processing and interpreting utterances. OLTC thus helps implement the straightforward idea mentioned in the introduction: the complexity and variants of lexical entries results from intersecting the information contained in abstract "blue-print" lexemes with the information contained in various word classes. The resulting architecture meets several of the demands on adequate theories of the lexicon. It possesses all the Hierarchical Lexicon's advantages when dealing with medium-size generalizations while providing a model of productivity that follows directly from the boolean structure of AND/OR nets. It furthermore eschews the shortcomings of lexical rule-based models. But OLTC does not constitute the full story. Because category intersection is an additive process, it cannot account for instances in which the information associated with the input of a putative rule is incompatible with that of the output, as for the verb 'play' and the noun 'player'. In fact, when discussing demotion processes in the previous chapter (passives or medio-passive reflexives), I already introduced more structure into lexical entries. For such cases, what is needed to maintain the hypothesis that all lexical processes are simply the result of category intersection is the presence of an internal structure in (a subset of) 'multimorphemic' words. The present chapter is devoted to this second component of lexical productivity.

My claim is that structural productivity is best modeled via a Typed and Construction-based Constituent structure Morphology (or TCCM).

Some of the material in this chapter was presented in Koenig et al. 1996.

By a constituent structure morphology I simply mean a representation of the structure of words through a hierarchical grouping of their subparts, that is an analysis of words that assigns an internal structure to 'played' as in (1):

(1)   [[play] ed]

The idea of using a constituent structure skeleton to model the internal structure of words dates back to the structuralists and is best represented among modern generative studies by the work of Lieber 1980, Selkirk 1982, Di Sciullo and Williams 1987, and Lieber 1992. But the specific morphological constituent structure which I advocate differs from the one found in these works. Firstly, it does not obey the X̄-theoretic format these scholars assume. In fact it is rather degenerate: the typical local tree configuration consists of a mother and a single daughter. Thus, the affix '-ed' in (1) is not a daughter, it is simply added to the phonology of the morphological mother, as indicated informally by the absence of brackets around it. The only real daughter is the root *play*. Secondly, the approach to word-internal structure I propose is construction-based rather than morpheme-based (see section 4.1 for more details on the difference). I still sometimes refer to my approach as context-free because of its similarities to well-known "syntactic" approaches to morphology. But the reader should keep in mind that when I use this traditional terminology, I simply mean that morphological structure is represented by a mechanism similar to that used for phrasal constituent structure. I do not presume a particular format for the context-free schemata involved.

In adapting a constituent structure skeleton to the representation of words in a Hierarchical Lexicon, I make use of ideas familiar from work in Lexical Phonology (see Kiparsky 1982a, Kiparsky 1982b, Kiparsky 1985, Mohanan 1986, and others). Part of the purpose of this chapter is to show how these ideas can be adapted to unification-based and type-based grammars, in particular to the Type Underpecified lexical architecture outlined in this book. But the emphasis of this chapter and the next is also on the particular contributions a TCCM approach can make to the study of morphological structures. To understand the nature of these contributions, I must first briefly summarize prior theories of morphological processes.

Traditional controversies on the appropriate representation of morphological processes in Generative Grammar typically assume the existence of only two basic methods of describing the structure of words, morpheme-based or realizational/word-based. The former is based on two assumptions:

- Words have an internal hierarchical structure similar to that found in syntactic phrases.
- Affixes are terminals of morphological trees.

Such an approach is epitomized by the title of Selkirk 1982's book *The Syntax of Words*. Words are built by context-free rules obeying an x̄ format, both bases and affixes are terminals, and the latter subcategorize for the former very much in the same way verbs subcategorize for their complements.

By contrast, realizational/word-based approaches to morphology (see Aronoff 1976, Zwicky 1991, or Anderson 1992 among others) are based on the assumption that words do not (typically) have internal structure, but are formed through the use of a special set of (Word Formation) rules. Whereas a morpheme-based approach assumes words are built through the same kind of mechanisms as phrases, a realizational approach postulates a special class of rules for morphological processes and challenges the claim that words have phrase-like internal structure. What the debate between morpheme-based and realizational approaches typically ignores is that many more possibilities are available. In particular, advocating a constituent structure-based morphology does not require adopting a morpheme-based theory. Indeed, the class of constituent structure-based morphologies can be divided in at least three groups as shown in figure 52. Furthermore, each can make use of types as I defined them in chapter 2.

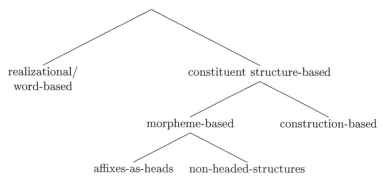

FIGURE 52 A classification of morphological theories

Only one of these six possible constituent structure-based morphologies corresponds to the currently prevailing view— an untyped, x̄-theoretic morphology in which affixes are head. Constituent structure-based morphologies need not assume that affixes are terminals of local morphological trees. Furthermore, if we assume they are, they need not be the head of the tree; it could be that either the base is or that morphological trees are unheaded. This limitation in what scholars consider possible constituent structure morphologies has had the unfortunate consequence that it is often presumed that arguments against a (particular kind of) morpheme-based approach apply to all versions of the hypothesis that words have internal structure. As we will see, this is not the case: a TCCM dodges the shortcomings of standard morpheme-based approaches to word structure and combines the positive aspects of both context-free and realizational/word-based morphologies. More specifically, I argue that it has three advantages to recommend itself.

- It avoids the drawbacks of morpheme-based approaches.
- It can restrict the application of general principles to the appropriate class of constructions.
- Most importantly, it uses a single mechanism to describe morphological operations which require several mechanisms in other theories. These include: subregularities and irregular inflections; stem selection and morpholexical rules (in the sense of Lieber 1980); cyclic *vs.* non-cyclic rule application; bound-roots; portemanteaux; and internal realization of inflection.

4.1 A typed constituent-structure morphology

4.1.1 Why we need a constituent structure

Let me first go back to an issue mentioned in the previous chapter and demonstrate that indeed type underspecification is not enough to model all morphological relations. I draw my arguments mainly from Krieger and Nerbonne 1993 who make a similar point. The need for a context-free morphology is seen most clearly in the case of category-changing affixation, as in the English triplet 'regress/regressive/regressiveness'.[1] Although related, the three lexemes belong to different categories: 'regress' is a verb, 'regressive' is an adjective, 'regressiveness' is a noun. In a typed system, this means we might classify (to simplify) 'regress' as a member of the *verb-class* category and let it inherit whatever properties are true of verbs. Similarly, 'regressive' and 'regressiveness' might be stipulated to be of category *adjective-class* and

---

[1] Arguments given in this section only show that within an unadorned TFS system, word-internal constituent structure is needed. We could of course add some other mechanism to Typed Feature Structures to achieve the same effect. For example, we could introduce ordered rules *à la* Anderson 1992. But all other mechanisms of which I am aware would require adding to the TFS theoretical apparatus. See section 5.5.2 for a discussion of realizational/word-based morphology.

noun-class respectively and inherit whatever properties are associated with adjectives and nouns. Verbs, adjectives, and nouns bear incompatible information. Nouns have case (that is, the attribute CASE is appropriate for nouns) whereas verbs do not. Reciprocally, verbs are specified for a verb form category (finite or infinitive, and so forth), that is, the attribute VFORM is appropriate for verbs. Crucially, if there is no internal structure to a word such as 'regressiveness', we cannot represent its relationship to both 'regress' and 'regressive' without appealing to lexical rules. Consider the simplified lexeme hierarchies in figures 53 and 54.

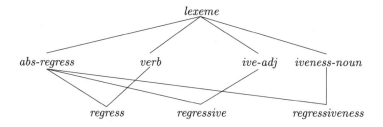

FIGURE 53 Representing shared information among lexemes I

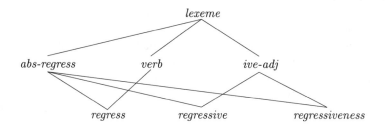

FIGURE 54 Representing shared information among lexemes II

The first figure captures the commonalities of 'regress', 'regressive', and 'regressiveness' through their inheritance of the information-structure of an abstract category *abs-regress*. But it does not represent the fact that 'regressive' and 'regressiveness' are directly related to each other independently of their common relation to 'regress'. The second figure encodes this relation: both lexemes inherit from a common *ive-adj* category. Unfortunately, this intuitively more satisfactory model is informationally incoherent. The figure is saying that *regressiveness* is an adjective (since it belongs to the class of *ive-adj*) when it must also be a noun (since it can pluralize, etc.). We end up ascribing inconsistent information to 'regressiveness'. As readers can easily convince themselves, no other reorganization of the hierarchy can simultaneously account for the perceived relations between the three words and be informationally consistent. A constituent structure approach to morphology avoids the problem by providing us with multiple levels of information structure, one for each node in a tree. By analyzing the structure of 'regressiveness' as in (2) we can state that the constituent in the innermost bracket is of type *verb-class*, the intermediate structure of type *adjective-class*, and the entire structure is of type *noun-class*. We can thus relate 'regressiveness' to both 'regress' and 'regressive' without fearing inconsistencies. The verbal root unifies with the daughter of the most deeply embedded local morphological tree for 'regressive'. The derived adjectival stem in turn unifies with the daughter of the least embedded local tree, while its mother node is nominal. No inconsistency arises. Each lexeme category characterizes different (sub)constituents of 'regressiveness'.

(2)   [[regress] ive] ness]

An obvious alternative to the introduction of a constituent structure skeleton is lexical rules that map a verb root onto an adjective stem, and an adjective stem onto a noun stem, a solution I rejected in chapter 2. In a typed feature structure system which does not make use of lexical rules, assuming a constituent structure skeleton to words like 'regressiveness' is a perspicuous way of insuring a consistent type for complex words.

Constituent structure is also needed to model the recursive application of morphological processes. Krieger and Nerbonne give the example of 'vor-' prefixation in German and the well-known 'anti-' prefixation in English. In both cases, we can use the prefix more than once with different results: an 'anticatholic' has different political convictions than an 'antianticatholic'. To account for the difference in meaning between the two words, we need to represent the presence of two 'anti-' prefixes in 'antianticatholic'— be it through the recursive application of Word Formation Rules or through the presence of an intermediate constituent structure corresponding to 'anticatholic'. If both words simply inherit from an *anti-N* type, we cannot represent the presence of two 'anti-' prefixes in one case; the difference in meaning between words that contain one and words that contain two occurrences of the prefix is lost.

Both of the arguments I just gave only apply to derivational morphology. Inflectional processes by definition do not change the category of words, nor do they typically change their meaning. The question is whether we should adopt the same constituent structure approach to inflectional morphology. Barring evidence to the contrary, both types of morphology should receive a similar treatment on Occamian grounds. Some independent evidence for this unified approach to morphological processes is adduced by Inkelas and Orgun (In press) in their work on Turkish morphology. They show how the difference between cyclic *vs.* non-cyclic phonology follows naturally from the hierarchical constituency of words. Now, the set of Turkish affixes on which their account is based involves both inflectional and derivational affixes. An account of cyclic *vs.* non-cyclic effects in Turkish morphology thus seems to require a parallel treatment of derivational and inflectional morphology. In what follows, I assume that both inflectional and derivational morphology involve word-internal constituent-structure even in languages such as English where inflectional morphology can be described without constituent structure skeletons by simply using two additional attributes representing the phonology of stems and suffixes respectively, as proposed in Krieger and Nerbonne 1993.

4.1.2   The lexeme hierarchy

Morphological constituent structure schemata in a TUHL. The previous section argued that in a lexical rule-less theory we need to include in our inventory of linguistic objects morphological as well as phrasal constituent structure constructions. In this section, I give an overview of the formal details of the various morphological constituent structure categories I hypothesize in the the rest of this book. But before going into the details of the relevant categories, let me expand on the difference between morpheme and construction-based approaches to morphological constituent structure. The distinction basically amounts to whether or not affixes are independent terminals of local morphological trees. It is illustrated in a simplified manner in figure 55.

The morphological tree on the left illustrates a traditional morpheme-based morphology. Both /pleɪ/ and /r/ are terminals of the tree and only terminals have a phonological representation. All non-terminal nodes carry syntactic (and optionally semantic) information, but no phonology (in the figure I have only represented minimal syntactic CAT(EGORY) information, for simplicity). In the tree on the right illustrative of a construction-based morphology, no terminal node exists for the affix. Moreover, all nodes in the tree, including non-terminal nodes, carry phonological information. The presence of phonological information on non-terminals in the right but not the left tree is not accidental. If

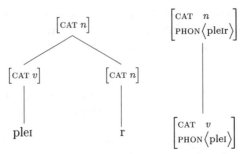

FIGURE 55 Morpheme- *vs.* Construction-based approaches

phonological information is not present on non-terminal nodes, a constituent structure-based morphology requires a traditional morpheme-based approach, simply to keep track of the phonological material contributed by each morphological local tree. If, on the other hand, phonological information is allowed on non-terminals, there is no need for terminals to record this information. As we will see throughout this chapter, an important consequence follows from not requiring affixal material to constitute a separate node: morphological constituent structure can be (partially) dissociated from morphophonological effects; word-internal structure can exist without phonological material being added to the base. Such a dissociation proves critical to answering realizational or word-based morphologists' concerns with word-internal constituent structure.

A representation of the general organization of the AND/OR net which underlies the hierarchy of signs I assume throughout the rest of this book is shown in figure 56.

Vertical dots connecting two types x and y indicate that x is not an immediate subcategory of y as between *cat* and *root* or *past* and *simple-word* for example. According to this network of categories, lexemes are classified along both a morphosyntactic and a morphophonological dimension (under *morph-syn* and *morph-phon* respectively in the diagram). I discuss each in turn in the next two subsections.

The morphosyntactic side of morphological constructions. The fundamental category of signs used to model the morphosyntactic properties of morphological processes is the *complex-lexeme* category, represented in the AVM in figure 57.

What characterizes complex lexemes is the presence of an internal constituent-structure which minimally consists of a mother and a daughter node. This lexeme-internal structure is represented in the diagram through the value of the μ-STRUC attribute. Such a representation of

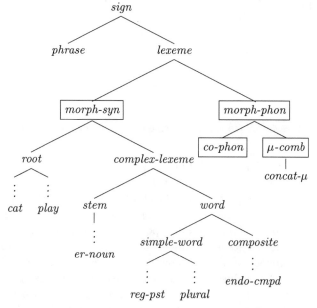

FIGURE 56 A hierarchy of signs (revised version)

FIGURE 57 The *complex-lexeme* category

morphological constituency follows HPSG's practice of encoding phrasal constituency through attributes. The value of the DAUGHTERS attributes encodes phrasal constituency in HPSG I and II (see the appendix A). The value of the proposed new μ-STRUC attribute encodes morphological constituency. The DGHTR attribute, in turn, represents the (morphological) daughter. Readers who are not familiar with this way of representing constituency can think of the definition of the category *complex-lexeme* in figure 57 as the featural equivalent of the more traditional tree-based representation in figure 58.

FIGURE 58   A tree-based representation of the *complex-lexeme* category

The function of the subhierarchy of lexemes rooted at *complex-lexeme* is to classify morphological constituent structure constructions— that is, the abstract templates needed to build up words such as 'player' or 'cats' from roots and stems such as *play* or *cat*. Particular constructions, such as *er-noun* or *plural* are subtypes of categories in the hierarchy which classify surface strings. The surface string 'cats', for example, belongs to the category of *plural* nouns; it is a *plural* noun whose morphological daughter (the value of the μ-STRUC|DGHTR path) is the root category *cat*. How such a "combination" of *plural* and *cat* proceeds is illustrated informally through a dashed arrow in figure 59.[2] The information structure associated with the root category *cat* is intersected with that of the value of the μ-STRUC|DGHTR path. In other words, to form 'cats' speakers must choose the *plural* noun category and intersect the category of its morphological daughter with the root *cat* whose minimal representation only includes phonological, semantic, and nominal category information— the values of the PHON|FORM, CONT, and CAT|HEAD attributes respectively. More technically, "combining" the word class *plural* and the root *cat* means that the value of the μ-STRUC|DGHTR of the former is the unification of the types *lexeme* and *cat*. The result of this combination is represented in figure 60. Building up more complex words such as 'players' proceeds in a similar manner. (3) informally summarizes the steps involved in generating or parsing 'players', assuming a top-down parser.

---

[2]Figure 59 is simplified for expository purposes. More details will be presented shortly. Simply note that suffixal material is encoded as the value of the path PHON|AFF|SUFF.

$$
\begin{bmatrix}
cat \\
\text{PHON} \begin{bmatrix} \text{FORM} \langle \text{kæt} \rangle \end{bmatrix} \\
\text{CONT} \begin{bmatrix} \text{INDEX } \boxed{1} \\ \text{RESTR} \left\{ \begin{bmatrix} cat \\ \text{INST } \boxed{1} \end{bmatrix} \right\} \end{bmatrix} \\
\text{CAT} \begin{bmatrix} \text{HEAD } noun \end{bmatrix}
\end{bmatrix}
$$

$$
\begin{bmatrix}
plural \\
\text{PHON} \begin{bmatrix} \text{AFF} \begin{bmatrix} \text{SUFF} \langle \text{s} \rangle \end{bmatrix} \end{bmatrix} \\
\mu\text{-STRUC} \begin{bmatrix} \mu\text{-struc} \\ \text{DGHTR } lexeme \end{bmatrix}
\end{bmatrix}
$$

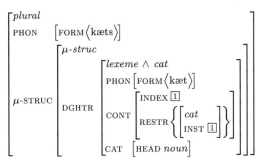

FIGURE 59 "Combining" *plural* and *cat*

$$
\begin{bmatrix}
plural \\
\text{PHON} \quad \begin{bmatrix} \text{FORM} \langle \text{kæts} \rangle \end{bmatrix} \\
\mu\text{-STRUC} \begin{bmatrix} \mu\text{-struc} \\ \text{DGHTR} \begin{bmatrix} lexeme \wedge cat \\ \text{PHON} \begin{bmatrix} \text{FORM} \langle \text{kæt} \rangle \end{bmatrix} \\ \text{CONT} \begin{bmatrix} \text{INDEX } \boxed{1} \\ \text{RESTR} \left\{ \begin{bmatrix} cat \\ \text{INST } \boxed{1} \end{bmatrix} \right\} \end{bmatrix} \\ \text{CAT} \begin{bmatrix} \text{HEAD } noun \end{bmatrix} \end{bmatrix}
\end{bmatrix}
\end{bmatrix}
$$

FIGURE 60 The result of "combining" *plural* and *cat*

(3)   1. Choose the *plural* noun category;
        2. Unify the value of its μ-STRUC|DGHTR attribute with the *er-noun* category;
        3. Unify the value of the latter's μ-STRUC|DGHTR attribute with the *play* root category.

This view of word internal structure amounts to treating plural words such as 'birds' as members of a category of lexemes which contain other lexemes as parts (in the case at hand, it contains the root category *bird*). Otherwise put, surface strings are members of categories such as *plural* or *past* which are (partly) characterized by their parts, themselves lexeme categories. To those readers who are puzzled by this approach to morphological constituent structure, note that it is quite natural under the hypothesis that lexical relations reduce to a boolean category network. If having a particular internal structure is just another kind of property on a par with phonological, syntactic, and semantic properties, categorizing lexemes in terms of their internal constituency is as natural as categorizing them on the basis of their semantics or part-of-speech.

(4) exemplifies the lexeme categories included in the hierarchy in figure 56. Subscripts name the category of the (sub)structure. The examples are simplified in many respects, in particular, as to the representation of affixes. Also included in (4) are examples of the category of *endocentric-compound* and *exocentric-compound* (*endo-cmpd* and *exo-cmpd* for short), two subtypes of *composite* lexemes discussed in section 5.4.

(4)   a. $[_{root}$ cat $]$
        b. $[_{root}$ play $]$
        c. $[_{stem}$ $[_{root}$ play$]$ er$]$
        d. $[_{simple\text{-}word}$ $[_{root}$ cat$]$ $]$
        e. $[_{simple\text{-}word}$ $[_{root}$ cat$]$ s $]$
        f. $[_{simple\text{-}word}$ $[_{root}$ play$]$ ed $]$
        g. $[_{simple\text{-}word}$ $[_{stem}$ $[_{root}$ play $]$ er $]$ s $]$
        h. $[_{word\text{-}particle}$ $[_{part}$ pre$]$ $[_{word}$ nuptial$]]$
        i. $[_{endo\text{-}cmpnd}$ $[_{root}$ mice$]$ $[_{simple\text{-}word}$ eater$]]$
        j. $[_{exo\text{-}cmpnd}$ $[_{word}$ porte$]$ $[_{simple\text{-}word}$couteaux$]]$

To the labeled bracketing representations in (4) corresponds the more accurate feature-based representations in figures 61 and 62 (for (4d) and (4f) respectively). As alluded to, the information structure associated with a mother node is represented in all the attributes rooted at the leftmost bracket; the information-structure associated with a daughter node is indicated by the values of the μ-STRUC|DGHTR path. The phonological suffixation induced by the relevant complex lexeme categories is recorded in the value of the path PHON|AFF|SUFF. Figure 61 thus says that the singular word 'cat' is derived from the root *cat* without the addition of any affixal material (see the *e-string* value of the suffix attribute).

$$
\begin{bmatrix}
\textit{sg-noun} \\
\text{PHON} \quad \begin{bmatrix} \text{AFF} \begin{bmatrix} \text{SUFF} \langle \textit{e-string} \rangle \end{bmatrix} \end{bmatrix} \\
\text{CAT} \quad \begin{bmatrix} \text{HEAD} \begin{bmatrix} \mu\text{-FEAT} \begin{bmatrix} \text{SGR} \mid \text{NUM } \textit{sg} \end{bmatrix} \end{bmatrix} \end{bmatrix} \\
\mu\text{-STRUC} \begin{bmatrix} \text{DGHTR } \textit{cat} \end{bmatrix}
\end{bmatrix}
$$

FIGURE 61   The internal constituency of the word 'cat'

$$
\begin{bmatrix}
\textit{past} \\
\text{PHON} \quad \begin{bmatrix} \text{AFF} \begin{bmatrix} \text{SUFF} \langle \text{d} \rangle \end{bmatrix} \end{bmatrix} \\
\text{CAT} \quad \begin{bmatrix} \text{HEAD} \begin{bmatrix} \text{VFORM } \textit{past} \end{bmatrix} \end{bmatrix} \\
\mu\text{-STRUC} \begin{bmatrix} \text{DGHTR } \textit{play} \end{bmatrix}
\end{bmatrix}
$$

FIGURE 62   The internal constituency of the word 'played'

The absence of suffix daughters in either figure 61 or 62 is a salient property of this representation of morphological structure. Affixes are treated as part of the phonology of the mother node. More precisely, they are phonological strings which serve as arguments of the phonological function mapping the phonology of the morphological daughter onto the phonology of the morphological mother (the list consisting of the empty-string in figure 61 and /d/ in figure 62). They merely mark morphological constructions and have no place in the lexeme network. In short, they are not signs or morphemes in the classical sense, only pieces of phonology introduced syncategorematically by the particular morphological construction on which they depend.[3] A consequence of this representation of affixes is that most derivational morphological constructions must *per force* be unheaded. Since the morphosyntactic category of the mother node of a derivational process is not identical

---

[3]This is true of most affixes. Some of the elements which are usually called affixes correspond to signs, though. "Affixes" such as 'pre-' or 'pro-', for example, present word-like characteristics. Bresnan and Mchombo 1995 note that such affixes coordinate ('pre- and post-WWII') and the lexeme to which they attach can be ellipsed ('I'm more interested in pre- than I am in post-World War II history', an example they attribute to Alsina). As for so-called bound roots such as the 'cran-' of 'cranberry', they are roots introduced by specific stem or word constructions, as discussed in section 5.3.

to that of its base and the base is typically the tree's unique daughter, the mother and (unique) daughter do not share syntactic category information. Hence morphological trees for derivational processes are not headed. As an example, consider the informal representation of the internal structure of the word 'player' in (5). The category of the whole complex lexeme is nominal, while that of its unique daughter is verbal. Clearly, this single daughter cannot be the head.

(5)   [N [V play] er]

The simplicity of the tree configuration in (5) embodies several hypotheses about the nature of morphology which are discussed in detail later on and are justified fully in section 5.5.2. I list them below for future reference.

- The constituent structure configurations relevant to morphology are not X̄-theoretic. Each local tree consists of a mother and (typically) a single daughter; it is (typically) not headed.

This hypothesis is indubitably true in the case of derivational morphology. The situation is more complex for inflectional morphology. It is tempting to assume they are universally headed, since morphosyntactic features are structure-shared between the daughter and mother nodes (see section 5.4). Turkish morphology, though, provides some evidence against the assumption that all inflectional constructions are headed. As mentioned above, it seems derivational and inflectional affixes can co-occur within a single local tree in Turkish. Since the former are not category preserving, the overall local tree cannot be, and we need to allow for the possibility that inflectional constructions are not associated with headed structures. I leave the resolution of this matter to further research and assume that inflectional constructions are headed in most languages, in particular English. (See section 5.4 for more details on morphological headedness and the Morphological Head-Feature Principle I take for granted in this book.)

- Affixes are not morphological daughters. They are only phonological objects and do not exist independently of the constituent structure construction itself.
- Affixes are never the heads of morphological constructions.

I now comment briefly on the lexeme subcategories included in the *morph-syn* dimension of figure 56, page 93. The most abstract lexical type in the hierarchy is the *lexeme* type. This type specifies properties common to all lexemes in a language. By lexeme I mean all linguistic signs smaller than or equal to a word: roots, stems, and words. There are two immediate subcategories of the type *lexeme* in the *morph-syn* dimension: the class of roots and the class of complex lexemes. Complex lexemes have internal constituent-structure, as shown in figure 57. Roots do not. They are minimal grammatical units and do not have internal constituency. They are our morphological atoms. Consequently, the attribute μ-STRUC which keeps a record of a lexeme's internal structure is only appropriate for members of the *complex-lexeme* category. Note that morphological daughters in the description of the *complex-lexeme* category represented in figure 57 are declared to be of type *lexeme*. Assigning the morphological daughter of complex lexemes to the *lexeme* category allows for recursivity in morphological constituent structure. A complex lexeme's daughter can itself be a complex lexeme, and so forth. Complex lexemes are divided into the classes of stems and words. Words are syntactic atoms selected by phrase structural schemata. Stems, on the other hand, are only defined negatively, as neither roots nor words. Given the absence of positive distinguishing traits, one might wonder whether positing a class of stem-forming constituent structure schemata is needed. It is.

To end our analysis of words into their component parts, we must set apart a class of lexemes which cannot be broken down further into simpler parts. This is the class of morphological atoms, the class of roots. We must also set apart a class of lexemes which are fit to enter into syntactic constructions, i.e. a class of syntactic atoms, to borrow a term from Di Sciullo and Williams 1987. Take again the Latin word 'amavissem' ('[I wish] I had loved'). We must distinguish between this word and an incompletely inflected lexeme such as 'amav-' or 'amavisse-'. Only fully inflected words can be daughters of phrasal structural schemata. The category *word* denotes these syntactic atoms.

For any language which contains more than two morphological levels (as in Turkish, according to Inkelas and Orgun 1995), there *must* be morphological objects which are neither morphological atoms— they have an internal morphological structure— nor syntactic atoms, they are not fully inflected.[4] Consider the Turkish word 'tebriklerimi' ('my congratulations') whose internal morphological structure is represented informally in (6) (from Inkelas and Orgun, op.cit.), where *root:1* stands for an object of type *root* and of level *1*)

(6) $[\ [[\text{tebrik}]_{root:1}\ \text{-ler}\ \text{-im}]_{stem:3}\ \text{- i}]_{word:4}$
      contratulation   PL   1SG.POSS   CASE

Both the plural and the possessive suffixes are level 3 affixes, that is, they are added to the morphology of the base at a point where level 3

---

[4]See the next section for a representation of levels within a TCCM. Whether these four levels are intrinsically or extrinsically ordered is irrelevant to the argument.

Turkish phonological constraints apply. The case affix applies at level 4, that is, it creates a word on which level 4 phonological constraints apply. The type of the innermost and outermost lexemes are known: they are of type *root* and *word*; they are our morphological and syntactic atoms respectively. The intermediate constituent cannot be either. It cannot be a root, since it is not morphologically atomic. It cannot be a word, since it cannot be inserted as is in the syntax ('*tebriklerim' is not a possible head noun). If we hypothesize, as this book does, that every linguistic object is assigned a type (belongs to a category), the inner constituent must be assigned to a category distinct from *root* or *word*. This is the category called *stem* in figure 56.

Finally, the category *word* is itself divided into simple words (corresponding to inflected words such as 'dog', 'dogs', 'played' ...) and composite words which comprise both words preceded by particles (such as 'withstand' in English) and compounds such as 'mountain-climber'. They both fall under the category of *composite* words (see section 5.4 for a discussion of composites).

The reader might legitimately ask at this point what is gained by organizing morphological processes and complex lexemes in a richly articulated hierarchy of categories rather than positing a handful of highly abstract constituent structure schemata, as is customary in x̄-theoretic approaches to morphology. Two classes of benefits accrue to this representation of the internal structure of words.

Firstly, a rich network of morphological categories affords us the benefits of the TUHL architecture discussed in chapter 3. It provides us with a flexible tool to capture common properties *and* differences among morphological processes. Like x̄-theoretic models, generalizations across morphological processes can be captured. Because all morphological constructions— individual roots as well as abstract morphological templates— belong to a single hierarchy, we can reuse shared properties in defining new morphological categories. The structural similarities between composite and simple words or between words and stems, for example, are abstracted into general categories. Each time a new subtype of word or morphological construction is isolated, we do not need to describe anew its entire structure. We only need specify the information which makes it different from other constructions, as when we distinguish between headed and non-headed morphological structures (see section 5.4). No generalization is lost by introducing different categories for particular affixation processes. What would be an abstract x̄ schema used to generate a complex word in a Selkirk or Lieber-like morphological analysis is now a very general category to which particular lexeme categories such as *plural* noun or *past* verb belong.

To illustrate, consider 'player' and played'. An X̄-theoretic approach to morphological processes would capture their parallel structure through their common use of a constituent structure rule or instantiation of universal principles, say:

(7) $X^n \longrightarrow \ldots Y^m + X^{af} \ldots$ $0 > n > m$

A TCCM approach captures their parallel structure through their membership in a common category. Two subcategories of complex lexemes are defined, the *plural* and *er-noun* categories. Each is a subclass of complex lexemes whose phonological form is built concatenatively. This shared information is represented informally in figure 63 (see next subsection for a more accurate description of the type *concat-μ*): both *plural* and *er-noun* are complex categories whose phonological form is the concatenation of their daughter's phonology with a suffix.

$$
\begin{bmatrix}
complex\text{-}lexeme \wedge concat\text{-}\mu \\
\text{PHON} \begin{bmatrix} \text{FORM} \boxed{1} \oplus \boxed{2} \\ \text{AFF} \begin{bmatrix} \text{SUFF} \boxed{2} \end{bmatrix} \end{bmatrix} \\
\mu\text{-STRUC} \begin{bmatrix} \text{DGHTR} \begin{bmatrix} \text{PHON} \boxed{1} \end{bmatrix} \end{bmatrix}
\end{bmatrix}
$$

FIGURE 63   The common information structure to *plural* and *er-noun*

Both proposals account for the structural parallelism between the two words. But treating those general morphological schemata as categories related through AND/OR nets has the additional benefit that we can cross-classify and describe them in as fine-grained a manner as required. We thus have an immediate model of the distinguishing properties of lexical relations on which this book concentrates (medium-size generalizations, exceptions, and subregularities) since morphological constituent structure schemata are now part of a Type Underspecified Hierarchical Lexicon (see chapter 3).

Secondly, organizing morphological processes into a hierarchy of lexeme categories accounts for several of their well-known properties. Briefly said, if morphological constituent structure configurations *are* categories that combine via On-Line Type Construction, we expect them to exhibit the properties characteristic of boolean category networks. The general hypothesis that morphological relations result from the boolean, hierarchical organization of lexeme categories would thus explain why morphological processes (including those requiring assigning an internal structure to words) bear traits typical of such networks. Hopefully, the rest of this book will illustrate this benefit to the satisfaction of the sceptical reader.

The morphophonological side of morphological constructions.
The previous discussion only considered the morphosyntactic properties of lexemes. No mention was made of their morphophonological
properties. It is time to turn our attention to this other component
of morphological processes. As usual, properties that characterize this
component are factored out into an AND/OR net of lexeme categories. In
fact, morphophonological categories are themselves classified along two
subdimensions, the μ-comb and co-phon dimensions (for *morphological combination* and *co-phonology* respectively).[5] The former classifies
morphological processes on the basis of the modes of combination of
the process' base and additional phonological material, the latter on the
basis of the phonological rules this combination entails. To explain how
both kinds of categories work, I must briefly digress into the phonological representations I take for granted. My account of morphophonology is based on Krieger et al. 1993's feature-based encoding of two-level
morphology. Since this book is not concerned with the details of morphophonological alternations, a comprehensive discussion of two-level
morphology is impossible; I content myself with a brief introduction (see
Koskenniemi 1983 and Koskenniemi 1997 for details and Sproat 1992 or
Karttunen 1993 for good, detailed introductions; see also Lakoff 1993 for
a more "cognitively" oriented approach to two-level morphology). The
leading idea behind two-level morphology is that morphophonological
processes can be modeled through the parallel application of declarative correspondence rules between a lexeme's lexical and surface forms.
The details of the implementation of each rule are not important for
our purposes; suffice it to say that a two-level rule can be seen as a
finite-state transducer between the input and output of a traditional
phonological rule. If each rule is a transducer, the set of rules that "derive" the surface form of words can be represented as a set of transducers
working in tandem, as illustrated informally in figure 64 adapted from
Karttunen 1993.

Two properties distinguish the variant of two-level morphology presented in this chapter. Firstly, the mapping between the two levels assumes a feature-based encoding of transducers, as presented in Krieger
et al.'s work. Secondly, and more importantly, I follow Orgun's lead and
assume the distinction between lexical and surface forms applies at each
local morphological tree rather than only once per word, whatever its
morphological complexity, as in Koskenniemi's work. In a form such as
'players', whose structure is $[_3 [_2 [_1 \text{play}]\ \text{er}]\ \text{s}]$, the mapping between

---

[5]I borrow the notion and term *co-phonology* from Inkelas and Orgun (In press).

surface form

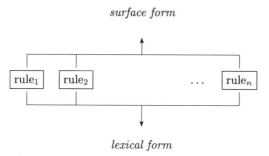

lexical form

FIGURE 64 Parallel application of "rules" in two-level morphology

lexical and surface forms applies to the local tree labeled 2 as well as the one labeled 3.[6] I discuss each property in turn.

Krieger et al. propose to effect the mapping between "lexical" and "surface" forms by treating phonological forms as sequences of elements taken out of an alphabet of so-called $\alpha\beta$ elements. Each such element consists in a lexical and surface segment, as represented in figure 65.

$$\begin{bmatrix} \alpha\beta \\ \text{SURF } segment \\ \text{LEX } \quad segment \end{bmatrix}$$

FIGURE 65 $\alpha\beta$ elements

The phonological form of strings (the values of the path PHON|FORM in figure 66) now involves lists of $\alpha\beta$ elements rather than lists of phonemes (or of autosegments in a more detailed representation of phonological strings). The value of the LEX attribute in an $\alpha\beta$ element is the equivalent of a segment in the "input" of phonological rules, the value of the SURF attribute is the equivalent of a segment in their "output". It is the LEX and SURF values of each $\alpha\beta$ element which phonological rules put into correspondence. More precisely, morphophonological "rules" are lexeme categories which constrain the correspondence between the values of the LEX and SURF attributes of $\alpha\beta$ elements on the mother node of morphological trees.

Consider the word 'played'. It is built out of the root *play* through an inflectional morphological category. The phonologically relevant information and its morphological structure are semi-formally represented in figure 66. The daughter's phonological form consists of a list of $\alpha\beta$ elements for /pleɪ/. Its lexical and surface forms are identical, assuming

---

[6]The mapping does not apply to roots, whose lexical and surface forms are identical.

$$
\left[\text{PHON} \begin{bmatrix} \text{FORM} \left\langle \begin{bmatrix} \text{SURF} - \\ \text{LEX} \boxed{1}\ p \end{bmatrix}, \begin{bmatrix} \text{SURF} - \\ \text{LEX} \boxed{2}\ 1 \end{bmatrix}, \begin{bmatrix} \text{SURF} - \\ \text{LEX} \boxed{3}\ eɪ \end{bmatrix} \begin{bmatrix} \text{SURF} - \\ \text{LEX} \boxed{4} \end{bmatrix} \right\rangle \\ \text{SUFF} \begin{bmatrix} \text{AFF} \left\langle \boxed{4}\ d \right\rangle \end{bmatrix} \end{bmatrix} \right]
$$

$$
\left[\text{PHON} \begin{bmatrix} \text{FORM} \left\langle \begin{bmatrix} \text{SURF} \boxed{1} \\ \text{LEX} \boxed{1}\ p \end{bmatrix}, \begin{bmatrix} \text{SURF} \boxed{2} \\ \text{LEX} \boxed{2}\ 1 \end{bmatrix}, \begin{bmatrix} \text{SURF} \boxed{3} \\ \text{LEX} \boxed{3}\ eɪ \end{bmatrix} \right\rangle \end{bmatrix} \right]
$$

FIGURE 66 The phonological build-up of 'played'

no phonological rules apply to roots. This necessary identity is indicated in the figure through the numbered tags $\boxed{1}$ through $\boxed{3}$. The mother's phonological form also consists of a list of $\alpha\beta$ elements. Its LEX attribute values correspond to the surface forms of the daughter followed by the suffix /d/, as indicated again by the tags $\boxed{1}$-$\boxed{4}$. In other words, the "input" to the phonological rules associated with the suffixation of /d/ comprises the surface form of the daughter and the additional suffixal (or prefixal) material.

The correspondence between the mother node's lexical and surface segments is not explicitly indicated in the figure and the values of the various SURF attributes are left blank, since the details of the morphophonology of English are irrelevant to my purposes. The important point is that the phonological effects of building a morphological tree are two-fold:

1. The surface form of the daughter is composed with some additional phonological material. The output of this composition is a phonological string that serves as input to (morpho)phonological rules. Typically, the additional material takes the form of affixal strings and the input to phonological rules is simply built out of the surface form of the daughter together with (possibly empty) lists of prefixal and suffixal strings.

2. The application of "phonological rules"— which simply constrain the correspondences between the values of the LEX and SURF attributes of the mother's phonological form.

These two kinds of effects of morphological processes are described by the various subcategories in the *μ-comp* and *co-phon* dimensions respectively. Members of the first dimension describe particular ways of combining the base and additional phonological material (concatenatively or non-concatenatively, for example).[7] Members of the second dimension describe the phonological "rules" that apply each time a derived lexeme is built. Figure 67 gives a more detailed representation of the *lexeme* AND/OR net which includes subtypes along both dimensions. Note that morphological categories in this more detailed network are defined as the intersection of three kinds of categories: the class of *ity-nouns*, for example, is defined as the intersection of (a subcategory of) *complex-lexeme* (*complex* for short), *concat-μ*, and *tri-laxing*.

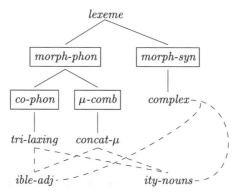

FIGURE 67 A more detailed hierarchy of lexemes

An example of a method of morphological composition is diagrammed in figure 68. The AVM describes the most general category for concatenatively composing morphological elements. Simply put, it says that the lexical form of the mother of a morphological tree is the concatenation of a string of prefixes, the surface form of its daughter and a string of suffixes.

$$
\begin{bmatrix}
concat\text{-}\mu \\
\text{PHON} \begin{bmatrix} \text{FORM } lex\text{-}append \ (sp(\boxed{1}), \ surf(\boxed{3}), \ sp(\boxed{2})) \\ \text{AFF} \begin{bmatrix} \text{PREF } \boxed{1}list(strings) \\ \text{SUFF } \boxed{2}list(strings) \end{bmatrix} \end{bmatrix} \\
\mu\text{-STRUC} \begin{bmatrix} \text{DGHTR} \begin{bmatrix} \text{PHON} \begin{bmatrix} \text{FORM} \boxed{3} \end{bmatrix} \end{bmatrix} \end{bmatrix}
\end{bmatrix}
$$

FIGURE 68 The concatenative morphology category

---

[7] I do not discuss non-concatenative morphology in this book. For a constraint-based approach to non-concatenative processes broadly compatible with the theory of morphology presented in this chapter, see Bird and Ellison 1994.

To implement this idea technically, three functions over lists of phonological strings and $\alpha\beta$ elements are introduced— *sp*, *surf*, and *lex-append*. Their definition is as follows. *Sp* when applied to a list of lists of strings returns the concatenation of their members, as illustrated in (8).

(8)   *sp* $\left(\left\langle\left\langle a,\, b\right\rangle,\left\langle c,\, d\right\rangle\right\rangle\right) = \left\langle a,\, b,\, c,\, d\right\rangle$

Lex-append concatenates its arguments and distributes them over the values of the LEX attibute in a sequence of $\alpha\beta$ elements, as illustrated in (9).

(9)   *lex-append* $\left(\left\langle a\right\rangle,\left\langle b\right\rangle,\left\langle c\right\rangle\right) = \left\langle\left[\text{LEX a}\right],\left[\text{LEX b}\right],\left[\text{LEX c}\right]\right\rangle$

Surf takes a list of $\alpha\beta$ elements and returns the list of values of their SURF attributes, as illustrated in (10).

(10)   *surf* $\left(\left\langle\left[\text{SURF a}\right],\left[\text{SURF b}\right],\left[\text{SURF c}\right]\right\rangle\right) = \left\langle a,\, b,\, c\right\rangle$

Given the definitions of the *sp*, *lex-append*, and *surf* functions, the net effect of the category described in figure 68 is that the lexical form of the mother node of concatenative morphological processes is the concatenation of a list of prefixes, the surface form of their single daughter, and a list of suffixes.[8]

I give a concrete example of the effects of the *concat-μ* category and these various operations on strings and lists of $\alpha\beta$ elements in the AVM for the word 'played' in figure 69. Note that indeed the mother's phonological form is a sequence of $\alpha\beta$ elements whose LEX values are (as a result of the *surf*, *sp*, and *lex-append* operations) the concatenation of the surface form of its daughter (the root *play*) and the suffix /d/.

$$
\begin{bmatrix}
\text{reg-pst} \\[4pt]
\text{PHON} & \begin{bmatrix}
\text{FORM} \left\langle\left[\text{LEX}\;\boxed{1}\;\text{p}\right],\left[\text{LEX}\;\boxed{2}\;\text{l}\right],\left[\text{LEX}\;\boxed{3}\;\text{eɪ}\right],\left[\text{LEX}\;\boxed{4}\right]\right\rangle \\
\text{AFF} & \left[\text{SUFF}\left\langle\boxed{4}\;\text{d}\right\rangle\right]
\end{bmatrix} \\[10pt]
\text{CAT} & \left[\text{HEAD}\left[\text{VFORM}\;past\right]\right] \\[6pt]
\text{μ-STRUC} & \begin{bmatrix}
\text{DGHTR} & \begin{bmatrix}
play \\
\text{PHON} & \left[\text{FORM}\left\langle\left[\text{SURF}\;\boxed{1}\;\text{p}\right],\left[\text{SURF}\;\boxed{2}\;\text{l}\right],\left[\text{SURF}\;\boxed{3}\;\text{eɪ}\right]\right\rangle\right]
\end{bmatrix}
\end{bmatrix}
\end{bmatrix}
$$

FIGURE 69 A more detailed representation of 'played'

Once so composed by a subtype of the *concat-μ* category, the re-

---

[8]The values of the attributes SUFF and PREF are *lists* of strings. I thus assume that a single local morphological tree can add more than one affix. For the most part, this assumption is orthogonal to the issues discussed in this chapter. See section 5.5.2 for justification of this assumption.

sponsibility for mapping the mother's lexical form onto its surface form falls upon phonological "rules", interpreted here as constraints on correspondences between the LEX and SURF values of $\alpha\beta$ elements. Such constraints are decribed by categories in the third lexemic dimension, the *co-phon* dimension.

Let me now briefly summarize the role of the three lexemic dimensions in figure 67, page 105, before presenting concrete examples of *co-phon* categories. Particular morphological constructions inherit constraints from subtypes in each of the three dimensions *morph-syn*, *µ-comb*, and *co-phon*. To continue with our previous example, the English past tense morphological category defines a particular class of complex lexemes— it is a subcategory of *complex-lexeme*. But it is also a certain kind of morpheme-composition process (in this case, suffixation). Finally, it triggers the application of a certain class of phonological rules. It is therefore defined as the intersection of a morphosyntactic category (the class of past-tense words) and a morphophonological category (the class of suffix-mediated morphophonological processes subject to a particular set of phonological rules). Concentrating for now on the first two kinds of properties, what regular past tense words share with all concatenative affixal morphology is captured in the *concat-µ* type; what they share with other inflected words is recorded in the *simple-word* type. What distinguish them is described in the *reg-pst* category represented in more detail in figure 70.[9]

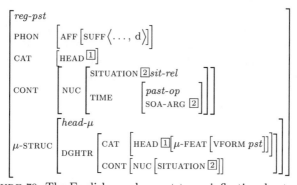

FIGURE 70 The English regular past-tense inflectional category

Although orthogonal to the main point of this section, I included for completeness a representation of the semantic contribution of the *reg-pst*

---

[9] For ease of reading, I have included in the diagram information the *reg-pst* category inherits from the more general *pst* category.

category in the value of the CONT|NUC path. The figure basically states that the verb denotes a situation (an entity of type *sit-rel*) and that this situation occurred in the past (as indicated by the value of the TIME attribute). Aside from its semantic contribution, the *reg-pst* category stipulates the following information. It is a subcategory of words (see its position in the AND/OR net in figure 56), since past verbs (its "output") can be inserted into phrase-structural positions. It also constrains the stem or root it includes to bear certain morphosyntactic features corresponding to the tense and mood of the form it derives (see the tag ⊡ and section 5.4 for a definition of the Head Feature Principle which ensures the head properties of the inflected word and its morphological base are identical). The relevant shared property here is the [VFORM *pst*] attribute/value pair which is part of the overall morphosyntactic head features encoded in the μ-FEAT attribute. Finally, the construction specifies the phonological material that marks its application, the presence of a /d/ suffix.

The type *reg-pst* inherits much information from its various superclasses. This inherited information represents the general properties the construction shares with other morphological processes. It inherits from the *complex-lexeme* category the existence of an internal constituent structure, represented by the μ-STRUC attribute in the diagram. It also inherits from the *concat-μ* category the constraint that the lexical form of its mother node is equal to the concatenation of the surface form of its daughter node and the value of its suffixes attribute (in this case, the single /d/), information which I left out for ease of reading. The word 'played', now, is formed by combining this *reg-pst* category and the root *play*, that is by choosing the *reg-pst* template and the root *play* as the value of the μ-STRUC|DGHTR attribute in the *reg-pst* template. The effect of this combination is shown in figure 71 (the phonological representation is simplified for perspicuity).

To sum up, by defining particular morphological processes as the intersection of categories in all three *morph-syn*, *μ-comb*, and *co-phon* dimensions, we can simultaneously represent three kinds of generalizations in which they participate:

1. The semantic and syntactic information they contribute;
2. The phonological method by which they mark this contribution;
3. The phonological processes they trigger.

We have already briefly discussed an example of the first two kinds of categories. I now turn to the third kind of generalization in which morphological processes can participate. As hinted at before, morphophonological rules in the model pursued here are treated as constraints on

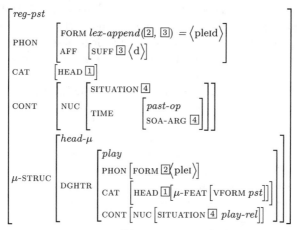

FIGURE 71 The past-tense of *play*

sequences of $\alpha\beta$ elements that are attached to particular categories of lexemes. In other words, they too are partial descriptions of classes of lexemes. By letting phonological rules be lexeme categories, we can represent the fact that different sets of morphophonological or allomorphic rules apply to distinct word classes. Consider the German schwa epenthesis allomorphy rule. It applies differently to verbs and adjectives, as the minimal data set in tables 1 and 2 indicates (adapted from Krieger et al.).

	'say'	'pray'	'free'
1sg pres ind	*sag+e*	*bet+e*	*befrei+e*
2sg pres ind	*sag+st*	*bet+est*	*befrei+st*
3sg pres ind	*sag+t*	*bet+et*	*befrei+t*

TABLE 1 German epenthesis (for verbs)

	'quick'	'free'	'intelligent'
positive	*schnell*	*frei*	*intelligent*
superlative	*schnell+ste*	*frei+este*	*intelligent+este*

TABLE 2 German epenthesis (for adjectives)

Whereas epenthesis is restricted to verbs whose stems end in either /d/ or /t/, it applies to adjectives whose stems end in a vowel, such as 'frei' ('free'). The absence of epenthesis for the de-adjectival verb 'be-frei' attests to the morphological conditioning of the epenthesis process. The dependency between epenthesis and lexical class is easily described if phonological effects of morphological processes are lexeme categories. As Krieger et al. suggest, at least three epenthesis constraints are needed for German allomorphy; they are (semi-informally) represented in figures 72-74.[10] The first constraint forbids words ending in either /t/ or /d/ to be followed by a /s/ or /t/ initial suffix. The second constraint restricts epenthesis to /s/ or /t/ initial suffixes. Finally, the constraint in figure 74 restricts epenthesis to stems ending in /t/ or /d/. As shown by the contrast between verbs and adjectives illustrated in tables 1 and 2 respectively, the first two constraints apply to adjectives and verbs equally, but the last constraint only applies to verbs.

$$
\begin{bmatrix}
\textit{epenth-1} \\
\text{PHON} \begin{bmatrix} \text{FORM} \ \neg \left(\langle \ldots \{t, d\} \rangle \oplus \left\langle [\,], \left[\text{LEX} \boxed{1} \{s, t\} \right] \ldots \right\rangle \right) \\ \text{AFF} \ \begin{bmatrix} \text{SUFF} \langle [\,], \boxed{1}, \ldots \rangle \end{bmatrix} \end{bmatrix}
\end{bmatrix}
$$

FIGURE 72   The first German epenthesis constraint

$$
\begin{bmatrix}
\textit{epenth-2} \\
\text{PHON} \begin{bmatrix} \text{FORM} \ \neg \left(\langle \ldots \rangle \oplus \left\langle \begin{bmatrix} \text{SURF} \ \partial \\ \text{LEX} \ \boxed{1} \ + \end{bmatrix}, \ \neg \left[\text{LEX} \boxed{2} \{s, t\} \right] \ldots \right\rangle \right) \\ \text{AFF} \ \begin{bmatrix} \text{SUFF} \langle \boxed{1}, \boxed{2}, \ldots \rangle \end{bmatrix} \end{bmatrix}
\end{bmatrix}
$$

FIGURE 73   The second German epenthesis constraint

With the help of these three constraints on epenthesis, representing similarities and differences among verbal and adjectival allomorphy becomes possible. The crucial constraints on lexeme class combinations are represented in figure 75 taken from Krieger et al's paper. The hierarchy states that epenthesis rules apply only to adjectives and verbs and that, moreover, of the three German epenthesis rules I just discussed, all three

---

[10]The three figures are adapted from Krieger et al.'s paper. To avoid confusion I use most of their conventions: {t, d} denotes $\alpha\beta$ elements whose lexical and surface values are either /t/ or /d/; [LEX {s, t}] denotes an $\alpha\beta$ element whose LEX value is either /s/ or /t/; '+' marks the beginning of all affixal material. This boundary marker surfaces as either the empty string or an epenthesis vowel. I use ¬ to represent the complement of the set of strings described by the expression to which it is prefixed. I use parentheses to mark the scope of ¬.

$$\begin{bmatrix} \textit{epenth-3} \\ \text{PHON} \begin{bmatrix} \text{FORM} \neg \left(\left\langle \ldots \neg \{ t, d \} \right\rangle \oplus \left\langle \begin{bmatrix} \text{SURF } \textschwa \\ \text{LEX } \boxed{1} + \end{bmatrix} \ldots \right\rangle \right) \\ \text{AFF} \begin{bmatrix} \text{SUFF} \left\langle \boxed{1}, \ldots \right\rangle \end{bmatrix} \end{bmatrix} \end{bmatrix}$$

FIGURE 74 The third German epenthesis constraint

apply to verbs, but only the first two to adjectives. Since adjectives are not forced to belong to the *epenth-3* category, epenthesis can apply to adjectives whose stems do not end in /t/ or /d/.

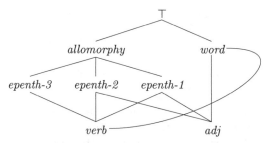

FIGURE 75 Krieger et al.'s approach to allomorphy

Krieger et al.'s treatment of German epenthesis ilustrates how integrating the morphophonological effects of morphological processes into our network of lexeme categories provides for a straightforward description of lexical class restrictions on allomorphy. The same is true of other phonological processes. Since I do not focus on the phonological side of morphology in this book, I only take a simple example due to Stump (In press). To understand this example, please note that Krieger et al's *allomorphy* category corresponds to the *co-phon* dimension of the AND/OR net represented in figure 56 on page 93, further detailed in figure 76 on the next page.

Categories along the *co-phon* subdimension record the allomorphy and phonological rules characteristic of classes of morphological processes. Stump notes that trisyllabic laxing in English applies to the suffixation of '-ible' and '-ity' (see 'divide' *vs.* 'divisible', 'divine' *vs.* 'divinity'), but not that of '-able' (see 'divide' *vs.* 'dividable'). Figure 76 represents this difference by letting only the first pair inherit from the *tri-laxing* category. Put succinctly, adjectives ending in '-ible' and nouns finishing in '-ity' are stipulated to be members of the category of lexemes undergoing tri-syllabic laxing. Of course, more than one phonological

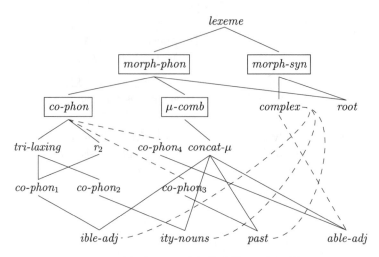

FIGURE 76 A more detailed hierarchy of lexemes

rule is typically associated with morphological processes, only some of which might be shared among two morphological processes. So, even-though *-ible* adjectives and *-ity* nouns both undergo tri-syllabic laxing, the former might undergo rules to which the latter is not subject. To indicate this possibility, I included in figure 76 a putative r_2 rule which only *-ible* adjectives undergo. More generally, morphological processes may share some, but not all phonological rules they trigger. If we call co-phonology the set of rules triggered by morphological composition, this observation amounts to saying that morphological processes might, but need not share their entire corresponding co-phonologies. The co-phonology associated with *-ible* adjectives, $co\text{-}phon_1$, for example, is defined as the conjunction of the tri-laxing constraint and the putative constraint r_2, whereas that associated with *-ity* nouns, $co\text{-}phon_2$, only inherits the tri-laxing rule.[11]

A criticism often leveled against two-level morphology (and more generally finite-state approaches to morphophonology) is their inability to represent differences in the surface form of words which arise from the derivational history of the way they were built, or, equivalently, from the word's internal structure. Consider a simple example from Shih 1986 and Sproat 1992, the Mandarin third-tone sandhi rule. An

---

[11]For ease of reading, figure 76 uses an hybrid style of representation between an AND/OR net and a type hierarchy.

informal statement of the rule is given in (11a), and (11b) provides an illustration (examples from Sproat, p.106).

(11) a. $3 \rightarrow 2/\underline{\quad}3$
      b. 'purple grass': zǐ cǎo → zí cǎo

'Zǐ' ('purple') low tone becomes a rising tone when followed by another low tone. Consider now the following compounds:

(12) a. ruǎn zí   cǎo
         soft purple grass
      b. [ruǎn [zǐ cǎo]] → [ruǎn [zí cǎo]]

(13) a. má   weí zǎo
         horse tail alga
      b. [[mǎ weǐ] zǎo]→ [[má weǐ] zǎo] → [[má weí] zǎo]

The contrast between the two outputs is easily explained as the result of a different order in which the two compounding operations are performed, as illustrated informally in (12b) and (13b). If we first apply the sandhi rule to the second and third elements of the compound, the rule's output, namely 'zí', blocks the application of the sandhi rule to the sequence 'ruǎn zí'. If on the other hand, we first apply the sandhi rule to the first and second elements of the compound yielding 'má weǐ', the rule can still apply to the second member of the compound, 'weǐ', leading to the surface form 'má weí zǎo'. Examples such as these have often been taken as evidence of the need for a cyclic application of phonological rules. But, as Orgun 1994 shows and as discussed by Koenig et al. 1996, the different order of cyclic rule application is mirrored by the compound's internal constituency (see the bracketing in (12b) and (13b)). To model the effect of cyclic rule application in a two-level morphology, we need only assume the sandhi rule applies each time morphological compounding occurs. The two corresponding constituent structures are shown in figures 77 and 78 respectively.[12]

By associating feature-based encoding of finite-state transducers with the mother node of each local morphological tree, we thus avoid the shortcomings of finite-state techniques in order-sensitive applications of phonological rules. We furthermore obtain the desired ordering effect within a declarative, constraint-based approach to morphological structure.

A final remark on this brief introduction to the phonological side of morphology is in order. The classification of lexemes assumed in figure 76 is based on the assumption that *stipulated* level ordering of

---

[12]The figures indicate the SURF and LEX attributes only when their values differ or are otherwise relevant.

$$\left[\text{PHON}\,|\,\text{FORM}\left\langle\text{r, u, }\begin{bmatrix}\text{LEX} & \text{ǎ}\\ \text{SURF} & \text{ǎ}\end{bmatrix}\text{, n, z, í, c, a, ǒ}\right\rangle\right]$$

$$\left[\text{PHON}\,|\,\text{FORM}\left\langle\text{r, u, ǎ, n}\right\rangle\right] \qquad \left[\text{PHON}\,|\,\text{FORM}\left\langle\text{z, }\begin{bmatrix}\text{LEX} & \text{ǐ}\\ \text{SURF} & \text{í}\end{bmatrix}\text{, c, a, ǒ}\right\rangle\right]$$

$$\left[\text{PHON}\,|\,\text{FORM}\left\langle\text{z, ǐ}\right\rangle\right] \qquad \left[\text{PHON}\,|\,\text{FORM}\left\langle\text{c, a, ǒ}\right\rangle\right]$$

FIGURE 77 Tone sandhi in Mandarin I

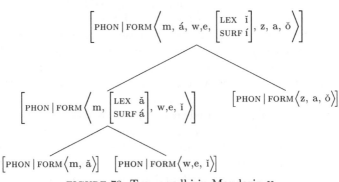

$$\left[\text{PHON}\,|\,\text{FORM}\left\langle\text{m, á, w,e, }\begin{bmatrix}\text{LEX} & \text{ǐ}\\ \text{SURF} & \text{í}\end{bmatrix}\text{, z, a, ǒ}\right\rangle\right]$$

$$\left[\text{PHON}\,|\,\text{FORM}\left\langle\text{m, }\begin{bmatrix}\text{LEX} & \text{ǎ}\\ \text{SURF} & \text{á}\end{bmatrix}\text{, w,e, ǐ}\right\rangle\right] \qquad \left[\text{PHON}\,|\,\text{FORM}\left\langle\text{z, a, ǒ}\right\rangle\right]$$

$$\left[\text{PHON}\,|\,\text{FORM}\left\langle\text{m, ǎ}\right\rangle\right] \qquad \left[\text{PHON}\,|\,\text{FORM}\left\langle\text{w,e, ǐ}\right\rangle\right]$$

FIGURE 78 Tone sandhi in Mandarin II

the kind found in traditional Lexical Phonology is not needed (see Kiparsky 1982a, Kiparsky 1985, Pulleyblank 1986 among others). Phonological levels are simply treated as co-phonologies— that is as a categorization of lexemes on the basis of the particular set of phonological rules they undergo. This analysis of non-extrinsically ordered levels is illustrated in figure 79, where I have represented a hypothetical language with four phonological rules. Lexeme categories which correspond to these rules are grouped into three different classes of co-phonologies, called *level-a*, *level-b*, and *level-c*. The classes of *3sg-word* and (nominal) *plural* select the set of phonological rules labeled *level-a*, the class of *nominalization* lexemes selects the set labeled *level-b*, and *possessive* lexemes the set labeled *level-c*. Put differently, third singular verbs and plural nouns are declared to be *level-a* lexemes, nominalized stems *level-b* lexemes, and possessives *level-c* lexemes.

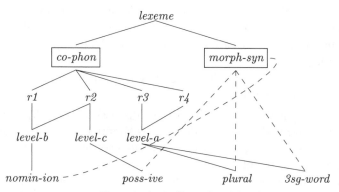

FIGURE 79 Non-extrinsically ordered levels in TCCM

$$\begin{bmatrix} possessive \\ \mu\text{-STRUC} \quad \begin{bmatrix} \text{DGHTR} \ level\text{-}b \end{bmatrix} \end{bmatrix}$$

FIGURE 80 The *possessive* category

But now each of these lexemes' morphological daughters can themselves be required to belong to particular levels. Consider the putative definition of the class of possessive words in figure 80. Its daughter is constrained to be of type *level-b*. This constraint insures that possessives are formed out of lexemes which have undergone *level-b* rules, that is, they belong to the class of *level-b* lexemes. Through such restrictions on the co-phonological class of a lexeme's morphological daughters, intrinsic level ordering is easily achieved:

(14)   *Level-a* is ordered "after" *level-b* iff *level-a* lexemes select *level-b* lexemes as their morphological daughters, but not the converse.

Synchronically valid clusters of properties that traditionally motivate the use of levels receive a similar analysis in an architecture that uses co-phonologies instead. Consider the traditional distinction between level 1 and level 2 affixes in English (assuming the distinction is warranted for purposes of exposition). Four properties at least distinguish the two classes of affixes (see the summary in Kenstowicz 1994, p.211sq).

1. Level 1 affixes precede level 2 affixes.
2. Only level 1 affixes affect accent placement and trigger trisyllabic laxing (compare the level one affix '-ous' to the level two affix '-ship' in 'hómonym'/'homónymous' *vs.* 'pártisan'/'pártisanship'; compare also the level one affix '-al' to '-ship' in 'nātion'/'nătional' *vs.* 'sēaman'/'sēamanship', data from Kenstowicz, op.cit.).
3. Only level 1 affixes attach to bound morphs (compare 'inept' and '*unept').
4. The meaning change effected by level 1 affixes is less compositional than that of level 2 affixes.

The first generalization parallels our discussion of the hypothetical language illustrated in figures 79-80: it is simply enforced by requiring constructions selecting a level one co-phonology to have roots or level one categories as daughters.[13]

The second generalization follows from the definition of levels as a class of morphological constituent structure constructions sharing a set of morphophonological processes (that is, as categories relating LEX and SURF forms of the mother node of morphological trees). All level one morphological constructions inherit from a *level-1* co-phonology cate-

---

[13]Since I did not introduce a numerical ordering on levels, we cannot represent universal conditions on the ordering of levels such as the strict layer hypothesis of Selkirk 1984. But Inkelas and Orgun 1995 present arguments against that hypothesis from level economy in Turkish. To include the strict layer hypothesis in the (universal) definition of the type *complex-lexeme*, we must add a constraint to the effect that the value of the LEVEL attribute of a mother must be superior by one to that of its daughter, as shown in the AVM below. (The formulation of this condition makes use of functional constraints on feature values of the kind discussed in Wittenburg 1993 and introduces an attribute LEVEL for all lexemes.)

$$\begin{bmatrix} \text{LEVEL} & n+1 \\ \mu\text{-STRUC} & \begin{bmatrix} \text{DGHTR} & \begin{bmatrix} \text{LEVEL} & n \end{bmatrix} \end{bmatrix} \end{bmatrix}$$

gory which is defined as the intersection of all the relevant co-phonology categories, including those describing stress assignment, trisyllabic laxing, and so forth. So-called level two processes simply inherit from a co-phonology category that does not include these phonological processes. The TCCM outlined in this chapter does not directly account for the third and fourth generalizations. But the synchronic status of these generalizations is unclear; they might simply be a reflection of the "historical layering" of affixes (see Bybee 1988). This is particularly true of the third generalization: bound morphs are typically relics of past morphology.

To summarize this brief phonological excursus, phonological rules are a categorization of morphological signs on the basis of the nature of the transducers that map LEX to SURF values of their phonological forms. Such "rules" apply at the mother node of each local morphological tree, mirroring cyclic effects through the inherent ordering induced by constituency. Phonological levels are conjunctions of such rules. To say, for example, that '-er' suffixation is a level 2 suffix in English is to say that the class of English '-er' stems belongs to the class of morphological objects to which level 2 rules apply. If r_1, r_2, and r_3 are the level 2 processes, this amounts to saying that the category of '-er' stems belongs to the class of r_1, r_2, and r_3 lexemes, since the class of level 2 lexemes is defined as the intersection of these three classes.

4.2 Morphological blocking

4.2.1 The obligatoriness of inflection

Although the description of the *reg-pst* construction I discussed in the previous section gives us a recipe for building inflected past verbs out of roots and stems, it does not address the question of its obligatory application, that is, why all syntactic atoms must belong to one of the set of English inflectional classes, *past, prst, 3sg, plural,* and so forth. The inflectional category gives us a recipe, it does not tell us why we *must* use it. If underspecified entries are free to combine with any compatible lexeme class, why is the surface form 'play' unable to express or realize the past tense of the root *play*, or the surface form 'bird' unable to realize the plural of the root *bird*? To illlustrate the nature of the problem, consider example (15).

(15) *The bird were flying over the field.

Intuitively, the ungrammaticality of (15) is due to the violation of the constraint imposed by 'were' that its subject be plural. The question is why is it violated? If we assume, as is natural in the approach taken here, that noun roots are underspecified for number, *bird* can satisfy the constraint imposed by 'were'. Since the root *bird* is underspecified for number, it ought to be able to combine with verbs that require either singular or plural subjects. The answer to this problem, of course, is that (15) is ungrammatical because the plural agreement feature of the noun is not "realized" by a relevant inflectional construction. The *plural* noun inflectional category should have been used. Lexeme type hierarchies such as those represented in figures 56 on page 93 or 76 on page 112 provide us with the appropriate logic to guarantee the application of inflectional constructions to underspecified roots.

Remember that syntactic atoms are of type *word* and morphological atoms are of type *root*. Since the two categories are incompatible, a word-forming construction must be used to turn roots such as *bird* into words such as 'bird'. The same reasoning applies to derived nominal stems, since they are of type *stem* and are not syntactic atoms. Inflectional categories serve the purpose of creating syntactic atoms: they apply to roots (or stems), and "derive" words, that is objects ready for syntactic manipulation. Their obligatory application follows from the categorial incompatibility between syntactic and morphological atoms (or stems). A consequence of this account of the obligatoriness of inflectional morphology is the presence of an internal morphological structure in all word forms in an inflectional paradigm, even those forms for which no phonological material is added to the root. The internal structure of the word 'sleep' in a sentence such as 'They sleep', for example, is as indicated in (16). The *word* 'sleep' belongs to the *non-3sg* complex-lexeme category whose morphological daughter is a *root* of type *sleep*.

(16) $[_{non\text{-}3sg} \quad [_{sleep} \quad \text{sleep}]]$

This explanation of the obligatoriness of inflectional morphology can be generalized to languages in which inflections can be added at various morphological levels. Take the case of Turkish noun morphology, where number is added at level 3 and case at level 4, as shown in example (6) above, repeated as (17) below. The general situation is represented informally in (18).

(17) $[\ [[\text{tebrik}]_{root:1} \quad \text{-ler} \quad \text{-im}]_{stem:3} \quad \text{-i}]_{word:4}$
     congratulation PL   1SG.POSS CASE

(18) $[[[\text{x}]_{root/level:1} \quad \text{NUM POSS}]_{stem/level:3} \quad \text{CASE}]_{word/level:4}$

The word level case-marking category requires its main daughter to be of level 3. Consequently, it cannot accept bare roots, which are of level 1. The level 3 number and possessive constructions must first map roots of level 1 onto level 3 lexemes.[14]

4.2.2   Irregular past tenses

The previous discussion showed how we can model the obligatoriness of inflectional processes through typing constraints: inflectional categories must be used for lexeme categories to bear the right type, *word, level:x,* and so forth. It is still incomplete. It does not account for a crucial property of inflectional systems: irregularly inflected forms block the application of regular processes. The existence of an irregular past tense 'took', for example, blocks forms such as '*taked' or '*tooked'. The observation of this interaction between irregular and regular forms goes back to Pāṇini, and is often called the Elsewhere Condition (henceforth EC, see Anderson 1969, Kiparsky 1973, Aronoff 1976, and Zwicky 1986 among others). The intuition behind the principle is that when two comparable patterns can apply, one of which is more specific than the other, the more specific applies.

FIGURE 81   Two subtypes of past word categories

Figure 81 represents the situation informally. It indicates that when inflecting English verbs for past-tense, we have a choice between two constructions (two types) *took-pst* and *reg-pst*. How do we choose which one applies in a given context? In general, barring stipulated disjointness, any two classes can equally combine with roots or stems that do not contain incompatible information. The problem posed by figure 81 is that it appears that both categories are informationally compatible with the root 'take'. The category *took-pst* is obviously compatible with the root *take* and the general *reg-pst* inflectional template applies to all verb roots or stems, including *take*, if not further stipulation is made. As is, the kind of AND/OR nets we have been discussing wrongly predicts that '*taked' is grammatical. Since only the choice of *took-pst* results in a grammatical form, the principles governing the choice of *took-pst* or *reg-pst* must differ from those governing conjunction or combination

---

[14]This simple-minded description of Turkish inflectional morphology does not take into account the phenomenon described as "level economy" in Inkelas and Orgun 1995. I leave a discussion of level economy to another occasion.

of categories in general: not all informationally consistent choices yield possible L-categories.

The gist of the EC is to provide speakers with a principle to guide their choice in situations where two morphological categories can be chosen and the general category intersection procedure discussed in chapter 3 is not sufficient. It can be summarized by the advice 'choose the most specific subcategory'. How can we implement such a principle in a TUHL? Three possible ways suggest themselves.

- A featural approach: include more information in the two types *took-pst* and *reg-pst* so that only one of the two is ever compatible with the various roots to which they apply.

- A logical approach: add a (non-declarative) constraint to the effect that a fully-specified lexeme can belong to the *reg-pst* category only if the same lexeme (modulo its phonology or orthography) cannot belong to the *took-pst* class.

- An extra-grammatical approach: leave out of the grammar the mechanism through which the choice between *took-pst* and *reg-pst* is made and assume it belongs to a general principle of knowledge use within the processing component.

In the rest of this section, I briefly describe the three approaches using the English past tense as an illustration. Despite their differences, all three approaches are similar in spirit. Blocking always depends on choosing among subtypes of a partition. The difference lies in how the choice is made. In a featural approach, the choice is imposed by the information structure contained in the category definitions. In the other two approaches, it is regulated by a general principle on the selection of a morphological category among types "in competition". All three approaches differ from a very popular approach to blocking within inheritance-based grammars.

Many systems assume that the ungrammaticality of forms such as '*taked' follows from a convention on inheritance of information (see Flickinger 1987 and Daelemans et al. 1992 for more details on the various approaches to blocking within inheritance-based frameworks). Typically, the general verb class is declared to take '-ed' as a past-tense and past participle suffix. Verbs such as *take* are declared to be subtypes of verbs but specify that their past-participle suffix is '-en'. In a default inheritance scheme, the presence of this conflicting information in a subclass prevents the inheritance of the information relative to the past-participle suffix. Blocking then follows from the adoption of a default inheritance scheme and the assumption that information contained in subclasses takes precedence over information contained in superclasses. This approach to blocking can be called vertical and partial inheritance-based. It relies on the relative position of the classes in the type hierarchy and an inheritance scheme where a type a can be a subtype of a supertype b without possessing all the properties characteristic of b. By contrast, the approach to blocking advocated in this section (whether we implement a general Elsewhere Condition or not) is partition-driven. It relies on two facts:

1. Sister subtypes (of an (exclusive) OR tree) form a partition of their supertype;
2. Combining types from an AND/OR tree through OLTC involves choosing among these subtypes.

A feature-based approach to blocking. A feature-based model of the EC solves the problem by making sure it never arises.[15] Enough information is added to the definition of inflectional categories to guarantee that a unique answer exists to the question of the category of any unambiguous word form. We are thus never required to choose between applying two past tense constructions equally compatible with the input root *take* because only the *took-pst* category is consistent with the root *take*. According to this view, no general Elsewhere Condition on the application of inflectional categories is needed. Each informationally consistent combination of types from the lexeme AND/OR net corresponds to a possible surface form.

To describe how a feature-based approach to the EC works, I must first introduce in more detail how roots are defined. Until now I have taken for granted that each word form has a single corresponding root placed at the fringe of the subhierarchy whose most general category is *root*. But in fact I propose to substitute a more complex object for the pre-theoretical notion of root: a bi-dimensional (sub)hierarchy of entries and forms. These bi-dimensional objects correspond roughly to what are called lexemes in the word-and-paradigm approach of Matthews 1974: abstract entities which subsume both more than one entry and more than one form.[16] The root *take*, for example, is now represented as a set of forms (*take-npst*, *take-ppt* and *take-pst-vb*) and a set of entries (*take-mvt* and *take-perc*). Figure 82 diagrams the relevant AND/OR net for the single root *take*. This bidimensional net expands the node *take* in the hierarchy in figure 83. Form categories (under *take-forms* in

---

[15] The account of blocking presented in this section bears some resemblance to so-called orthogonal inheritance approaches to blocking. See Daelemans et al. 1992 for more details.

[16] This more traditional notion of lexeme is not to be confused with the type *lexeme* I use throughout this book as a cover term for words, roots, and stems.

figure 82) record the various (irregular) forms associated with the root *take* while entry categories (under *take-synsem* in the figure) record the various combinations of semantic and syntactic information associated with any member of the set of root forms (see Brugman 1988b for an early proposal in that direction within CG).

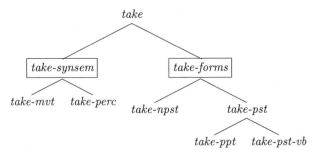

FIGURE 82 The subcategories of the root *take*

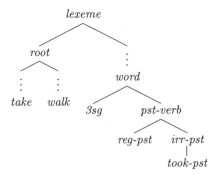

FIGURE 83 The position of the root *take* in the lexeme hierarchy

Examples (19a)-(19b) illustrate two entries for the English verb 'take'. One expresses a relation of caused-motion; I call the entry *take-mvt*. The other expresses some metaphorical extension of this sense, where 'take' means something like perceive; I call this entry *take-perc* (see Norvig and Lakoff 1987 for a much more refined analysis of the various entries for 'take').

(19) a. I took the book from Mary.

    b. He never takes a look at what he is doing.

The two entries not only have different but related meanings, they also differ in their subcategorization properties. *Take-mvt* subcategorizes for two NPs and a locational PP, whereas *take-perc* subcategorizes for two NPs. Despite their syntactic and semantic differences, both entries are associated with the same set of idiosyncratic morphological forms. The past tense and past participle of both are 'took' and 'taken' respectively. It is the orthogonality of these two kinds of information which the more complex description of the root *take* in figure 82 represents. Two dimensions of categorization of the root *take* are posited, one for each class of properties. Note that we have an AND branch between the entries and forms for *take*; any instantiation of the root is therefore specified along both dimensions. By contrast, we have OR branches between the form categories as well as between the entry categories; any instantiation of the root belongs to only one form and one entry. In brief, any word formed on the root *take* must be based on one of the three root forms *take-npst*, *take-ppt*, or *take-pst-vb* and one of the two entries *take-mvt* or *take-perc*.[17] To form the past tense word 'took' as used in (19a), one must first choose the entry *take-mvt* and the form *take-pst-vb*. To form the third person singular word 'takes' as used in (19b), one must first choose the entry *take-perc* and the form *take-npst*.

Given such bidimensional representations of roots, blocking ungrammatical past-tense forms amounts to properly matching the choice of root form and the choice of inflectional template by disallowing the combination of the general *reg-pst* category and the *take-pst-vb* or *take-npst* root forms to yield '*tooked' and '*taked' respectively. In a feature-based approach to the EC, the presence of incompatible information is the only mechanism that can prevent combinations of categories which do not result in grammatical forms (aside from the general incompability of subcategories under the same OR branch). Some explicit information must therefore be present in the categories *take-pst-vb* and *take-npst* to block their combined use with *reg-pst*. In the case at hand, two pieces of information block these combinations, as illustrated in figures 84-88 which define some of the categories listed in figure 82.[18]

---

[17]The *take-forms* dimension is a rough equivalent of the notion of stem-set in Anderson 1992 and the set of stems related by morpholexical rules in Lieber 1980. By opposition to both of these, though, no new theoretical construct is required in a TUHL to represent the relations between these forms. I only apply the usual AND/OR net logic to the representation of roots.

[18]All figures in the rest of this chapter simplify the representation of phonological strings by assuming whenever possible they are lists of segments rather than lists of $\alpha\beta$ elements. Note also that the *reg-pst* category has been stripped of much of its non-phonological information. Since this information is common to both regular and irregular past tense formation, it is abstracted away into the supercategory of *past* words. I only included the inherited VFORM information for clarity.

$$
\begin{bmatrix}
take\text{-}npst \\
\text{PHON} \begin{bmatrix} \text{FORM} \langle \text{teɪk} \rangle \end{bmatrix} \\
\text{CAT} \begin{bmatrix} \text{HEAD} \begin{bmatrix} \mu\text{-FEAT} \begin{bmatrix} \text{VFORM} \neg \; pst \\ \text{CLASS} \;\; base \end{bmatrix} \end{bmatrix} \end{bmatrix}
\end{bmatrix}
$$

FIGURE 84 The 'take' form of *take*

$$
\begin{bmatrix}
take\text{-}pst\text{-}vb \\
\text{PHON} \begin{bmatrix} \text{FORM} \langle \text{tʊk} \rangle \end{bmatrix} \\
\text{CAT} \begin{bmatrix} \text{HEAD} \begin{bmatrix} \mu\text{-FEAT} \begin{bmatrix} \text{VFORM} \; pst \\ \text{CLASS} \;\; restr \end{bmatrix} \end{bmatrix} \end{bmatrix}
\end{bmatrix}
$$

FIGURE 85 The 'took' form of *take*

$$
\begin{bmatrix}
reg\text{-}pst \\
\text{PHON} \quad \begin{bmatrix} \text{AFF} \begin{bmatrix} \text{SUFFIX} \langle \text{d} \rangle \end{bmatrix} \end{bmatrix} \\
\mu\text{-STRUC} \begin{bmatrix} \text{DGHTR} \begin{bmatrix} \text{CAT} \mid \text{HEAD} \begin{bmatrix} \mu\text{-FEAT} \begin{bmatrix} \text{VFORM} \; pst \\ \text{CLASS} \;\; base \end{bmatrix} \end{bmatrix} \end{bmatrix} \end{bmatrix}
\end{bmatrix}
$$

FIGURE 86 The *regular-past* category

$$
\begin{bmatrix}
irr\text{-}pst \\
\mu\text{-STRUC} \begin{bmatrix} \text{DGHTR} \begin{bmatrix} \text{CAT} \mid \text{HEAD} \begin{bmatrix} \mu\text{-FEAT} \begin{bmatrix} \text{CLASS} \; restr \end{bmatrix} \end{bmatrix} \end{bmatrix} \end{bmatrix}
\end{bmatrix}
$$

FIGURE 87 The general *irregular-past* category

$$
\begin{bmatrix}
took\text{-}pst \\
\text{PHON} \quad \begin{bmatrix} \text{AFF} \begin{bmatrix} \text{SUFF} \; elist \end{bmatrix} \end{bmatrix} \\
\mu\text{-STRUC} \begin{bmatrix} \text{DGHTR} \; take \end{bmatrix}
\end{bmatrix}
$$

FIGURE 88 The *took-past* subcategory of irregular past words

The inclusion of the attribute-value pair [VFORM ¬*pst*] in the root-form *take-npst* in figure 84 blocks the combination of the *reg-pst* category and the root form category for /teɪk/ since the VFORM specification of the latter directly contradicts that of the former (see figure 86): words formed on the root-form *take-npst* are explicitly restricted to non-past contexts. '*Taked' is appropriately ruled out. Now, to block the combination of the *reg-pst* category and *take-pst-vb*— that is the root form category for /tʊk/— a CLASS attribute is included in the definition of each root form. The two possible values of this attribute are *base* and *restricted*. By including this information in both root forms and inflectional categories we can insure their proper pairing. Regular templates select *base* root daughters while irregular templates select *restricted* root daughters. Since the root CLASS of *take-pst-vb* is *restricted*, the selection of *take-pst-vb* as the morphological daughter of *reg-pst* (leading to '*tooked') is properly excluded. The former category's CLASS value is *restricted* while the latter requires its morphological daughter to bear a *base* CLASS value. This featural clash forbids the combination of categories.

As the reader can see, a featural approach to blocking requires the addition of a significant amount of information to each category. Fortunately, this added complexity is mainly located in irregular roots. We can underspecify this information in the type declaration for regular roots. A regular root such as *walk* need not specify the value of its CLASS attribute. The *reg-pst* or any other regular inflectional category can still select it as its morphological daughter, since the underspecified CLASS attribute of *walk* is compatible with the value *base* which regular templates include. The *took-pst* or any other irregular template, on the other hand, cannot select *walk*, since they select a particular root (*take* in the case of *took-pst*): the stipulation of which individual roots can serve as their base is what makes irregular past tense inflectional categories unproductive. The class of roots which satisfy the constraints they impose on their daughters is explicitly listed.[19]

To summarize, a feature-based approach to the EC relies on three ideas:

1. Irregular roots are represented as a bi-dimensional subhierarchy of entries and forms. Regular roots consist of a uni-dimensional subhierarchy of entries.

2. Specification of the morphosyntactic environments in which root-forms of irregular roots can occur is stipulated.

---

[19]For a discussion of subregularities within irregular past tense forms, see section 4.2.3.

3. Each root form of irregular roots is stipulated to be either a base or restricted form.

Two aspects of a feature-based approach to blocking are positive. Firstly, regular roots do not need any special marking; their representation is less complex than that of irregular roots, as one would expect. Secondly, because the CLASS attribute is part of the morphosyntactic head features of a root, it is not transmitted to new roots by category-changing derivational processes. Nouns formed from verbs, for example, do not inherit the inflectional properties of their base verbs (including their CLASS value). Consequently, they do not share the form properties of the root on which they are formed in very much the same way they do not inherit its other inflectional attributes. We can thus account for the well-known fact that roots derived from irregular verbs are not themselves irregular (see Kiparsky 1982a and Kim et al. 1991): the past tense of 'to fly out'— which is based on the noun 'fly (ball)', itself based on the irregular verb 'to fly'— is the regular 'flied out' and not the irregular 'flew out' (see Kim et al. for more examples of the same kind, as well as psychological experiments showing the reality of this effect. See also Marcus et al. 1995 for similar data from German).

Still, featural encoding of the EC is not particularly elegant. We must classify irregular roots into base and restricted root forms, and there is no easy way to automatically infer which root forms are base or restricted roots.[20] Furthermore, we must explicitly specify the environments in which the base root form of an irregular verb occurs. We cannot express the general principle governing their morphosyntactic contexts of occurrence, namely that base root forms occur in the complement set of environments where restricted root forms occur.

Other approaches to the Elsewhere Condition. The second and third approaches are more direct implementations of the idea of an Elsewhere Condition which answer these critiques. Both allow for automatic inference of which root form or inflectional category is the "default", the fall-back category used when more restricted categories cannot apply. The second approach still makes the mechanism that allows us to choose which past-tense construction to apply part of the grammatical component, that is, part of the grammatical knowledge of native speakers. But by contrast to the feature-based strategy, it achieves the effect of the EC

---

[20]Although inelegant, the stipulation that certain root forms are marked as base while others as restricted is not necessarily implausible from a morphological perspective. After all, many inflectional systems group verbs or nouns into arbitrary inflectional classes. The selection by regular and irregular past-verb categories of base and restricted root forms, respectively, thus resembles the selection of particular verb classes by inflectional endings in many Indo-European languages.

without requiring stipulations in the definition of individual inflectional categories. It follows from a general filter on the set of well-formed lexemes. Several implementations of this idea exist within unification-based, lexicalist theories (see Andrews 1990, Briscoe et al. 1995, and Blevins 1995, for example). I adapt their formulation and propose the following principle:

(20)   a. MORPHOLOGICAL BLOCKING PRINCIPLE

   A L-category l_1 of type *word* is ungrammatical if it contains (or one of its subconstituents contains) a basic type τ_1 that unilaterally subsumes a *lexical competitor* τ_2 (type and phonological information aside).

   b. Two basic categories of an AND/OR net are *lexical competitors* iff:

   1. They are maximally specific types of the net (they do not have subtypes in the net);
   2. They are mutually exclusive (they belong to an OR division in the net);
   3. One unilaterally subsumes the other (is informationally less specific than the other), when their phonological and own type information is left aside.

I illustrate how the Morphological Blocking Principle (hereafter MBP) works on *take*, whose subcategories were listed in figure 82. Figures 89 through 92 are the new relevant type declarations needed for a lexical architecture which uses the MBP. They should be compared to figures 84 through 88.

$$\begin{bmatrix} take\text{-}npst \\ \text{PHON} \begin{bmatrix} \text{FORM} \langle \text{teɪk} \rangle \end{bmatrix} \end{bmatrix}$$

FIGURE 89   The 'take' form of *take*

$$\begin{bmatrix} take\text{-}pst\text{-}vb \\ \text{PHON} \begin{bmatrix} \text{FORM} \langle \text{tʊk} \rangle \end{bmatrix} \\ \text{CAT} \begin{bmatrix} \text{HEAD} \begin{bmatrix} \mu\text{-FEAT} \begin{bmatrix} \text{VFORM } pst \end{bmatrix} \end{bmatrix} \end{bmatrix} \end{bmatrix}$$

FIGURE 90   The 'took' form of *take*

We can infer from these type declarations and the AND/OR nets represented in figures 82 and 83, page 122, that the two pairs of type <*take-*

$$\begin{bmatrix} reg\text{-}pst \\ \text{PHON} \quad \begin{bmatrix} \text{AFF} \begin{bmatrix} \text{SUFFIX} \langle \text{d} \rangle \end{bmatrix} \end{bmatrix} \\ \mu\text{-STRUC} \begin{bmatrix} \text{DGHTR} \begin{bmatrix} \text{CAT} \begin{bmatrix} \text{HEAD} \begin{bmatrix} \mu\text{-FEAT} \mid \text{VFORM } past \end{bmatrix} \end{bmatrix} \end{bmatrix} \end{bmatrix} \end{bmatrix}$$

FIGURE 91 The *regular-past* category

$$\begin{bmatrix} took\text{-}pst \\ \text{PHON} \quad \begin{bmatrix} \text{AFF} \begin{bmatrix} \text{SUFF } elist \end{bmatrix} \end{bmatrix} \\ \mu\text{-STRUC} \begin{bmatrix} \text{DGHTR } take \end{bmatrix} \end{bmatrix}$$

FIGURE 92 The *took-pst* subcategory of irregular past words

npst, take-pst-vb> and *<reg-pst, took-pst>* are lexical competitors. The argument runs as follows.

1. These categories do not have subcategories within the AND/OR net represented in figure 82 and 83; they are maximally specific types.
2. The members of each pair are exclusive of each other since they belong to the same dimension.
3. When stripped of their phonological and type information, the *take-npst* category unilaterally subsumes the *take-pst-vb* category since the latter, but not the former, is restricted to past contexts. Similarly, *reg-pst* unilaterally subsumes *took-pst*. Any lexeme can be the morphological daughter of the former; only the root *take* will do for the latter.

The MBP now explains the ungrammaticality of (21a) and (21b). In the case of (21a), '*tooked' is of category *reg-pst* which— phonology and type aside— unilaterally subsumes its *took-pst* lexical competitor in violation of the MBP. In the case of (21b), the daughter of '*taked' is of category *take-npst* which— phonology and type aside— unilaterally subsumes its lexical competitor *take-pst-vb*, again in violation of the MBP.

(21) a.*Susan tooked the train.
      b.*Susan taked the train.

Like Andrews 1990's, the formulation in (20) runs afoul of the pro-claimed monotonicity of HPSG and unification-based grammars. What is a possible combination at one point in the processing of a sentence turns out to be illicit later on. Note that the principle does not exclude the combination of the *take-npst* and *reg-pst* categories; it merely precludes any fully type-specified L-category to include both types since the former unilaterally subsumes its *take-pst-vb* lexical competitor. In other words, the MBP is a constraint on L-categories, not on type combination.[21] A consequence of its "filtering" nature is that what is a possible combination of information at one point in the processing of a sentence or word can turn out to be illicit later on. Processing is not anymore an additive matter. The MBP clearly differs in that respect from run-of-the-mill grammatical principles such as HPSG's head-feature or valence principles (see appendix A for a definition of these principles). Such principles are both local and behave in a "satisfied once, always satisfied" manner. Whether such a breach of monotonicity is worrisome partly depends on various implementation issues which I cannot tackle here.

Until now I have treated the MBP as a grammar internal principle But it need not receive such an interpretation. We can adopt the third strategy to the EC I mentioned above and move the problem out of the grammatical component altogether by placing it in the performance or processing component. As in the previous approach, the third approach proposes a general condition that insures the "right" choice of category. But this principle is now seen as outside the declarative knowledge of language native speakers possess. It is a condition on the *use* of this knowledge. Support for this position comes from the need of very similar principles in non-linguistic areas of cognition. Researchers in knowledge representation have sometimes used extra-grammatical principles similar to the Elsewhere Condition to model the use to which a non-linguistic knowledge base can be put. Witness Wilensky 1983's First Law of Knowledge Application:

'Always apply the most specific pieces of knowledge available.' (p.25)

The principle formulated in (20) is a special case of knowledge use which targets linguistic information. Such an interpretation of the EC would seem more in keeping with the shift of type combination to the processing component that distinguishes the TUHL architecture outlined in chapter 3.

---

[21]Some readers might wonder why I chose to make the MBP a constraint on L-categories of type *word* rather than a condition on category combination. The reason is simple: the inclusion of the most specific subtype in a lexeme category is only appropriate when the "relevant" category combination is under consideration. So, the inclusion of the more specific *take-pst-vb* over the more general *take-npst* is appropriate if the combination under consideration is that of a root form of *take* and an inflectional construction, not if it is that of a root form of *take* and, say, a *trans* or *intrans* category before an inflectional category is selected. Defining the notion of "relevant" category combination proves difficult, however. The simplest way out is to assume the principle constrains L-categories of type *word*. Since L-categories are fully type-specified, they *per force* include all the "relevant" category combinations.

Whether we choose a logic- or extra-grammatical approach to the
EC is irrelevant for the main point of this chapter. In both cases, we
rely on a general principle to choose between the two possible past tense
constructions: select the category whose information structure matches
better that of the root. We are not required to include in the definition
of individual types enough information to force the choice between regular and irregular past tense constructions. The result is simpler type
declarations. We need not specify in the root forms of 'take' whether
they are a base or restricted CLASS or have particular classes of past
tenses select for base or restricted roots so as to induce the proper pairing of root forms to morphosyntactic environments. We can also leave
out of the default form its morphosyntactic context of occurrence; the
MBP insures it is used in the complement set of contexts of other root
forms. We only need posit two classes of past-tense constructions, corresponding to regular and irregular past tenses. A general EC insures
that if we build the past tense of the *take-pst-vb* root form, the *took-pst*
subtype of *pst-verb* constructions is chosen, since only this choice satisfies the Morphological Blocking Principle. Implementing a general EC
thus results in a significant simplification of the type declarations. In
the rest of this book, I assume the existence of the principle defined in
(20) and interpret it as an extra-grammatical condition on the use of
grammatical information.

4.2.3 Subregularities

As mentioned in chapter 3, On-Line Type Construction represents both
productive and non-productive subregularities with the help of a single formal mechanism, basically class abstraction. Subregularities are
simply classes whose members are also listed. We can use this property of OLTC to our benefit in modeling subregularities in English past
tense formation. It has been noticed for a long time that irregular past
tenses fall into small subgroups. Moreover, Bybee and Slobin 1982 and
Bybee and Moder 1983 show that irregular past tenses can sometimes be
extended to new or nonce verbs that are phonologically similar to members of a subgroup. Although it is possible that even for those speakers
who extend irregular past tense formation, the extension is computed
on the fly through analogy and does not rely on a pre-existing class, it
is at least plausible to hypothesize that some speakers might have abstracted the partial similarities between roots whose past tense forms
are similar. The TUHL architecture easily models such abstraction of
unproductive classes (see Jurafsky 1991 for a similar point): we simply
define in both an extensional and an intensional manner categories for
verb roots whose irregular past-tense forms are similar.

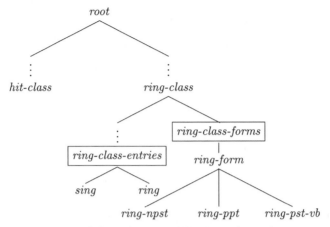

FIGURE 93 Subregularities within irregular verbs

Figure 93 diagrams some more root subcategories whose past forms are irregular. These additional types help describe subregularities in the past tense of verbs such as 'ring'. All *ring*-like roots are grouped in a general *ring-class* subclass of roots. Entries that belong to the class such as *sing, ring* ... are listed under the *ring-class-entries* dimension. The subcategories within the *ring-class-forms* subdimension represent the similarities in the shape of their various root forms. The definitions of the relevant categories are diagrammed in figures 94 through 96.

$$\begin{bmatrix} \textit{ring-form} \\ \text{PHON} \mid \text{FORM} \left\langle \dots \eta \right\rangle \end{bmatrix}$$

FIGURE 94 The general *ring-form* class

$$\begin{bmatrix} \textit{ring-npst} \\ \text{PHON} \mid \text{FORM} \left\langle \dots, \text{i}, [\,] \right\rangle \end{bmatrix}$$

FIGURE 95 The non-past *ring*-form class

As in the case of 'take', each root entry of the *ring-class* employed in the production of an utterance must combine with one of the three abstract root forms mentioned in the *ring-class-forms* subdimension. Each form abstracts the common phonological properties to the class of ring entries, including the ablaut process marking these verbs' past

$$\begin{bmatrix} \textit{ring-pst-vb} \\ \text{PHON} \mid \text{FORM} \quad \left\langle \dots, \text{æ}, [\,] \right\rangle \\ \text{SYSEM} \mid \text{LOCAL} \begin{bmatrix} \text{CAT} \mid \text{HEAD} \begin{bmatrix} \text{VFORM } \textit{pst} \end{bmatrix} \end{bmatrix} \end{bmatrix}$$

FIGURE 96 The past *ring*-form class

tense root forms. (Note the differences in the (abbreviated) $\alpha\beta$ element preceding the final /ŋ/ in figures 95 and 96.) Through abstraction of a (partially) extensionally defined class, we represent the common phonological properties of this subgroup of English irregular verbs and provide a basis for the pattern's analogical extension. Furthermore, contrary to what happens in both traditional rule- and representation-based models of lexical relations (to borrow the terminology of Bybee 1988), these similarities are captured through the same mechanisms used for productive processes: class abstraction and the organization of categories into AND/OR nets. The contrast reduces to the presence or absence of a list of members of the abstracted classes. The presence of the categories *sing* and *ring* under the *ring-class-entries* dimension in figure 94 entails that members of the *ring-class* must be either the root of the word 'sing' OR the root of the word 'ring', by the definition of OR branches. Any other root would falsify the constraint encoded in the OR branch that the entries *sing* and *ring* partition the *ring-class-entries* dimension.

Whether the ensuing theoretical uniformity is a plus might be questioned in light of the arguments presented in Pinker and Prince 1988, Marcus et al. 1995, and Jaeger et al. 1996 that productive and unproductive morphological processes differ in kind. Pinker and Prince convincingly argue that regular and irregular past tense formation behave differently psycholinguistically *contra* the implicit hypothesis underlying many recent connectionist accounts. Fortunately, the account proposed in this section is not affected by their criticisms. For one thing, regular and irregular past tense forms are still distinct: irregular inflectional categories are (partly) extensionally defined classes; regular inflectional categories are intensionally defined. Moreover, English irregular past tense formation is based on the presence and retrieval of special root forms. Regular past tenses are computed on-line by combining roots with abstract templates. Since retrieval of forms and on-line type construction are plausibly implemented through two different neural processes, processing of regular past tense forms can be impaired without the retrieval of exceptional root forms being affected. Speakers might lose the ability to combine categories and use the regular past tense construction to derive words from roots, but still be able to retrieve irregular root forms. Such speakers would use the *root forms* of irregularly inflected past tense words without reliably producing inflected *past tense words*. The account of irregular inflection presented in this section is thus compatible with the evidence presented in Pinker and Prince and Jaeger et al. that regularly and irregularly inflected forms differ in kind both psychologically and neurally.

4.3 Summary

Theories of morphological relations fall into two groups we can conveniently label representational and generative. The first group is characterized by its inclusion in the description of lexical knowledge of a static representation of morphological relations among lexemes; the second group is distinguished by its use of rules or principles to generatively derive complex lexemes from simpler ones. I briefly mentioned at the beginning of the last chapter why static representations are, by themselves, insufficient to model productivity. The bulk of chapter 2 examined attempts at turning lexical redundancy rules into a generative device and pointed out their shortcomings. The present chapter concentrated on generative models of morphology. As I mentioned at the outset, proponents of a generative approach to word structure often assume that only two choices are available to them. Morphological relations must be described through a set of morphology-specific Word Formation Rules or a set of x̄ rules (or principles) that generate words and phrases alike. I argued in this chapter that other choices are possible and proposed a Typed, Construction-based Constituent structure Morphology which differs from both traditional morpheme-based and realizational/word-based theories. Unlike the former, it does not assume that affixes are signs (morphemes) and that one affix is added per local tree. Unlike the latter, it assumes complex words have internal structure.

Morphological processes in the theory I advocate are categories which describe lexemes in terms of their (lexemic) subparts. The presence of subparts in the definition of the category *complex-lexeme* parallels the internal constituency induced by context-free rules. But the word structure it induces is degenerate; it typically consists of a mother and single daughter. I furthermore suggested that the information structure associated with categories describing complex lexemes can be profitably factored out into three classes, morphosynctactic and morphosemantic effects, mode of composition of the base and the additional phonological material, and finally the morphophonological effects the combination induces. Individual categories (say the category of *-ity* or *-er* nouns) inherit from subclasses along all three dimensions. The initial motivation for the TCCM approach was mostly theory-internal: not all morphological relations can be adequately described through the application of the On-Line Type Construction method I defined in chapter 3. Intersecting categories is not enough to describe morphological relations which are not information-preserving. Assuming the presence of internal structure in such cases salvages the monotonic stance of our category-based conception of lexical relations. Despite its modest origins, this view of the nature of word structure presents several advantages of its own. Some of the benefits were briefly touched upon in this chapter (see the discussion of subregularities in English past-tense formation or of morphologically conditioned epenthesis in German). But the most convincing argument in favor of this morphological theory is that many salient traits of morphological processes follow naturally from the AND/OR net organization of the category network of which they are part. The next chapter details these properties.

5

The AND/OR nature of morphological processes

The last chapter introduced the idea of a Typed Construction-based Constituent structure Morphology; this chapter concentrates on its benefits. A recurring theme will be that several important properties of morphological processes fall out of the nature of AND/OR nets of which word-structure categories are now a part. The chapter is organized as follows. Section 5.1 returns to the issue of stem selection discussed in chapter 2 and shows how the hypothesis that morphological processes are lexeme categories makes for an immediate account of stem selection. Section 5.2 pursues this theme further and returns to Latin inflectional morphology discussed briefly in chapter 3. As I suggested at that time, the notion of disjunctive *vs.* conjunctive rule blocks reduces to the logic of linguistic categories. Section 5.2 demonstrates that the same argument applies if words are assigned internal structure, provided morphological constituent structure configurations are themselves lexeme categories. Section 5.3 deals with subregularities and so-called "cranberry" morphemes. Section 5.4 discusses morphological headedness. I show that the treatment of stem selection discussed in section 5.1 and a general Morphological Head Feature Principle accounts for the internal realization of inflections in compounds. Finally, section 5.5 briefly compares TCCMs to both morpheme-based and realizational/word-based approaches.

5.1 Stem selection and disjunctive *vs.* conjunctive rule application

One of the salient benefits of the TCCM analysis of morphologically complex lexemes is that we can use the usual AND/OR logic of type construction to account for the many instances where morphological objects need to be cross-classified. When discussing irregular past tenses, I proposed a bi-dimensional representation of roots to model the common observation that the identification of lexemes by their morphosyntactic properties does not necessarily correlate with their morphophonological identity: the same set of exceptional root forms can be attached to entries that differ morphosyntactically or semantically. By cross-classifying roots we can define the morphological identity of, say, 'take'— what Matthews 1974 would call the lexeme *take*— in terms of a bi-dimensional array of entries and forms. The fact that any well-formed fully specified lexeme based on this array must include one member from each of the two dimensions then simply results from the definition of On-Line Type Construction.

More generally, the ability to cross-classify morphological objects that distinguishes the TCCM approach allows for a direct account of three common properties of inflectional morphology:

1. Stem selection;
2. Inflectional "paradigms" or cross-classification of forms along several inflectional dimensions;
3. Many-to-many relations between inflectional properties and their phonological marks (their "realization" in Zwicky's terminology).

By contrast, other theories of morphology, be they morpheme-based or realizational/word-based, require some additional mechanisms to describe what follows here from the logic of linguistic categorization. A typed, construction-based morphology frees us from *ad hoc* devices including stem-sets, morpholexical rules, or conjunctively *vs.* disjunctively ordered rule blocks, to name a few.

5.1.1 Suppletive stems and morpholexical rules

Suppletive stems: French 'aller' revisited. The representation of roots as bi-dimensional subhierarchies of entries and forms can be profitably employed to model suppletive stem selection which I briefly discussed in chapter 2, section 2.2.2. As mentioned there, the French verb 'aller' possesses four different suppletive stems as shown below in (1), repeated from chapter 2.

(1)   a. Marc est   allé   à   Paris.
          Marc be-PR go-PPT to Paris
          'Marc went to Paris.'

       b. Marc s'   en   ira.
          Marc 3.REFL of.it go-FUT
          'Marc will leave.'

   c. Ce   costume te va   bien.
      This suit   you go-PR well
      'This suit becomes you.' (lit. goes well to you)
   d. Il faut que j' y   aille.
      It must that I to.there go-SUBJ.PR
      'I must go there.'

Despite the existence of several suppletive stems, most forms of 'aller' exhibit regular inflectional endings. (Exceptions are restricted to some of the forms based on the *v*- root.) What is exceptional is the existence of several bases onto which regular endings attach. We can take advantage of the same bi-dimensional representation of roots I used for English irregular past tenses to describe the inflectional paradigm of 'aller.' The relevant hierarchy for the root *aller* is diagramed in figure 97.

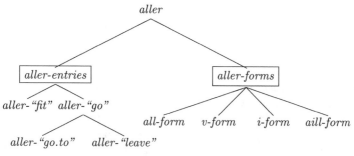

FIGURE 97 The French root *aller*

    To build words out of the root *aller*, we proceed as we did for English past tense verbs: any root form or entry can be the value of the μ-STRUC|DGHTR attribute of any compatible inflectional template. Take a form such as 'irai' ('I will go'). It is "derived" by using the *i-form* category as value of the μ-STRUCT|DGHTR attribute in the inflectional *1sg-fut* construction diagrammed in figure 98.

    The *1sg-fut* category specifies that the class of words that are in the first person of the future must have /re/ as a suffix. Moreover, as other inflectional constructions, it is headed; its head properties are therefore identical to those of its morphological daughter, as indicated in the figure by the tag ①. Hence, the [TNS *fut*] and [MOOD *ind*] VFORM properties of *1sg-fut* words are shared between first singular future or conditional words and the roots or stems on which they are based. Through the specification of its VFORM properties, the *1sg-fut* inflectional category appropriately restricts the choice of root form of its base. No other

$$
\begin{bmatrix}
\textit{1sg-fut} \\[4pt]
\text{CAT} \quad \begin{bmatrix} \text{HEAD}\,\boxed{1} & \begin{bmatrix} \text{VFORM} & \begin{bmatrix} \text{TNS} & \textit{fut} \\ \text{MOOD} & \textit{ind} \end{bmatrix} \\[6pt] \text{AGR} & \begin{bmatrix} \text{PERS } \textit{1} \\ \text{NUM } \textit{sg} \end{bmatrix} \end{bmatrix} \end{bmatrix} \\[10pt]
\text{PHON} \quad \begin{bmatrix} \text{AFF} \begin{bmatrix} \text{SUFF} \langle \text{re} \rangle \end{bmatrix} \end{bmatrix} \\[6pt]
\mu\text{-STRUC} \begin{bmatrix} \text{DGHTR} \begin{bmatrix} \text{CAT} \begin{bmatrix} \text{HEAD}\,\boxed{1} \end{bmatrix} \end{bmatrix} \end{bmatrix}
\end{bmatrix}
$$

FIGURE 98 The *1sg-fut* verb category

$$
\begin{bmatrix}
\textit{i-form} \\[4pt]
\text{CAT} \quad \begin{bmatrix} \text{HEAD} \boxed{1} \begin{bmatrix} \text{VFORM} \begin{bmatrix} \text{TNS} \textit{fut} \vee \textit{cond} \end{bmatrix} \end{bmatrix} \end{bmatrix} \\[8pt]
\mu\text{-STRC} \begin{bmatrix} \text{DGHTR} \begin{bmatrix} \text{PHON} \begin{bmatrix} \text{FORM} \langle \text{i} \rangle \end{bmatrix} \\[4pt] \text{CAT} \begin{bmatrix} \text{HEAD} \boxed{1} \end{bmatrix} \end{bmatrix} \end{bmatrix}
\end{bmatrix}
$$

FIGURE 99 The *i-form* of *aller*

choice but the *i-form* root form category will do as the daughter of *1sg-fut* when it combines with the root *aller*. The inflectional properties of all other forms clash with its own. Reciprocally, choosing the *i-form* of *aller* forces us to build a *1sg-fut* word, since its morphosyntactic features restrict its occurrence to conditional or future contexts, that is, to inflectional categories whose morphosyntactic features do not conflict with future or conditional tenses. By contrast to a lexical rule approach which required the introduction of a redundant listing of stem forms and their morphosyntactic features in the definition of *aller*, the logic of AND/OR nets and the assumption that inflectional constructions are headed suffice to account for stem selection.

No appeal to a new class of linguistic objects like Anderson 1992's stem sets is necessary either. Anderson proposes to attach to lexical items sets of stems which particular inflectional processes select according to the principle in (2).

(2)   'In interpreting a given Morphosyntactic representation M, from among the stems in the lexical set S of a given lexical item, only that stem S_1 which is characterized for the maximal subset of the features compatible with M may serve as the basis of an inflected form $\{S, M\}$.' (p.133)

Stem selection is clearly similar in spirit to the effects of our AND/OR logic on bi-dimensional descriptions of roots. But whereas the notion of stem-set and stem-selection is not independently motivated and requires the addition of new principles such as (2), multi-dimensional subhierarchies and the logic of AND/OR nets which underlies them are the bread and butter of Typed Feature Structure systems. To the extent that the effects of stem selection follow from the organization of lexeme categories, the central claim of this book that lexical productivity reduces to category intersection is supported: *if* (underspecified) category intersection is the source of lexical productivity, principles like (2) need not be stipulated.

Productive stem selection: Czech nominal declension. English irregular verbs exemplify (exceptional) roots that have several morphosyntactically restricted forms to which no regular inflectional endings attach. French 'aller' illustrates (exceptional) roots which possess several morphosyntactically restricted suppletive forms to which regular endings attach. In both cases, the selection of the appropriate root form by inflectional constructions follows from a bi-dimensional description of roots and ordinary OLTC. This account can be generalized to situations in which classes of roots share partially similar sets of root forms to which regular endings attach— the very circumstances where morpholexical rules have been invoked since Lieber 1980. Spencer 1988 proposes, for example, to use such rules in his model of stem alternations in Czech nominal declension. Czech nominal stems are grouped into two basic classes, "hard" and "soft." Certain affixes select "hard" stems; others "soft" stems. More interestingly, certain affixes seem not only to select "soft" stems, but to create soft allomorphs out of hard stems by palatalizing their final consonant.

The prepositional plural allomorph '-ích', for example, only attaches to soft stems, whereas the allomorphs '-ech' and '-ách' attach to hard stems. But '-ích' can also attach to a subset of hard stems and select their palatalized, soft allomorph. The hard stem 'zvuk-' ('sound'), for example, takes the hard suffix '-u' in the genitive singular to produce the surface form 'zvuku'. But it also takes the soft suffix '-ích' in the prepositional plural, which then attaches to the stem's soft allomorph, 'zvuc-', resulting in the surface form 'zvucích', with palatalization of the final stem consonant. The suffix '-ích' requires a soft stem or induces a "softening" of the hard stems to which it affixes.

Spencer argues convincingly that the choice of allomorph is not phonologically conditioned or the result of a productive synchronic phonological rule, even though the alternation of hard and soft allomorphs is productive in modern Czech. Stems ending in *p, b, f, v, m, t, d, n, r, k, g, ch, h* are hard, whereas stems ending in *c, č, š, ž, ř, ť, ň, j* are soft. But the classification of stems into hard and soft stems— based in most cases on the phonological class of the stem-ending consonant— is sometimes arbitrary, as is the case for stems ending in l, s, and z which sometimes are hard and sometimes soft. Although Spencer adduces the Czech secondary palatalization data specifically to argue in favor of morpholexical rules in the sense of Lieber 1980, bi-dimensional descriptions of roots and OLTC are all that is required. The addition of morpholexical rules in our morphological toolkit is superfluous. To account for the Czech data, I generalize the treatment of *aller* presented in the last section and associate a set of root forms with a category of velar roots rather than a single root, as shown in figure 100. To model the regularities found in the definition of soft and hard roots noticed by Spencer, two subclasses of both soft and hard roots are posited in the diagram. One class is (partially) described by the phonological form of the last segment of their FORM attribute. These are the hard-final-consonant and soft-final-consonant classes of roots (*hd-C* and *sft-C* respectively in figure 100). Another class is defined by sheer listing of its idiosyncratically hard and soft members (*lex-hd* and *lex-sft* respectively in figure 100).[1]

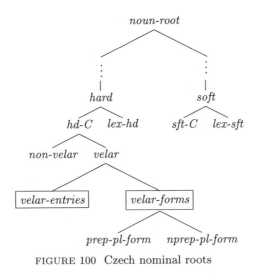

FIGURE 100 Czech nominal roots

The *velar* subclass of final-hard-consonant hard roots consists of a bi-

---

[1]I assume for purposes of exposition that Czech secondary palatalization only applies to underived roots. If the same alternation applies to derived stems, we must simply move the subhierarchy of nominal roots to another location in the hierarchy of Czech lexemes.

dimensional classification of its members in a list of entries and a list of form categories. To form words out of velar roots one must choose both a specific *velar* entry and one of the two abstract root form categories, *prep-pl-form* or *n-prep-pl-form*. Figures 101 and 102 define each.

$$
\begin{bmatrix}
\textit{prep-pl-form} \\
\text{μ-STRUC}
\begin{bmatrix}
\text{DGHTR}
\begin{bmatrix}
\text{PHON} \begin{bmatrix} \text{FORM} \langle ..., \; +\textit{palatal} \rangle \end{bmatrix} \\
\text{CAT} \begin{bmatrix} \text{HEAD} \begin{bmatrix} \text{μ-FEAT} \begin{bmatrix} \text{CASE } \textit{prep} \\ \text{AGR} \begin{bmatrix} \text{NUM } \textit{plur} \end{bmatrix} \end{bmatrix} \end{bmatrix} \end{bmatrix}
\end{bmatrix}
\end{bmatrix}
\end{bmatrix}
$$

FIGURE 101 The *prepositional-plural* form of nominal roots

$$
\begin{bmatrix}
\textit{n-prep-pl-form} \\
\text{μ-STRUC} \begin{bmatrix} \text{DGHTR} \begin{bmatrix} \text{PHON} \mid \text{FORM} \langle ..., \; +\textit{velar} \rangle \end{bmatrix} \end{bmatrix}
\end{bmatrix}
$$

FIGURE 102 The *non-prepositional-plural* form of nominal roots

Both categories include phonological conditions on their last consonant. The former is restricted to prepositional plural contexts and has a palatal consonant as its last segment. The latter can occur in all other contexts (thanks to the absence of any case or number specification and the Morphological Blocking Principle) and has a velar consonant as its last segment.[2] The relationship between the two classes of forms and their appropriate selection by inflectional categories are handled in the usual manner: any category can be the daughter of an inflectional category unless this results in inconsistent information. This general principle of category combination, not morphology specific rules, insures the selection of a *prep-pl-form* form of velar nominal roots when a *ích*-suffixed noun is built, since members of this root form category alone are consistent with the definition of *ích*-suffixed nouns in figure 103 (witness the [CASE *prep*], [NUM *plur*] feature specifications).

The treatment of Czech secondary palatalization I just presented is similar to that of stem alternations in the paradigm of the French verb 'aller'. Ordinary inflectional categories select different forms of the root on the basis of the morphosyntactic features they "realize". In the Czech case, though, the two different roots are similar phonologically; they differ only by a single phonological feature. Moreover, the set of

---

[2]I use a shorthand representation of segmental features in the diagrams for expository purposes. See Bird and Klein 1994 for a representation of phonological features within HPSG.

$$\begin{bmatrix} \textit{ich-nouns} & & \\ \text{PHON} & \begin{bmatrix} \text{AFF} \begin{bmatrix} \text{SUFF} \langle \text{i, č} \rangle \end{bmatrix} \end{bmatrix} \\ \text{CAT} & \begin{bmatrix} \text{HEAD}\boxed{1} \begin{bmatrix} \mu\text{-FEAT} \begin{bmatrix} \text{CASE } \textit{prep} \\ \text{AGR } \begin{bmatrix} \text{NUM } \textit{plur} \end{bmatrix} \end{bmatrix} \end{bmatrix} \end{bmatrix} \\ \mu\text{-STRUC} \begin{bmatrix} \text{DGHTR} \begin{bmatrix} \text{PHON} \begin{bmatrix} \text{FORM} \langle ..., +\textit{palatal} \rangle \end{bmatrix} \\ \text{CAT} \begin{bmatrix} \text{HEAD } \boxed{1} \end{bmatrix} \end{bmatrix} \end{bmatrix} \end{bmatrix}$$

FIGURE 103 *ich*-suffixed nouns

root forms is not associated with a single root; it applies to an open-ended class of nominal roots. The conclusions are still the same: stem selection receives an immediate model through the use of lexeme classes and AND/OR logic. We can avoid *ad hoc* mechanisms such as stem-sets (Anderson 1992) or morpholexical rules (Lieber 1980, Spencer 1988).

5.2 Latin verbal morphology

Until now, the uses of multi-dimensional classifications which I illustrated were restricted to morphological atoms, that is, roots or sets of roots. But, in fact, one of the major benefits of a TCCM is that all morphological constituent structure constructions (morphological processes in general) are so classified. In this section, I argue that this property of morphological constructions under a TCCM provides an immediate model of what Anderson calls conjunctive *vs.* disjunctive rule application. The theme has a well-known flavor by now: what are in other approaches stipulated properties of the application of morphological processes follows from the fact that lexical productivity reduces to category intersection in a TUHL architecture.

To illustrate my point, I return to the Latin verbal morphology briefly discussed in chapters 2 and 3. A sample of Latin verb forms is presented in tables 3 and 4. The upper halves of the tables contain first person singular forms, the lower halves contain second person singular forms. (For ease of exposition, I make use of the traditional term "perfect" in the following discussion regardless of the true aspectual value of these forms. The person attribute is irrelevant for the perfect passive participle. Vowel length is marked when relevant.)

	Present of the indicative active	Present of the indicative passive	Imperfect of the indicative active
amare 'love'	am-o	am-or	am-ā-ba-m
delere 'destroy'	del-ē-o	del-ē-or	del-ē-ba-m
legere 'read'	leg-o	leg-or	leg-ĕ-ba-m
amare 'love'	am-ā-s	am-ā-ris	am-ā-ba-s
delere 'destroy'	del-ē-s	del-ē-ris	del-ē-ba-s
legere 'read'	leg-i-s	leg-ĕ-ris	leg-ĕ-bas

TABLE 3 Latin imperfective verb forms

	Perfect of the indicative active	Perfect participle
amare 'love'	am-ā-v-ī	am-ā-t-s
delere 'destroy'	del-ē-v-ī	del-ē-t-us
legere 'read'	leg-i	lec-t-us
amare 'love'	am-ā-v-isti	
delere 'destroy'	del-ē-v-isti	
legere 'read'	leg-i-sti	

TABLE 4 Latin perfect verb forms

A few important aspects of Latin verbal inflections are illustrated in the forms in tables 3 and 4. Firstly, except for the first person present of the indicative, most verbal forms have what is traditionally called a thematic vowel— a vowel tagged onto the end of the root (or stem) before aspect, tense, and person markings. Distinct classes of verbs select different thematic vowels. For verbs such as 'amāre' the added vowel is /ā/. For 'delēre', it is /ē/, and for 'legĕre,' it is /ĕ/. Secondly, perfect tenses and moods are built on a stem which typically consists of the root, the theme vowel, and /v/ in that order.

The basic organization of the tense/mood and agreement Latin inflectional categories is represented in figure 104 on page 144. Only a few of the set of inflectional categories are mentioned for clarity. The same analysis applies to others. According to this hierarchy, a Latin verb form such as 'amavissem' ('[I wish] I had loved') is built in two steps. The root 'ama-' combines first with a perfect-stem forming construction to create the stem 'amav-'. The perfect stem 'amav-' combines then with both tense/mood and person/voice constructions to yield the surface form 'amavissem'.

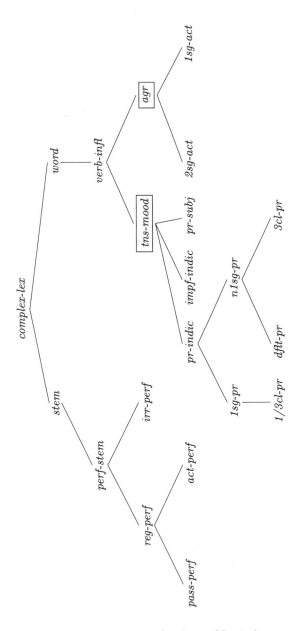

FIGURE 104 A subset of Latin lexeme categories

The constituent structure schemata building up perfect stems are represented in figures 105, 106, and 108. These schemata build up a *stem* to which tense and mood inflections attach. The common superclass *perf-stem* in figure 105 simply specifies the perfect aspectual class of its members.[3]

$$
\begin{bmatrix}
\textit{perf-stem} \\
\text{CAT} \begin{bmatrix} \text{HEAD} \begin{bmatrix} \mu\text{-FEAT} \begin{bmatrix} \text{VFORM} \mid \text{ASP } \textit{perf} \end{bmatrix} \end{bmatrix} \end{bmatrix}
\end{bmatrix}
$$

FIGURE 105 The general *perfect-verb-stem* category

Its *act-perf* subclass in figure 106 specifies that the second suffix (after the theme vowel) for active forms must be /v/. The application of this construction to the root *amare* is diagrammed in figure 107 (see appendix A for a definition of the attribute LXM).

$$
\begin{bmatrix}
\textit{act-perf} \\
\text{PHON} \quad \begin{bmatrix} \text{AFF} \begin{bmatrix} \text{SUFF} \langle \boxed{1}, \text{v} \rangle \end{bmatrix} \end{bmatrix} \\
\text{CAT} \quad \begin{bmatrix} \text{HEAD} \begin{bmatrix} \mu\text{-FEAT} \begin{bmatrix} \text{VFORM} \begin{bmatrix} \text{VOICE } \textit{act} \end{bmatrix} \\ \text{LXM} \begin{bmatrix} \text{THEME-V} \boxed{1} \end{bmatrix} \end{bmatrix} \end{bmatrix} \end{bmatrix}
\end{bmatrix}
$$

FIGURE 106 The regular *active-perfect* stem category

The *irr-perf* subclass of perfect stem constructions is represented in figure 108. The construction specifies that the second suffix to be added to the stem is the empty-string; in other words, irregular perfects do not make use of a root-extending /v/. Note that imperfective verbal forms are not created by a constituent structure schema. Imperfective aspectual information is carried exclusively by tense/mood affixes. I thus assume there is a difference in complexity in Latin verbal forms. Perfect forms have one more layer of internal structure than imperfective forms, as indicated by the difference in bracketing of (3) and (4).

---

[3]Morphological feature information— which is specified on mother nodes in the diagrams— is shared among mothers and daughters *per* the Morphological Head Feature Principle defined in (8) in section 5.4. The definition of the *perf-stem* category in figure 105 is therefore equivalent to the following definition:

$$
\begin{bmatrix}
\textit{perf-stem} \\
\text{CAT} \quad \begin{bmatrix} \text{HEAD} \boxed{1} \end{bmatrix} \\
\mu\text{-STRUC} \quad \begin{bmatrix} \text{DGHTR} \begin{bmatrix} \text{CAT} \begin{bmatrix} \text{HEAD} \boxed{1} \begin{bmatrix} \mu\text{-FEAT} \begin{bmatrix} \text{VFORM} \mid \text{ASP } \textit{perf} \end{bmatrix} \end{bmatrix} \end{bmatrix} \end{bmatrix} \end{bmatrix}
\end{bmatrix}
$$

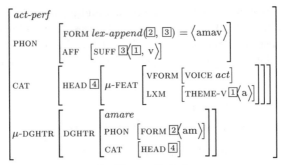

$$
\begin{bmatrix}
\textit{act-perf} \\[2pt]
\text{PHON} \begin{bmatrix} \text{FORM } \textit{lex-append}(\boxed{2},\, \boxed{3}) = \langle \text{amav} \rangle \\ \text{AFF } [\text{SUFF } \boxed{3}\langle \boxed{1},\, \text{v} \rangle] \end{bmatrix} \\[10pt]
\text{CAT} \begin{bmatrix} \text{HEAD } \boxed{4} \begin{bmatrix} \mu\text{-FEAT} \begin{bmatrix} \text{VFORM} [\text{VOICE } \textit{act}] \\ \text{LXM} [\text{THEME-V } \boxed{1}\langle a \rangle] \end{bmatrix} \end{bmatrix} \end{bmatrix} \\[10pt]
\mu\text{-DGHTR} \begin{bmatrix} \text{DGHTR} \begin{bmatrix} \textit{amare} \\ \text{PHON } [\text{FORM } \boxed{2}\langle \text{am} \rangle] \\ \text{CAT } [\text{HEAD } \boxed{4}] \end{bmatrix} \end{bmatrix}
\end{bmatrix}
$$

FIGURE 107 The perfect stem *amav-*

(3) [[ama] ba-m] 'I loved (impf)'

(4) [[[ama] v] isse-m] '[I wish] I had loved'

We can avoid a vacuous imperfective stem construction in the case of Latin verbal morphology because tense-mood and agreement endings of perfect forms are disjoint from those of imperfective forms. The use of each class of tense/mood and agreement affixes can therefore be restricted to words bearing perfect and imperfective aspect by appropriately constraining the value of the μ-STRUC|DGHTR attribute. Only the former class of affixes requires its value to belong to the category of *perf-stem*, thereby inducing the "application" of one of the stem-forming morphological constructions. We thus do not need all Latin verbal forms to go through an aspect construction, the default assumption in the absence of any evidence to the contrary.

$$
\begin{bmatrix}
\textit{irr-perf} \\[2pt]
\text{PHON} \begin{bmatrix} \text{AFF} [\text{SUFF} \langle \ldots,\, \textit{elist} \rangle] \end{bmatrix} \\[6pt]
\text{CAT} \begin{bmatrix} \text{HEAD} [\mu\text{-FEAT} [\text{VFORM} [\text{VOICE } \textit{act}]]] \end{bmatrix}
\end{bmatrix}
$$

FIGURE 108 The *irregular-perfect* stem category

Turning now to tense/mood and person marking, the subpart of the Latin *word* hierarchy relevant to verbal inflectional morphology is dominated by the type *verb-infl*. Verbal inflectional templates in Latin fall into two subdimensions and Latin verbs must be defined along both. A fully specified Latin verb like 'delēs' ('you destroy'), for example, is both a second person singular active verb and a present of the indicative verb. It is the result of:

1. Intersecting two inflectional categories along the *tns-mood* and

agr dimensions, the *dflt-pr* category (for default-present-of-the-indicative) and the *2sg-act* category (for second-person-singular-active);

2. Choosing the root *delere* as the daughter of both categories.

The *dflt-pr* category is represented in figure 109. It stipulates that present of the indicative verbs have their theme vowel as the first element of their suffix list and no characteristic consonant, as indicated by the fact that the list of suffixes has an empty-list as second element. The *2sg-act* category represented in figure 110 stipulates that second person singular active verbs have /s/ as the third element on their suffix list.

$$
\begin{bmatrix}
\textit{dflt-pr} \\
\text{PHON} & \begin{bmatrix} \text{AFF} \begin{bmatrix} \text{SUFF} \langle \boxed{1}, elist, \dots \rangle \end{bmatrix} \end{bmatrix} \\
\text{CAT} & \begin{bmatrix} \text{HEAD} \begin{bmatrix} \mu\text{-FEAT} \begin{bmatrix} \text{LXM} \begin{bmatrix} \text{THEME-V} \boxed{1} \end{bmatrix} \end{bmatrix} \end{bmatrix} \end{bmatrix}
\end{bmatrix}
$$

FIGURE 109 The *default-present* inflectional category

$$
\begin{bmatrix}
\textit{2sg-act} \\
\text{PHON} & \begin{bmatrix} \text{AFF} \begin{bmatrix} \text{SUFF} \langle \dots, \dots, s \rangle \end{bmatrix} \end{bmatrix} \\
\text{CAT} & \begin{bmatrix} \text{HEAD} \begin{bmatrix} \mu\text{-FEAT} \begin{bmatrix} \begin{bmatrix} \text{VFORM} \begin{bmatrix} \text{VOICE } \textit{act} \end{bmatrix} \end{bmatrix} \\ \text{AGR} \begin{bmatrix} \text{PERSON } \textit{2} \\ \text{NUM } \quad \textit{sg} \end{bmatrix} \end{bmatrix} \end{bmatrix} \end{bmatrix}
\end{bmatrix}
$$

FIGURE 110 The *second-singular-active* inflectional category

The structure of the form 'delēs' is thus as in (5), where /ē/, the so-called thematic vowel, is added to the root before any tense/mood or person/voice ending. A more precise representation is given in figure 111. Note that the lexical phonological form of the mother node is /delēs/ ($\alpha\beta$ elements aside.) The absence of any phonological mark of the present of the indicative (indicated by the *elist* in the second position of the SUFF list) has no effect on the output of *lex-append*, since the empty-list is the identity element of the concatenation operation.

(5) [$_{dflt-pr \wedge 2sg-act}$ [$_{delere}$ del] ē-s]

Other verb forms can be described out of the same or other roots by choosing other types in each of the dimensions of the *verb-infl* subpart of the net. The first person of the present of the indicative of a verb such as 'amāre', for example, differs from the present of the indicative of

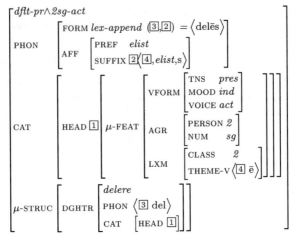

FIGURE 111 The word 'delēs'

other verbs, as well as from its other tenses and moods in not exhibiting a theme vowel (see table 3). Hence, the *1/3cl-pr* category which it instantiates and is represented in figure 112 has an empty first suffix.[4]

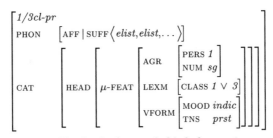

FIGURE 112 The Latin first and third classes *1sg* present

The *1/3cl-pr* category illustrates an important property of typed con-

---

[4]The diagram includes for clarity tense and mood information borne by members of the category, even though this information is inherited from its *pr-indic* superclass. I also assume that the 'legĕre' verb class has a short /ĕ/ as thematic vowel and that it is irregular in all of its present of the indicative forms in having either no thematic vowel or a vowel other than its thematic vowel between the bare root and the agreement affix. Lieber 1980 argues that the form 'legĕre' is regular, if we hypothesize the existence of an otherwise invisible underlying segment. Although possible, her analysis does not rely on any synchronic data. Nothing crucial as to the overall organization of Latin inflectional morphology hinges on the particular analysis I chose.

stituent and construction-based morphologies: inflectional constituent structure constructions can constrain the morphological features of verbs to which they apply without "realizing" these features— intuitively, without discharging their need for a phonological mark. The inflectional category *1/3cl-pr* restricts the person/voice contexts with which it is compatible— namely first person singular active words, as indicated by the featural content of the template (notice the [PERS *1*] and [NUM *sg*] attribute/value pairs). By pre-specifying the values of the PERS and NUM attributes, it constrains the person/number ending categories with which it can conjoin. The *2sg-act* inflectional category is, for example, excluded since its intersection with the *1/3cl-pr* class would be empty. But despite the combinatorial restrictions it effects, the *1/3cl-pr* class is not the "realization" of first person singular morphosyntactic feature specifications. The feature values [PERS *1*] and [NUM *sg*] must also be "realized" by the *1sg-act* category in the *agr* dimension. By distinguishing between constraining and realizing morphological specifications, a TCCM crucially differs from morpheme-based approaches to inflection rightly criticized in Matthews 1974 and Anderson 1992. A single inflectional category, the *1/3cl-pr*, can both constrain the tense/mood *and* the person/number morphosyntactic features borne by its members and only "realize" the former (i.e. discharge its need for a phonological mark).

Figure 112 and the form 'amo' ('I love') illustrate another difference between TCCMs and traditional morpheme-based morphology. The form contains two pieces of inflectional information: (i) the verb is in the present of the indicative; (ii) the verb is in the first person singular active form. To these two pieces of information correspond two different types in the type hierarchy, the types *1/3cl-pr* and *1sg-act*. But only the second of these two constructions is the analogue of a classical morpheme, i.e. a correlation between a phonological substring and the presence of some morphosyntactic or semantic information. The first construction specifies part of the information structure associated with the form, but does not correlate with the presence of specific affixal material.[5] Most of Anderson's attacks against morpheme-based views of morphology (including Lieber's framework) have therefore no bearing against a TCCM. Although our morphological constituent structure constructions are typically marked by the addition of some phonological material to their base, they need not be. Furthermore, a single category, although "realizing" a particular set of morphological features ([[MOOD *indic*],

---

[5]The reader should keep in mind that in the approach to morphology I advocate, the '-o' "affix" which marks the application of the *1sg-act* construction is not *stricto sensu* a morpheme either, since '-o' is not a sign but a mere phonological string added to the morphological base.

[TENSE *prt*]]), can constrain or pre-specify other morphological features, thus limiting the range of other constructions with which a *1/3cl-pr* word can combine. The fact that the mapping between sets of morphological features and affixes is many-to-many, as stressed by Matthews and Anderson, is thus easily explained once cross-classifying constituent structure categories are substituted for traditional morphemes.

5.3   Subregularities in derivational morphology

A hallmark of the TUHL architecture is that all lexical relations reduce to lexemic categorization. The difference between productive and non-productive relations boils down to the manner in which categories are defined (through their sole intension or through both their intension and extension). One of the claimed benefits of this view is that both kinds of processes receive an adequate analysis. Now that the tools necessary to the description of the internal structure of words are introduced, we can assess the validity of this claim on the very processes which Jackendoff 1975 used to justify his introduction of lexical redundancy rules.

Take the celebrated example of 'aggressive' and 'aggression' which satisfy the constraints on the class of *-ive* adjectives and *-ion* nouns respectively, but whose putative base— the verb '*aggress*'— does not exist in the dialect of many English speakers. My proposal is that bound-roots are constructionally introduced roots, that is, roots syncategorematically embedded in particular constituent structure categories. Consider the category hierarchy of *ive-adj* in figure 113. Both *aggressive* and *regressive* are listed as subtypes of *ive-adj*. The need for such listing is obvious. The *ive-adj* construction is not productive; it does not apply to verbs like 'confess' or 'suppress' (cf. '*confessive*', '*suppressive*'). To capture the common properties of *ive-adj* without overgenerating, we must specify the roots to which the construction can apply even when the root exists independently as in the case of 'regress'. Both words must constitute a particular subtype of the general *ive-adj* category. If both *aggressive* and *regressive* are pre-typed to the *ive-adj* category, what explains the nonexistence of a base root for the former? Crucially, 'aggressive'— but not 'regressive'— is not based on an independent '*aggress*' root. Rather its root form is introduced by the *aggressive* category itself.

(6)   [$_{word}$ [$_{root}$ aggress] ive]

The situation is illustrated in (6) and figures 114 and 115 (I leave out of the diagrams the semantic and subcategorization effects of '-ive' suf-

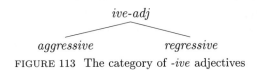

FIGURE 113 The category of *-ive* adjectives

$$
\begin{bmatrix}
\textit{ive-adj} \\
\text{PHON} & \begin{bmatrix} \text{AFF} \begin{bmatrix} \text{SUFF} \langle \text{IV} \rangle \end{bmatrix} \end{bmatrix} \\
\text{CAT} & \begin{bmatrix} \text{HEAD } \textit{adj} \end{bmatrix} \\
\mu\text{-STRUC} & \begin{bmatrix} \text{DGHTR} \begin{bmatrix} \text{CAT} \begin{bmatrix} \text{HEAD } \textit{verb} \end{bmatrix} \end{bmatrix} \end{bmatrix}
\end{bmatrix}
$$

FIGURE 114 The general *ive-adjective* category

$$
\begin{bmatrix}
\textit{aggressive} \\
\mu\text{-STRUC} & \begin{bmatrix} \text{DGHTR} & \begin{bmatrix} \textit{generic-root} \\ \text{PHON} \begin{bmatrix} \text{FORM} \langle \text{ægrɛs} \rangle \end{bmatrix} \end{bmatrix} \end{bmatrix}
\end{bmatrix}
$$

FIGURE 115 The word *aggressive*

$$
\begin{bmatrix}
\textit{regressive} \\
\mu\text{-STRUC} & \begin{bmatrix} \text{DGHTR } \textit{regress} \end{bmatrix}
\end{bmatrix}
$$

FIGURE 116 The word *regressive*

fixation since they are irrelevant to my point).[6] Although the structure in (6) implies that there is a root whose form is /ægrɛs/, no category *aggress* is listed under the *root* subhierarchy of lexemes. The properties of the root instantiated in 'aggressive' are induced by the stem construction represented in figure 115; they are not associated with a subcategory of roots corresponding to the base of 'aggressive'. In other words, the root on which 'aggressive' is based does not exist outside of this constituent structure construction; it is bound to the *ive-adj* subtype. By contrast, the root *regress* is listed independently as a subcategory of roots. More technically, the only difference between 'regressive' and 'aggressive' lies in the different type of their daughter. 'Regressive' requires its daughter to be of type *regress*, whereas 'aggressive' requires it to be of type *generic-root*, the informationally non-specific type for all "bound roots". Most properties of the root daughter of 'aggressive' are thus syncategorematically determined, through inheritance of information that defines the *ive-adj* category. Other cases of so-called *cranberry* morphemes or bound roots would be treated in a similar fashion.[7]

This approach to unproductive derivational processes can be generalized to all situations in which lexical patterns fall into two subgroups, one productive, the other unproductive. Consider the suffix '-ity', which as Bochner 1993 notes after Aronoff is typically not productive in English, except when following the '-able' suffix. We thus have 'serenity', but not '*effectivity'. Putative nonce forms such as 'xeroxability', on the other hand, are perfectly grammatical. To model the dual behavior of the *-ity* category, I propose to divide *-ity* nouns into at least two subclasses, as indicated in figure 117. Figure 118 includes definitions of two relevant subclasses.

Although both subclasses share syntactic and semantic information, they differ in how their membership is defined. One subclass (the *unprod-ity* class) individually lists its members (only *vivacity* and *serenity* are explicitly mentioned in the diagram for clarity). Since bases to which the

---

[6]Inkelas 1989 proposes that bound roots be treated via prosodic subcategorization frames. In her approach too, a record of their c-structural context of occurrence is associated with each bound root.

[7]As pointed out to me by Karin Michelson, this analysis of the pair 'aggressive' and 'aggression' does not explicitly represent the similarity of their bound base: both contain the substring /ægrɛs/. Their constructionally-induced bases are *de facto* identical, but nowhere in the grammar is this fact directly represented. Similarly, the lexeme hierarchy contains no explicit representation of the substring /grɛs/ common to 'aggressive' and 'regressive'. Whether either fact should count against my analysis is unclear. I do not know of any fact which depends on the explicit representation of the relationship between the two bases. See chapter 6 for suggestions as to how to overcome this potential drawback.

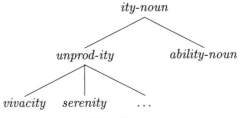

FIGURE 117 The -*ity* nouns category

FIGURE 118 Two subclasses of -*ity* nouns

pattern applies are daughters of explicitly listed stems, the subcategory forms a closed class: by the definition of OR branches, any member of the *ity-noun* category which does not end in '-ability' must be *vivacity* OR *serenity* OR ... The other subcategory merely requires its morphological daughter to be an *able-adj*. Any *able-adj* can thus fill the category's daughter slot. Since all adjectives which end in '-able' are not enumerated, the category is open-ended to the extent that the class of *able-adj* is. Typing our morphological templates thus allows for a simple representation of productive and unproductive subpatterns of a common morphological process. By recognizing a general *ity-noun* pattern we capture whatever generalizations are common to all English -*ity* nouns. By distinguishing between *serenity*-like individual noun stems and the *ability-noun* class, we model the difference in productivity of the two kinds of -*ity* nouns. Only the latter defines its base strictly intensionally and thus categorizes an open-ended set of -*ity* nouns.

5.4 Headed words and other mice-eater problems

At various points in this chapter I indicated that a subset of morphological constituent structure categories are headed, suggesting in particular that by contrast to derivational categories inflectional processes are headed. It is time to be more precise about what I mean by a headed morphological constituent structure schema. To discuss some of the issues involved, I use as my main example endocentric compounds (a subcategory of *composite-word*). I choose this class of morphological structures for illustrative purposes. It provides a good example of how the hypothesis that some morphological structures are headed enables a TCCM to explain seemingly puzzling properties of compounds. My foray into morphological headedness begins with Stump 1991's discussion of Breton compounds.

One of the main issues on which Stump focuses is the internal realization of inflectional categories, that is, instances in which the inflectional features of words are not realized on their "outermost layer", but on some of their internal parts. He discusses at length a particularly interesting example of this phenomenon in Breton nominal compounds. The basic facts of relevance are illustrated in the following set of Breton singular and plural forms.

(7)

singular	Plural	Gloss
mamm-gozh [lit. mother-old]	mamoù-kozh	'grand-mother'
ki-dour [lit.dog-water]	chas-dour	'otter'
mamm	mamoù	'mother'
ki	chas	'dog'

Two important facts for our purposes are illustrated in this small data set. Firstly, the plural affix applies "semantically" to the nominal compound as a whole and not to its parts, since the plural forms present the same semantic idiosyncrasies as the singular. *Chas-dour* means 'otters' not 'dogs of water'. Secondly, the plural inflectional rule is realized on the first member of the compound, not on the overall word. Note in particular that when the first member's plural form is suppletive, as with 'ki' in 'ki-dour,' it is this suppletive form which occurs in the plural form of the compound, confirming that the plural feature is realized on the compound's first member.

Both facts follow from the assumption that endocentric compounds are headed and irregular roots are stored as a bi-dimensional array of forms and entries, as we have been assuming through sections 4.2 and 5.1. The relevant portion of the Breton lexeme hierarchy is diagrammed in figure 119.

The general endocentric compound construction is defined in figure 120.

Its distinguishing properties are its headedness, the presence of two daughters in the local morphological tree it defines, and the mode of combination of the two bases. The last property is inherited from the *compound* subcategory of μ-*comb*: the lexical phonological form of a compound's mother node is the concatenation of the surface forms of its two daughters. Each of the first two properties is characteristic of one separate class of internal morphological structures (that is, values of μ-STRUC), namely *headed-μ-struc* and *composite-μ-struc*. The category *composite-μ-struc* describes binary morphological trees (hence the two attributes DGHTR and DGHTR2). The category *headed-μ-struc* groups to-

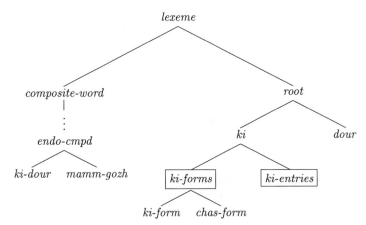

lexeme

composite-word   *root*

⋮

endo-cmpd   *ki*   *dour*

ki-dour *mamm-gozh*   ki-forms   ki-entries

ki-form *chas-form*

FIGURE 119 A portion of the Breton lexeme network

$$\begin{bmatrix} endo\text{-}cmpd \\ \text{PHON} \quad \begin{bmatrix} \text{FORM } lex\text{-}append \ (surf(\boxed{1}), surf(\boxed{2})) \end{bmatrix} \\ \mu\text{-STRUC} \begin{bmatrix} head\text{-}\mu\text{-}struc \wedge composite\text{-}\mu\text{-}struc \\ \text{DGHTR} \begin{bmatrix} \text{PHON} \mid \text{FORM } \boxed{1} \end{bmatrix} \\ \text{DGHTR2} \begin{bmatrix} \text{PHON} \mid \text{FORM } \boxed{2} \end{bmatrix} \end{bmatrix} \end{bmatrix}$$

FIGURE 120 The *endocentric-compound* category

gether the morphological constituent structure configurations to which
the Morphological Head Feature Principle applies. Finally, since compounding combines two lexemes together, we must decide on the category of the values of the DGHTR and DGHTR2 attributes. Stump 1993
shows that the head member of compounds can be either a root or a
word, depending on the construction, and that language-specific stipulations regarding the morphological category of the other daughter cannot
be avoided. I assume that in the case of Breton compounds, the compound's head is a fully inflected word and the second member a stem
(or root).

The *ki-dour* subcategory of endocentric compounds (see figure 121
for its definition) specifies the 'non-compositional' meaning of the compound (it denotes members of the otter category) and its lexemic make-
up: one of its daughters is the root *dour*, the other is a word formed on
the root *ki*.

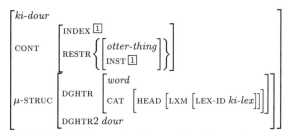

FIGURE 121 The *ki-dour* subcategory of endocentric compounds

The diagram includes the new lexemic, head attribute LEX-ID. The
use of this feature is motivated independently of its use in compounding.
Take the crown example of non-compositional idioms, 'kick the bucket'.
An economical representation of this idiom would posit the existence
of a particular lexical entry for 'kick' which subcategorizes for a direct
object whose head is the word 'bucket' and whose specifier is the definite
article. By localizing the idiom's idiosyncrasy in a specific word, we can
abstract from its representation what can be inferred from our theory
of headed phrases: the head of the VP is the verb, its form is similar to
that of other verbs, the direct object corresponds to a subcategorization
requirement of the head, and so forth. But, then, we need to find a
way to encode into this entry for 'kick' the lexical identity of the head
of its direct object, namely 'bucket'. We cannot use typing and say
that idiomatic *kick* subcategorizes for a phrase whose head is of type
bucket. For one thing, the type *bucket* is a subtype of *root*; it is not the

category of the *word* 'bucket'. Moreover, heads in HPSG subcategorize for the syntactic and semantic information of their sisters (the values of their SYNSEM attributes), not whole signs (see Pollard and Sag 1994 for justifications). Since lexeme categories are signs, the lexeme category of 'bucket' is *per force* invisible to the valence information of 'kick'. In the absence of individuation through typing, we must introduce an attribute whose value is specific to each lexeme. This is the function of the attribute LEX-ID. It uniquely identifies the lexeme of which it is part and, because it is a head feature, its value is shared by words and their stems. With its help, we can now model idioms within a restrictive theory of subcategorization: the relevant entry for 'kick' subcategorizes for a direct object NP whose LEX-ID value is *bucket-lex*. Through the application of phrasal and morphological Head Feature Principles, this information perlocates down to the root of the direct object's head and insures that that root is the one on which the word 'bucket' is based.

A similar reasoning applies in the case of Breton compounds. The key to explaining the "internal" inflection of Breton compounds exemplified in (7) lies in the Morphological Head Feature Principle stated in (8) which parallels the Head Feature Principle of Pollard and Sag 1994 for phrases.[8]

(8)   *Morphological Head Feature Principle*
      In a headed morphological structure— that is, for complex lexemes whose μ-STRUC value is of type *headed-μ-struc*— the value of the head feature of the mother is token-identical to the value of the head feature of the head daughter. More technically:

      μ-STRUC|DGHTR|SYNSEM|LOCAL|CAT|HEAD =
      SYNSEM|LOCAL|CAT|HEAD

Since the lexeme *ki-dour* described in figure 121 is a subtype of endocentric compounds (whose μ-STRUC values are of type *headed-μ-struc*), it is subject to the Morphological Head Feature Principle: its DGHTR's head features are its head features. Now, head features include categorial information as well as morphosyntactic features; consequently, the morphosyntactic features of the compound as a whole are (token) identical to those of its head daughter. Furthermore, the head-daughter of *ki-dour* is a fully inflected word based on the lexeme (and indirectly on the root) *ki*, according to the type declaration for *ki-dour* in figure 121. Together, these two facts insure that when the compound is pluralized, the head daughter is a plural noun formed on the *ki* root: if the com-

---

[8]The principle, as stated, is adapted from Krieger and Nerbonne 1993. Its application is wider in their approach, though, since they assume that derivational affixes head the morphological structures which include them.

pound is marked for plurality, so is the head daughter in accordance with the Morphological Head Feature Principle. But the root *ki* is an irregular root. Its 'ki' form is restricted to singular contexts while its plural is based on the suppletive 'chas' form. Both are defined in figures 122, and 123 respectively.

$$
\begin{bmatrix}
\textit{ki-form} \\
\text{PHON} \begin{bmatrix} \text{FORM} \langle \text{ki} \rangle \end{bmatrix} \\
\text{CAT} \begin{bmatrix} \text{HEAD} \begin{bmatrix} \mu\text{-FEAT} \begin{bmatrix} \text{AGR} \begin{bmatrix} \text{NUM } sg \end{bmatrix} \end{bmatrix} \end{bmatrix} \end{bmatrix}
\end{bmatrix}
$$

FIGURE 122 The *ki-form* of the root for 'dog'

$$
\begin{bmatrix}
\textit{chas-form} \\
\text{PHON} \begin{bmatrix} \text{FORM} \langle \text{xas} \rangle \end{bmatrix} \\
\text{CAT} \begin{bmatrix} \text{HEAD} \begin{bmatrix} \mu\text{-FEAT} \begin{bmatrix} \text{AGR} \begin{bmatrix} \text{NUM } pl \end{bmatrix} \end{bmatrix} \end{bmatrix} \end{bmatrix}
\end{bmatrix}
$$

FIGURE 123 The *chas-form* of the root for 'dog'

By the same reasoning we used in section 4.2.2 for English 'take' and in 5.1.1 for French 'aller' and Czech secondary palatalization, the fully inflected plural form of *ki* must be based on the root form *chas*; it is the only form whose informational content is compatible with plural contexts. When the compound is plural, the head daughter must therefore surface as 'chas.' Hence the pattern in (7).

Importantly, the "internal" realization of inflection in endocentric compounds (including suppletive realization of inflectional features) does not require the invocation of principles specific to inflection. It is a direct consequence of the bi-dimensional classification of irregular roots presented in sections 4.2.2 and 5.1.1 and a universal principle of headed constituents, be they phrasal or word-internal. By contrast, Stump's paradigm function theory approach— which excludes any word internal constituency— cannot rely on general principles of constituent structure and requires the addition of an otherwise unmotivated inflection-specific principle according to which, in morphologically headed structures the values of morpholexical rules realizing the entire word's morphosyntactic features are equal to the values of morpholexical rules realizing the same features on the head.[9]

---

[9]Stump's morpholexical rules are meant to model the phonological correlate of a morphological distinction (such as 'concatenate <r> to the phonology of the base'). They differ from Lieber's morpholexical rules to which I alluded before.

General properties of morphological structure also explain why the same morphosyntactic features are typically not realized on the overall compound— that is why a form like (9) is ungrammatical. By definition, a *word* is a fully inflected lexeme. All inflections must therefore be realized internal to the *word* level. They cannot apply (externally) to words, as they do in (9).

(9) *[[[mamoù]-[kozh]]où]   'grand-mothers'

(10) *[[mamoù]-[[kozh]où]]   'grand-mothers'

Why can't we realize the plural morpheme on the second member of the compound, though? Why is the same form but with the bracketing in (10) also ungrammatical? The answer is construction-specific: *mamm-gozh* is an instance of a $[[_{word} \; x] \; [_{stem} \; y]]$ endocentric schema. Since the second-member of the compound must be a stem (or root), not a word, it cannot receive nominal inflection. Breton compounds thus differ from English *X-self* compounds where both members are inflected for number and the first member, as a pronominal, is also inflected for gender and case.[10]

The same analysis carries over to English nominal compounds. Consider the well-known contrast between 'mice-eater' and 'rat-eater' (see Kiparsky 1982a, as well as Gordon 1985 and Kim et al. 1991 for developmental data on the early acquisition of such patterns cross-linguistically). If we simply assume that the English endocentric nominal compound construction requires its non-head daughter to be a root (or stem), we directly account for the contrast. From the knowledge that the first member is a *root* (or *stem*), we can infer that plural inflection cannot apply to it. Since English inflectional categories are subclasses of words, their output is simply incompatible with the constraint on the non-head daughter of the compound. The ungrammaticality of '*rats-eater' is explained.[11]

---

[10]The fact that no case-marking or preposition occurs on either element argues against the putative claim that *X-self* is a phrase whose head is either *self* or *X*. Such juxtaposition is unheard of in English nominal syntax. By contrast, no comparable complication is necessary if we assume that *X-self* constitutes an endocentric compound whose two members are words and the second member must agree with the first in morphosyntactic features.

[11]As many scholars have noted (see Anderson 1992, for example), numerous apparent exceptions to this constraint exist, such as 'grants secretary' or 'parks superintendent'. I assume the compound construction mentioned in the text is different from that illustrated in 'grants secretary', as their semantics suggest. The non-head daughter of 'mice-eater' realizes an internal argument of the verbal base, whereas the non-head daughter of 'grants secretary' encodes something like an adjunct purposive role. We can account for the different inflectional behavior of the two compounds by assuming that the first compound construction requires its non-head daughter to

The grammaticality of 'mice-eater', on the other hand, is a direct consequence of the by-now familiar bi-dimensional representation of irregular roots. As with French 'aller' or Breton 'ki', two suppletive root forms are associated with the root *mouse*, one restricted to singular, the other to plural contexts. Since these two forms are subtypes of *root*, the nominal compound construction can select either one. Assuming the English nominal compound requires the first members of the compound to be roots and stems bearing a plural number feature (a natural assumption, given the very possibility of 'mice-eater'), the root form *mice* must be selected. The difference between 'mice-eater' and '*rats-eater', I thus suggest, is not due to the fact that irregular plural inflection is a level 1 process and regular inflection a level 3 process, as proposed in Kiparsky 1982a. Rather, 'mice', as an irregularly inflected word, is built out of a restricted root form. Although 'mice' in 'mice-eater' has the same phonological and graphemic form as a plural word, it is not a plural word. It is one of the two forms of the root *mouse*, the root form restricted to plural contexts.

Words such as 'mice-eater' illustrate once more the crucial difference between the realization of features and constraints on features, a cornerstone of the morphological theory proposed in this chapter. The root form corresponding to 'mice' bears the attribute value pair [NUM *plur*] and is consequently restricted to the daughter node of plural word templates. But it does not "realize" the plural inflection; it is not classified as a *plural* word. Hence it can appear as the daughter of a compound construction which requires its first daughter to be a root. Conversely, in a word like 'rats-eater', 'rat' is not a singular word: it bears the same attribute-value pair [NUM *plu*] as 'mice' in 'mice-eater', even though it too is not a *plural* word, but a bare root.

5.5 Comparison with other approaches to morphology

My introduction to a category-based model of lexical productivity is now finished; both categorial and structural productivity have been outlined. It might be useful at this point to compare the overall model with other proposals regarding the nature of morphological relations. To some degree, the approach to word structure outlined in the last two chapters simply incorporates into a TUHL architecture some of the familiar results of morphological theory. But, as I have insisted at various points, the incorporation of these results into an on-line typing system presents

---

be of type *root/stem*, while the other requires its non-head daughter to be of type *word*. The difference between the two kinds of compounds boils down to a stipulated difference in the category of the non-head daughter.

advantages of its own. Treating morphological processes as categories subject to the logic of OLTC solves several difficulties that plague other theories. To name a few:

- Both partial regularities and productive morphological processes can be described through a single mechanism: category abstraction and intersection.

- Morphological cross-classifications which are required to represent stem selection and conjunctive *vs.* disjunctive rule application are examples of the overarching AND/OR logic which underlies all lexical relations.

- The restriction of general morphological principles such as the Morphological Head Feature Principle to subsets of morphological constructions can be modeled in a principled manner by referring to various subclasses of lexemes.

- The many-to-many relations between morphosyntactic categories and their morphophonological markings can be accommodated without losing the advantages of a constituent structure approach to morphology.

The rest of this section provides an explicit albeit brief comparison between the theory I outlined in the last two chapters and other modern generative theories of morphology. Generative morphological theories fall into two basic groups, word-based or realizational and constituent structure based. In the first approach, advocated by Zwicky, Anderson, and dating back at least to Aronoff 1976, morphological processes are viewed as rules mapping existing words (or stems) onto new words (or stems). Affixes are introduced by the rules themselves and do not have independent existence. The word 'played', for example, derives from the stem 'play' by a rule concatenating the string /d/ to the phonological value of 'play', when its morphological features contain the information [TENSE *past*]. Nowhere in the grammar is the affix /d/ represented; it only exists as a by-product of a morphophonological operation.

In the most common form of the second approach, advocated by Selkirk, Lieber, and DiSciullo and Williams *inter alia*, both the suffix '-ed' and the base stem 'play-' are independent grammatical objects which combine through constituent structure rules. The approach I outlined in the previous section is a variant of the second approach to morphology, in that morphological operations introduce internal structure in words. But, as I suggested at various points in the last two chapters, it differs from it in crucial respects and agrees with "realizational" approaches on many points. Two properties distinguish it from ordinary morpheme-based theories:

1. It is construction-based rather than morpheme-based; no requirement that a morphological construction be associated with a specific phonological mark is imposed on morphological processes.

2. It rejects common hypotheses among advocates of context-free morphology concerning the nature of morphological constituent structure: it allows for more than one affix to be added at each (morphological) local tree and denies that (derivational) affixes are the head of their local tree. In other words, morphological constituent structure constructions do not obey a $\bar{X}$ format.[12]

Because of these two differences, a TCCM is not subject to the criticisms of context-free morphology presented in work by Zwicky, Anderson, and others. Their critique only applies to morpheme-based theories. In fact, as I now show, a TCCM compares favorably to both morpheme-based and realizational/word-based approaches.

5.5.1 Are affixes heads of morphological structures?

It is often assumed that affixes (especially derivational affixes) are the heads of their local tree (see Selkirk 1982, Lieber 1980, Lieber 1992). By letting affixes be heads which subcategorize for their bases, we can reduce the ways in which morphemes can combine to a minimum number of abstract $\bar{X}$ schemata. We are not forced to introduce a different *base + affix* rule for each affix. Despite its elegance, several reasons militate against this widely accepted hypothesis. The most important is that it entails either assuming the existence of numerous different types of zero affixes or positing new *ad hoc* morphological processes for all instances in which derivational processes are not marked by the addition of phonological material. Take the well-known conversion of verbs into nouns in English, the process relating the noun 'a throw' to the verb 'to throw'. If the head of derivational structures are affixes, we must posit a zero affix to derive the former from the latter, since the nominalization does not add phonological material. The resulting structure for the noun 'throw' is shown in (11):

(11) $[_N [_V \text{ throw}] \; e]$

(12) $[_V \text{ throw}] \longleftrightarrow [_N \text{ throw}]$

Such an approach, as Lieber 1980 argues convincingly, leads one to hypothesize many zero affixes across and within a single language. Furthermore, such putative zero heads differ from ordinary empty categories. Whereas the number and type of empty categories is severely re-

---

[12]The rejection of the second assumption is partially dependent on the rejection of the first: if affixes are heads of their local tree, only one affix can be added at a time, assuming that local trees only have one head.

stricted by universal grammar, as discussed in Chomsky 1982, there is no limit on null affixes, and idiosyncratic semantics and subcategorization requirements must be attached to different null affixes. An application of the affix-as-head motto to such instances leads to an unconstrained theory of inaudible categories.

Lieber proposes to avoid this unwelcome consequence by assuming the noun 'throw' is not constituent structurally related to the verb 'throw'. Rather, both [N throw] and [V throw] exist independently in the lexicon and are related by a redundancy rule *à la* Jackendoff, as indicated in (12). But Lieber does not give independent evidence that the [N throw]/[V throw] alternation behaves differently from affix-mediated processes— that is, independent of her assumption that affixes are heads. Her model of these morphological patterns thus requires the introduction of otherwise unmotivated mechanisms.

Moreover, because redundancy rules are in essence symmetrical, she must acknowledge that her proposal cannot explain the semantic directionality typically exhibited by such rules; in the pair 'to throw'/ 'a throw', for example, the intuition is that 'throw' is first semantically a verb.[13] To account for such semantic asymmetries, Lieber is forced to supplement symmetrical redundancy rules with asymmetrical semantic rules.

By contrast, if we agree that words have internal structure and are built via constituent structure schemata, but do not make the further hypothesis that derivational affixes are heads, we need not resort to redundancy rules each time a morphological process does not add phonological material. We can then directly account for the semantic directionality of verb to noun and noun to verb conversions. Pairs like 'to throw'/ 'a throw' can be related via a constituent structure construction as shown informally in (13) without fearing an excess of empty categories, since positing a structural relation does not entail the postulation of an empty affix head.[14]

(13) [N [V throw]]

A more interesting argument against the hypothesis that affixes are heads comes from a cross-linguistic comparison of inchoativization processes. Consider the following sentences from French, English, and Chicheŵa respectively (Chicheŵa data from Mchombo 1993).

---

[13]Those intuitions are based on Canonical Realization Principles linking verbs to situations and nouns to entities (see Pesetzky 1982, Langacker 1987).

[14]I thus agree with Williams 1981 that morphological conversion is unheaded and does not involve a zero morpheme. But, contrary to what Williams assumes, morphological conversion is the rule, not the exception. Derivational processes are (typically) unheaded and do not involve affixal *morphemes*.

(14) a. Le chef a plié le panier.
      the chief have.PR bend.PPT the basket
      'The leader bent the basket.'

    b. Le panier s' est plié.
      the basket 3.REFL be.PR bend.PPT
      'The basket bent.'

(15) a. The leader bent the basket.
    b. The basket bent.

(16) a. Mtsogoleri a-na-pínd-á dengu.
      1:leader 1SM-PST-bend-FV 5:basket
      'The leader bent the basket.'

    b. Dengu li-na-pínd-ĭk-á.
      5:basket 5SM-PST-bend-STAT-FV
      'The basket bent.'

The lexical process illustrated in (14) is highly productive in French. It applies to most causative verbs whose caused event is a state, and it derives verbs with inchoative meaning (approximately 700 verbs fall into this category). The equivalent English valence alternation is illustrated in (15) (see Zubizarreta 1987 and Levin and Rappaport 1994 for arguments that the English construction takes a causative stem and derives an inchoative stem rather than the other way around). Finally, the corresponding Chicheŵa construction is exemplified in (16). What is significant for our purposes is that the morphophonological effects of the inchoative alternation are cross-linguistically variable. The Chicheŵa construction is a run-of-the-mill derivational construction. The French construction has morphological consequences (the addition of a "reflexive" affix onto a verb), although its morphological consequences are indirect (the affix can be added to a verb which is not the verb stem to which the inchoative construction applies, as shown in (14b), where 'se' attaches to 'est' and not to 'plié'). The English construction is not morphophonologically marked at all.[15]

By not assuming affixes are the heads of derivational morphological processes, we can capture the common properties of these processes despite their distinct morphophonological realizations without committing ourselves to otherwise unmotivated zeros. The common morphosyn-

---

[15]The morphophonological marking of inchoativization processes is even variable in a single language. French, for example, also uses in a restricted set of cases an English style inchoative construction, typically with verbs of the second group, as traditional grammars call them. (Witness 'bleuir'—'to become blue' or 'to cause to be blue', or 'vieillir'— 'to become old' or 'to cause to be old'.)

tactic inchoative construction for all three languages is represented in figure 124.

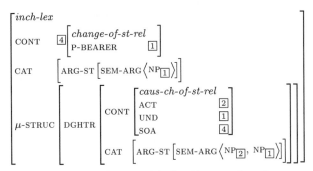

FIGURE 124 A general inchoative construction

The description of the inchoative construction is similar to that given in Grimshaw 1982 by means of a lexical rule. The construction says that stems with inchoative semantics (whose semantic content is of category *change-of-st-rel*) can be formed from roots or stems which denote causal events that result in a change of state (whose semantic content is of type *cause-ch-of-st-rel*). The derived stems denote a change-of-state identical to the caused situation of the causal event described by the base. The construction also suppresses the subcategorization requirement corresponding to the causal force (as indicated in the figure by leaving out of the mother's SEM-ARG list the NP whose semantics correspond to the value of the ACT attribute).[16]

Positing a general lexeme-to-lexeme construction for all three cases, including those in which no overt morphophonological effect is visible, results in a unified description of such alternations whatever their morphophonological spell-out. The differences between the inchoative constructions in the three languages is then minimal:

1. The affix-list of the morphological construction is empty in both English and French, but contains <ĭk> in Chicheŵa;
2. No "reflexive" affix (realized locally or non-locally) is present in English or Chicheŵa.[17]

The category diagrammed in figure 124 captures the convincing intuition of the structuralist practice of adding a "zero morpheme" in cases

---

[16]For detailed definitions of the ACT(OR), UND(ERGOER), S(TATE)-O(F)-A(FFAIRS), and P(ROPERTY)-BEARER attributes, see Davis 1996 and Davis and Koenig 1997.

[17]For a detailed treatment of so-called French object clitics in HPSG, see Miller and Sag 1997.

like the English inchoative construction without requiring us to make a commitment to inaudible phonological entities.

Each language adds particular morphophonological information to this common morphosyntactic and semantic information. The Chicheŵa construction, for example, adds information to the effect that the inchoative stem category is also a subclass of concatenative morphological processes and that the affixal material to concatenate is the suffix /ĭk/, as shown in figure 125 (irrelevant details omitted). If we had chosen to make derivational affixes the head, as is common in work which follows Lieber 1980 or Selkirk 1982's lead, the three inchoative constructions could not have received a unified treatment without zero affixes and (reflexive) affix movement to faithfully reflect their different morphophonological markings.

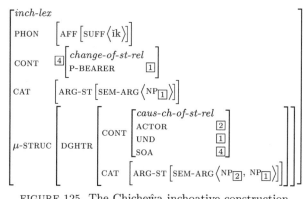

FIGURE 125   The Chicheŵa inchoative construction

The drawback of the affix-as-head hypothesis would be acceptable if some generalizations were exclusively accounted for by the assumption that derivational affixes head the morphological constituent structures of which they are a part. But this is not the case. For one thing, Zwicky 1985 and Zwicky 1991 argue persuasively that syntactic heads differ enough from putative morphological affixal heads to question calling them both heads. Among his arguments are the following: no agreement ever exist between putative morphological heads and their arguments by opposition to what frequently happens in syntax; heads are often ellipsed in syntax, but never in morphology, and so forth. Given the existence of such differences, we cannot justify adopting the affix-as-head hypothesis on grounds of theoretical parsimony. If affixal morphological and syntactic heads behave differently, we cannot rely on the well-known independent motivation for syntactic heads in our justification of affixal morphological heads.

A further argument against the notion that syntactic and affixal morphological heads are similar can be found in the behavior of morphological feature percolation conventions. By opposition to syntactic head feature principles, the various (morphological) head percolation conventions that have been proposed for derivational processes do not simplify our grammar. Since no affix combines with more than one element in those morphological theories which adopt the affix-as-head hypothesis, associating the relevant features with the affix daughter node and percolating them is no simpler than directly associating the same features with the mother node. Moreover, the various percolation conventions proposed by Selkirk or Lieber work quite differently from their putative parallel syntactic principles. Lieber 1992, p.92, for example, assumes the following two percolation conventions (slight rephrasing mine):

(17) a. *Head percolation*
          Morphosyntactic features are passed from the head morpheme to the mother node.

      b. *Back-up percolation*
          If the mother node remains unmarked for a given feature after head percolation, a value for that feature is percolated from a non-head daughter marked for that feature.

Back-up percolation makes morphological percolation conventions quite unusual. Syntactic head features' percolation never undergoes back-up percolation. Features never percolate from the complements of verbs, for example. Furthermore, in the absence of any constraint on which morphosyntactic features are open to back-up percolation, the empirical significance of head percolation is seriously weakened. The convention admits potential affixes which are the heads of their local trees without contributing any feature to their mother nodes!

Finally, the affix-as-head hypothesis is not necessary to capture what is common to classes of morphological constructions— i.e., the general schema they instantiate. In the approach outlined in this book, particular constituent structure templates such as the English [[V] *er*] construction are subtypes of abstract morphological schemata. They therefore inherit all that is shared among members of the general category.

Consider the category of *er-noun* represented in figure 126. The construction takes a verb denoting an event and turns it into a noun denoting the individual corresponding to the logical subject of the situation described by the verb. (I leave out of the statement of the construction the argument-structure of the derived nominal stem as well as the

$$
\begin{bmatrix}
\textit{er-noun} \\
\text{PHON} \quad \begin{bmatrix} \text{AFF} \begin{bmatrix} \text{SUFF} \langle r \rangle \end{bmatrix} \end{bmatrix} \\
\text{CONT} \quad \begin{bmatrix} \text{NUC} \begin{bmatrix} \text{INDEX} \boxed{1} \\ \text{RESTR} \{ \boxed{2} \} \end{bmatrix} \end{bmatrix} \\
\text{CAT} \quad \begin{bmatrix} \text{HEAD } \textit{noun} \end{bmatrix} \\
\mu\text{-STRUC} \quad \begin{bmatrix} \text{DGHTR} \begin{bmatrix} \text{CONT} \begin{bmatrix} \text{NUC} \quad\quad \boxed{2} \\ \text{DESIG-ARG} \boxed{1} \end{bmatrix} \\ \text{CAT} \begin{bmatrix} \text{HEAD } \textit{verb} \end{bmatrix} \end{bmatrix} \end{bmatrix}
\end{bmatrix}
$$

FIGURE 126 The *er-noun* stem category

constraint discussed in Rappaport and Levin 1992 that *-er* nominalization does not apply to unaccusative verbs.) Furthermore, the *er-noun*
category is a subtype of *concat-μ* and *stem* and inherits all the properties common to members of those categories, including the existence of a
(morphological) daughter and a suffix list, the general type of the daughter, the way the daughter's phonological form is composed with affixal
material, and so forth. Only information specific to the *er-noun* subcategory needs additional stipulation. This includes the syntactic category
of the daughter, the syntactic category of the mother, the form of the affixal material, the semantic effects of the morphological construction, as
well as the fact that the construction applies to stems and roots (but not
words). This is exactly the information that the '-er' suffix contains in
frameworks that assume it is the head of words like 'player'. Abandoning
the assumption that (derivational) affixes are heads does not therefore
result in a multiplication of idiosyncratic constructions. As long as a
TCCM is part of a category network, we can capture the properties common to large classes of constituent structure schemata. The motivation
for the affix-as-head hypothesis disappears. Both approaches are equally
apt at representing what is common among morphological structures.[18]

An affix-as-head framework abstracts the common properties of
morphological constructions in the constituent structure component
of morphology. Language-specific information from which the constituent structure is projected is then recorded in entries for individual affixes. A TCCM captures the same difference between general

---

[18]The constructional treatment of *-er* affixation appears to require the additional
statement that the *er-noun* category is a subtype of *stem*. But if all linguistic objects
are typed, corresponding statements would have to be included if we treated '-er' as
an independent morpheme (i.e., as a sign). Statements to the effect that *er-nouns*
are subtypes of *stem* are no more costly than corresponding (implicit) statements
necessary if we adopt the affix-as-head hypothesis, namely that '-er' is an *affix*.

and language-specific information vertically, by abstracting away from language-specific morphological patterns into a general category what is common to all constructions and letting language-specific (morphological) structures inherit these abstract categories. But if both approaches are equally capable of capturing the commonalities among morphological structures, they are still not equivalent. Only a typed approach avoids an unconstrained theory of empty heads, can model medium-size generalizations, non-productive and regular processes as well as true productivity, and so forth.

To summarize, assuming (derivational) affixes are not the heads of the morphological trees which introduce them does not lead to less economical grammars. Metatheoretically, the notion of head relevant in derivational morphology is sufficiently different from the notion of syntactic head that the availability of a unified "syntax" for both phrases and lexemes is very much in question. Moreover, the integration of a TCCM and a TFS system enables us to gather the common properties of morphological patterns in the definition of general categories without the need to posit affixes as bearers of all language-specific properties. By so doing, we avoid the need to postulate zero-affixes and, as I demonstrate in the next section, account for the observation stressed by proponents of "realizational" or process-based approaches that the relation between morphosyntactic feature specifications and their morphophonological realizations is many-to-many rather than one-to-one.

5.5.2 Morpheme *vs.* construction-based constituent-structure morphology

Not all arguments against the view that morphology is the syntax of words depend on the assumption that affixes are heads. Zwicky 1991 and Anderson 1992, after Matthews 1974, point out that sets of (inflectional) features and morphemes do not typically line up in a one-to-one fashion, so that a morphology that is made up of schemata of the form in (18) leads to many inelegances indicative of a wrong-headed theory.

(18) $[_{X^n} \; Y^m \; X^{af}]$

Most of their argumentation, though, relies on two assumptions rejected in the proposal put forth in the last two chapters:

1. At most one affix is added by each morphological constituent structure construction;
2. At least one affix is added by each morphological constituent structure construction.

In a construction-based approach to morphology, although many morphological constructions must be marked by adding single affixes, the addition of an affix is not a necessary correlate of the application of a process. Affixes only serve as arguments of the phonological function which derives the phonology of the mother node. Nothing prevents one of the arguments of this function from being an empty string, an empty list of strings, or a list of more than one string. In fact, given the usual definition of the type list in HPSG, *elist*, the empty-list, is expected to be a possible subtype of the suffixes attribute.[19] Similarly, not all morphological constructions need introduce a new constituent structure level (see the case of Turkish in section 4.1.1). Morphological constructions can "realize" morphosyntactic features without the addition of constituent structure bracketing. The only requirement imposed by a TCCM is that a difference between roots and words be posited (i.e., at least two levels of structure are recognized). Given that word-and-paradigm approaches like Anderson's also recognize as theoretical entities both words and stems (which are defined as words minus inflections), this minimum requirement seems rather uncontroversial.

Because of this partial dissociation between the morphosyntax and morphophonology of lexical processes, a TCCM is not subject to the same difficulties as morpheme-based theories. I illustrate this point with examples involving both multiple exponence (cases where the same feature is realized by more than one affix) and portmanteaux (cases where more than one morphological distinction is realized by a single affix). My data come from Zwicky 1991's discussion of Swahili verbal morphology which he intended as an illustration of the difficulties that plague context-free morphologies.

The basic structure of Swahili verb forms is given in (19). The crucial examples are given in (20). Since I only discuss the Swahili data for purposes of illustration, my analysis will be simplified in several respects.

(19) (NEG)-SUBJ-T/A-(OBJ)-stem-FV

(20) wa-ta-[som-a]   ha-wa-ta-[som-a]
      'they will read'   'they won't read'
      wa-li-[som-a]   ha-wa-ku-[som-a]
      'they did read'   'they didn't read'
      wa-me-[som-a]   ha-wa-ja-[som-a]
      'they have read'   'they haven't read'
      w-a-[som-a]   ha-wa-[som-i]
      'they do read'   'they don't read'

---

[19]Empty string arguments of a string concatenation function are not zero affixes. They are not part of the Hierarchical Lexicon like putative zero affixes in morpheme-based theories. They are a kind of string, like empty sets are a kind of set. Furthermore, they are only used in the computation of the phonological form of the mother node. No morphological object has the empty string as its actual phonological form.

w-a-[som-a]   ha-wa-[som-i]
'they are reading'   'they aren't reading'
ni-ta-[som-a]   si-ta-[som-a]
'I will read'   'I won't read'

Swahili's negative past and negative perfect forms require special tense-aspect markers in the third slot ('-ku-' and '-ja-' vs. '-li-' and '-me-' respectively). Zwicky claims that a realizational framework, but not context-free approaches, can easily describe such discontinuous dependencies between affixes filling the first and third slot: 'ha-' in the first slot realizes [+NEG], whereas '-ku-' and '-ja-' in the third realize [T/A:PST, +NEG] and [T/A:PERF, +NEG] respectively. In other words, more than one realization rule can refer to the same [+NEG] morphosyntactic feature.

A TCCM equally easily describes such dependencies. The notion of "slot" in the structure of Swahili verbs corresponds to a dimension of the relevant morphological constructions hierarchy. "Filling" the third slot means being the third element on the prefix list. To model the (discontinuous) dependency between the tense-aspect affixes and the presence of a negative prefix in the first slot we only need introduce two subtypes of past verb classes along the third "slot" dimension and have each subtype idiosyncratically pre-specify some of the morphosyntactic features of verb forms it describes.

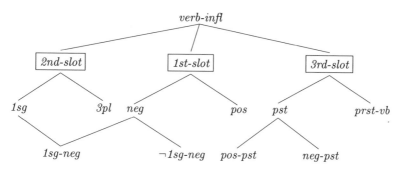

FIGURE 127 A portion of the Swahili verbal inflection network

The relevant portion of the Swahili verbal inflectional categories is represented in figure 127. Swahili verbs are built by combining together a morphological type from each of the three dimensions in figure 127. A well-formed fully inflected verb form (i.e. any member of the category *verb-infl*) is a lexeme built by choosing one category along each dimension.[20] The word 'ha-wa-ku-som-a' ('they didn't read'), for example, is derived by intersecting the categories ¬-*1sg-neg*, *3pl*, and *neg-pst* in the *1st-slot*, *2nd-slot*, and *3rd-slot* dimensions respectively and by having the root *som-* be the value of the μ-STRUC|DGHTR path for each of these three inflectional types.

The apparent discontinuous dependency between 'ha-' and '-ku-' disappears once we allow single morphological trees to be cross-classified, that is, once the same morphological constituent structure schema that maps stems (or roots) onto words can belong to more than one inflectional category. Each dimension along which the constituent structure is classified independently constrains a common set of Swahili morphosyntactic features. Because all verbal inflectional categories have access to the same features, they can constrain each other through restrictions on the morphosyntactic environments of roots or stems with which they combine. Take the *neg-pst* construction. It only applies if the verb is in the negative form, as indicated in figure 128. The pre-specification of the verb's polarity rules out the conjunction of categories *neg-pst* ∧ *pos*, forcing the choice of the type *neg* verb within the 1st-slot dimension. Even though the *neg-pst* category does not by itself mark negation, its featural information insures that the local morphological tree it defines belongs to the *neg* category.

$$
\begin{bmatrix}
neg\text{-}pst \\
\text{PHON} \begin{bmatrix} \text{AFF} \begin{bmatrix} \text{PREF} \langle \ldots, \ldots, \text{ku} \rangle \end{bmatrix} \end{bmatrix} \\
\text{CAT} \begin{bmatrix} \text{HEAD} \begin{bmatrix} \mu\text{-FEAT} \begin{bmatrix} \text{NEG} + \end{bmatrix} \end{bmatrix} \end{bmatrix}
\end{bmatrix}
$$

FIGURE 128 The *negative-past* category

$$
\begin{bmatrix}
pos\text{-}pst \\
\text{PHON} \begin{bmatrix} \text{AFF} \begin{bmatrix} \text{PREF} \langle \ldots, \ldots, \text{li} \rangle \end{bmatrix} \end{bmatrix} \\
\text{CAT} \begin{bmatrix} \text{HEAD} \begin{bmatrix} \mu\text{-FEAT} \begin{bmatrix} \text{NEG} - \end{bmatrix} \end{bmatrix} \end{bmatrix}
\end{bmatrix}
$$

FIGURE 129 The *positive-past* verbal category

The same basic analysis applies to the case of portmanteaux morphs, such as the first singular negative prefix, which is 'si-', instead of the

---

[20]I assume all verbal affixes belong to the same constituent structure level in the figure for ease of exposition. Nothing substantive for the present discussion hinges on this assumption.

$$\begin{bmatrix} pst \\ \text{CAT} \begin{bmatrix} \text{HEAD} \begin{bmatrix} \mu\text{-FEAT} \begin{bmatrix} \text{TNS } pst \end{bmatrix} \end{bmatrix} \end{bmatrix} \end{bmatrix}$$

FIGURE 130 The *past* category

expected 'ha-ni-' (see (20)). We simply divide both the *neg* and *1sg* categories into two subtypes and have them join in a special *1st-neg* construction. This joined category specifies that when the verb is both of negative polarity and has a first person singular subject, the prefix list begins with *si-* and has the empty string as second element, as shown in figure 131.

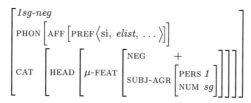

FIGURE 131 The *1sg-negative* verbal category

What makes portmanteaux and multiple exponents easy to represent is the distinction between inflectional constituent structure constructions as lexeme classes and phonological marking of these classes. Inflectional constructions are simply constraints on lexemes (typically of type *word*). They can, but need not, be marked by an affix. The type *pos*, for example, represents a class of Swahili verbs (corresponding to the fact that the inflectional morphology of Swahili is sensitive to a verb's polarity), but is not marked by a special affix. Since no one-to-one mapping between morphological constructions and sequences of affixes is assumed, instances of multiple exponences, zero exponence, and portmanteaux do not present any particular difficulty.[21]

---

[21] One inelegance of morpheme-based approaches carries over to TCCMs. At least one level of constituent structure between morphological atoms (or stems) and syntactic atoms must exist. It entails that a form such as 'walk' in 'they walk' involves an inflectional constituent structure construction which builds up a word from a root or stem. The existence of such affix-deprived constituent structure constructions is necessary since roots, by contrast to words, do not bear the DGHTR attribute. Zwicky 1991 argues that a realizational framework is not subject to this liability and can rely on a general default convention to the effect that, in the absence of a more specific rule, the unmodified stem "realizes" a given set of morphological features. Whether this type of "default" can be implemented in a declarative approach to morphology, such as the one presented here, remains to be seen.

Until now, I have argued that a typed construction-based morphology is not subject to most of the objections leveled against strictly morpheme-based theories. I did not motivate the rejection of realizational or word-based approaches. Some of the motivations for adopting a TCCM are metatheoretical. Whereas realizational/word-based theories require the introduction of new mechanisms such as sets of rules applying conjunctively or disjunctively or stem sets (see Anderson 1992), a TCCM derives the behavior of rule blocks and stem selection from the independently motivated logic of AND/OR nets.[22]

Morphophonological cyclicity and the "hierarchical behavior" of morphological processes provide more empirical reasons to prefer a TCCM. A realizational/word-based framework cannot naturally describe the difference between cyclic and non-cyclic affixation processes, that is, the difference between instances where adding some phonological material leads to an application of cyclic phonological rules and instances where it does not. Non-cyclicity does not follow from the "format of the rule", it must be stipulated. By contrast, the formal analysis of the structure of words in a TCCM mirrors the distinct behavior of these two classes of "rules". As shown in Orgun 1994, the difference is a natural consequence of the claim that words are internally organized in constituent structure trees. We only need assume that phonological rules apply each time a local morphological tree is built. Cyclic application of phonological rules then reflects the internal constituent structure of words. If we make the further assumption that more than one affix can be added each time a local morphological tree is built (or equivalently, in a TCCM, more than one morphological category can describe a single local tree), we can correlate non-cyclic effects with the simultaneous membership of a local tree in several constituent structure categories. Since a single application of phonological rules occurs for all the added affixal material, all but one of the added affixes behave as if they were non-cyclic.[23]

By contrast to Word Formation Rules, constituent structure trees do not require a one-to-one correlation between the syntactic/semantic effects of a morphological process and the application of phonological rules. Phonological rules apply once per morphological tree. Se-

---

[22] Anderson's rule blocks also include extrinsic orderings between rules which lie outside the purview of the logic of AND/OR nets. But, as pointed out by Pullum and Zwicky 1991, this aspect of Anderson's framework— which is not inherent to realizational/word-based theories— is not an advantage. It forces linguists to always order rules, even when there can be no empirical consequence to their various orderings.

[23] Orgun 1995 gives independent syntactic evidence for the claim that more than one morphological construction can apply per local morphological tree. I refer the reader to his paper for more details.

mantic/syntactic effects characterize mappings between the information structure of the daughter and mother of a local tree. Now, since categories in a Hierarchical Lexicon are typically cross-classified, the same local tree can be described by more than one category. To a single phonological mapping between a daughter and mother node can therefore correspond more than one *morph-syn* category. The existence of both so-called cyclic and non-cyclic affixes thus ties in with the general architecture of morphological constructions: *if* phonological rules and syntactic/semantic effects are "unpaired," the possibility of a many-to-one relation between the latter and the former is predicted.[24]

Finally, a TCCM is ideally suited to the "hierarchical" nature of morphological processes— i.e., to the fact that processes often have several subclasses whose productivity differs, as we saw with English '-ity' in section 5.4. Since morphological processes are lexical categories, their organization is expected to be similar to that of other linguistic categories. In hierarchical grammars such as CG, HPSG, or COGGR, this organization is basically that of an AND/OR network. Capturing similarities and differences between subclasses of a process is no more difficult than capturing other lexical and phrasal generalizations; it involves the same categorization of linguistic knowledge. Realizational/word-based approaches do not provide an explanation for this "hierarchical" behavior of morphological processes, nor do they provide tools for its modeling.

5.5.3 Recent approaches to morphology within HPSG

The model of morphology outlined in the last two chapters is closest in spirit to other recent work within HPSG. In fact, several scholars have independently developed theories similar to the one presented here. Krieger and Nerbonne 1993, for example, also proposes a typed constituent structure-based approach to derivational morphology. By contrast to the approach I advocate, though, they assume, with Lieber, Selkirk, Williams, and others that derivational affixes head their morphological constituent structure. In other words, their theory is morpheme-based, not construction-based; it is subject to all the objections mentioned in sections 5.5.1 and 5.5.2. Their model of morphological processes suffers other drawbacks not incurred by more traditional morpheme-based theories. This section focuses on these additional shortcomings. Riehemann 1993 abandons the hypothesis that affixes

---

[24]This benefit is not unique to the approach to morphology presented in the last two chapters. It also inheres in morphological theories in which affixes are morphemes, provided more than one affix can be added per local tree and phonological rules are constraints on the phonological form of mother nodes.

are heads and her model is very close to the one outlined in the last two chapters. The only substantive difference is the absence of roots in her lexical hierarchy. Although lexical entries contain something akin to an internal morphological constituent structure, no linguistic objects in the type hierarchy correspond to our morphological atoms. The internal structure of words is therefore not built up at parse-time and roots cannot serve as independently existing building blocks in the formation of internally complex words. Because subparts of words are not listed independently of words of which they are part, it is unclear how Riehemann's system can model productive derivational processes. In fact, in more recent work Riehemann (p.c.) has revised this assumption and she now assumes that roots are listed independently of words in which they are included. Her revised approach to derivational morphology is, as far as I can see, basically equivalent to the one proposed here (modulo the absence of On-Line Type Construction).

By contrast to their analysis of derivational morphology, a constituent structure skeleton does not form the basis of inflectional processes in Krieger and Nerbonne 1993. They rely rather on abstract disjunctions of features which specific entries inherit. Figure 132 presents (part) of the abstract disjunction of feature structures associated with German verbs. Values surrounded by braces in the figure are to be understood as disjunctions. Braces followed by identical *$number* signs are interpreted as co-varying disjunctions, such that if the first element of one set is chosen, the first element of co-numbered sets must be chosen; similarly for the second, third element, and so forth. In the example represented in the diagram, if the first value of the ending set *e* is selected, the *1st* and *sg* feature values must be selected in the set of values for the person and number attributes.[25]

$$\left[\begin{array}{l} \text{MORPH} \left[\begin{array}{l} \text{STEM} \\ \text{ENDING} \left\{ \$1 \ \text{``e'', ``st'', ``t'', ``n''} \right\} \end{array} \right] \\ \text{CAT} \left[\text{HEAD} \left[\text{AGR} \left[\begin{array}{l} \text{PERS} \left\{ \$1 \ \text{1ST,2ND}, \left\{ \$2 \ \text{3RD,2ND} \right\}, \left\{ \$2 \ \text{1ST,3RD} \right\} \right\} \\ \text{NUM} \left\{ \$1 \ \text{SG,SG}, \left\{ \$2 \ \text{SG,PL} \right\}, \text{PL} \right\} \end{array} \right] \right] \right] \end{array} \right]$$

FIGURE 132 German verbs

Intuitively, one can think of each disjunct in such distributed disjunc-

[25]Such representations are called distributed disjunctions, because the disjunction between the entire feature structures associated with verbs has been distributed on the specific attributes whose values differ. See Krieger and Nerbonne (op. cit.) for more details.

tions as the equivalent of a slot in the inflectional paradigm for German verbs. Actual lexical entries are defined as subtypes of this abstract lexical category and inherit the entire disjunction (modulo default inheritance.) Each disjunct, when combined with the information added by specific verbs, corresponds to the surface form of a German verb.

Several difficulties plague Krieger and Nerbonne's treatment of inflectional morphology. They all stem from the fact that distributed disjunctions are simply a convenient notation for the various slots in a word's paradigm and do not allow cross-classifications of the same set of morphological features, something which is clearly needed, as we saw in the case of Swahili verbal morphology. The distributed disjunction technique requires that co-varying disjunction sets be aligned: the first element in one set corresponds to the first element in each co-numbered set, the second to the second, and so forth. It is therefore impossible to refer to a word's morphosyntactic features as a whole. We can only correlate root forms or affixes to features by associating a particular root form or affix with particular members of disjunction sets which specify morphosyntactic information. This restriction severely limits the expressive power of distributed disjunctions: they cannot cover instances in which a verbs' morphological features are constrained differently by two sets of affixes or a set of affixes and their base. French 'aller' is an example of the second situation, Swahili verbal morphology an example of the first.

The stem 'all-' of the French verb 'aller' is used for the 1st or 2nd person plural of the present of the indicative, for the "imparfait" of the indicative, the participle, and infinitive. One member of the set of stems associated with the entry for French 'aller' must therefore covary with this complex morphosyntactic feature bundle. Tense-moods endings, on the other hand, group the same morphosyntactic features of verbs differently; '-ent', for example, is common to the third person plural present of the indicative and subjunctive, and other tenses. No tense-mood ending selects the morphosyntactic features targeted by the stem 'all-'. A single distributed disjunction over morphosyntactic features, tense-mood affixes, and stem-forms cannot therefore account for the various forms of 'aller'. The only possibility open to the distributed disjunction method is to stipulatively posit different morphological feature attributes that enter into two distributed disjunctions, one with the set of stem forms and one with the tense-mood affixes. Such duplication of a word's inflectional features is of course *ad hoc*.

Swahili verbal morphology poses a similar problem. The "first slot" prefix 'ha-', for example, constrains the verb to be negative, whereas the "third slot" prefix '-ku-' constrains the verb to be both negative and in the past tense. In a TCCM approach, each affix constrains the same set of morphosyntactic features. But in the distributed disjunction approach no single such set exists. To model the difference between '-ku-', which is restricted to negative past tenses, and '-li-', which is restricted to positive past tenses, we need to put in co-varying disjunction the tense and polarity attributes. But given such co-variation, we now cannot represent the fact that the suffix 'ha-' is used to mark negation whatever the value of the tense attribute. The existence of a co-variation between tense and polarity in the case of '-ku-' prevents us from being able to refer to negative verbs *simpliciter*. Like French 'aller', Swahili verbal morphology clearly illustrates the shortcomings of a distributed disjunction approach to inflectional morphology: features must be duplicated every time two classes of affixes (or the affix and the base) group morphosyntactic information differently.

5.6   Summary

Two of the motivations underlying arguments against generalizing the notion of constituent structure from syntax to morphology have been the existence of so many more unproductive or semi-productive patterns in morphology than in syntax as well as the absence of a one-to-one correlation between affixes and what they are meant to mark. Why adopt an architecture devised for modeling syntactic creativity when so much of lexical structure is exceptional and must be learnt on the basis of positive evidence? Why assume a *[base + affix]* constituent structure is present in derived stems or words when so often such a correlation between affixes and morphological trees is absent? This chapter demonstrates that adopting constituent structure configurations for morphological analysis does not force us to ignore the particularities of lexical patterns. By availing ourselves of the ability to categorize constituent structure templates and rejecting the assumption that affixes are signs (morphemes), we can do justice to the observations of realizational/word-based morphologists while reaping the benefits of constituent structure representations. We can put forth a constituent structure-based theory of morphological processes which does not run afoul of the observation that the correlation between morphosyntactic properties and their phonological marks is typically many-to-many. We are then not forced to add new generative mechanisms above constituent structure schemata for fear of missing out on the particular character of morphological structure.

But a more positive argument in favor of a TCCM theory resides in the number of salient behavioral properties which find a natural explanation in terms of AND/OR nets and a boolean category structure:

stem-selection, exceptional or unattested roots, morphological subpat-
terning, many-to-many relationships between morphosyntactic features
and morphophonological marks. Phenomena whose treatments require
ad hoc apparatus in other theories exhibit expected formal properties,
given the logic of linguistic categorization which underlies a TCCM and
the TUHL architecture.

6

Conclusion

Lexical knowledge is a Janus: it exhibits some of the productivity and creativity of syntax while being the repository of the inescapable idiosyncrasies of natural languages. Previous theories have had difficulties with either of its two faces. Rule-based approaches stress the parallels between syntactic and lexical knowledge. By relying on rules, they account for lexical productivity, but not for output properties which are neither present in the input nor contributed by rules. Because analyzability of a form is equated with its derivation, whenever unpredictable information requires storage of the output, a form must be left unanalyzed. *A contrario* representational theories stress the organization of lexical knowledge and the presence of static relations among existing entries. They have no difficulty handling unproductive relations or "output" properties, since lexical relations apply to stored items and the existence of a relation does not preclude storage of the relata. Analyzability is not equated with derivation, but with the presence of static links between stored items. Unfortunately, the success of representation-based theories in modeling unpredictable "output" properties does not extend to truly productive processes. Static relations cannot model the dynamic creation of new entries on the fly. How to adapt representation-based systems so as to cover productive morphological relations is left unclear. Either the problem is not explicitly recognized (as in Bochner 1993) or scholars rely on some unspecified process of analogy (as in Langacker 1987 or Bybee 1988). The similarities between the productive aspects of lexical and syntactic knowledge are left unexplained.

This book has outlined a unified architecture for the organization of lexical knowledge that combines the advantages of both rule- and representation-based approaches to lexical relations. The basic idea is simple:

1. All lexical relations reduce to categorization (to the membership of the two related lexemes in a common category or to the inclusion of a lexeme category in the definition of another lexeme category);
2. Lexical items can be stored partially underspecified as to their category membership;
3. Category intersection is the only mechanism required to describe lexical relations (provided some lexeme categories have internal structure).

The resulting architecture straddles the boundary between rule- and representation-based approaches: the network of categories encompasses representations of both individual roots *and* relationships between lexemes. The claim is that, properly used, class abstraction can reconcile these two views of lexical knowledge and reduce rule application to conjoining categories.

Because the model is category-based, analyzability of a form does not preclude storage of the "output" whenever it is needed. Analyzability is defined as membership in a (constituent structure) category and is orthogonal to the issue of when membership is computed— that is, whether it is derived on-line or stored in the mental lexicon. We thus need not answer the question of whether or not derived forms are listed; they can be, but need not be. Leaving this question unanswered *linguistically* is the best solution. Bybee 1988 and others have demonstrated that assuming derived forms *can* be stored is advantageous when explaining well-known cross-linguistic generalizations. But not all derived forms can be stored, if we wish to provide for rule-like behavior; many derived words are created spontaneously. The TUHL allows both kinds of word analysis.

The implementation of the hypothesis that all lexical relations reduce to categorization started with Hierarchical Lexicons as currently used in HPSG. The organization of categories inherent in this representation of lexical knowledge is well-suited to classificatory relations and their characteristic medium-size. But, chapter 2 demonstrated that ordinary HLs cannot describe productive morphological relations. To account for the the latter, they need to resort to lexical rules, a less than optimal solution, as I argued in detail in that chapter. Chapter 3 revised the HL architecture and introduced the notion of a Type Underspecified Hierarchical Lexicon which preserves the advantages of HLs or usage-based models, but does not falter on lexical creativity. To preserve the flexibility of HLs, the lexicon still consists of a system of categories organized in a multiple inheritance hierarchy.   But to model productivity, lexical entries are not simply retrieved from a stored hierarchy; they are constructed on the fly by intersecting underspecified classes.

Two changes to the HL were necessary: lexical underspecification and a typed constituent structure-based morphology. With these two modifications all lexical relations, productive and unproductive, classificatory and morphological, are uniformly captured through a single mechanism. Aside from the conceptual simplification that results from this move, I have shown it presents several empirical and theoretical benefits.

Firstly, we obviate the objections leveled against a context-free morphology by scholars such as Anderson and Zwicky. The many-to-many correlations between morphosyntactic (or morphosemantic) properties of lexemes and their morphophonological expressions cease to be a problem: morphological constituency does not entail the phonological combination of a base with a single affix. Secondly, we can represent the cross-linguistic similarities of several lexical phenomena whose morphophonological manifestations differ, as I suggested in the case of inchoativization in chapter 5. Thirdly, we account for what I call "medium-size" generalizations: their presence falls out of the integration of an underspecified lexicon in a category-based lexical network. Fourthly, many salient traits of morphological processes reduce to inherent, formal properties of the TUHL. To the extent that a match between observed linguistic generalizations and behavior predicted from the formal properties of a grammatical architecture counts as strong evidence in favor of this architecture, this last advantage is significant. It suggests the fundamental soundness of the TUHL. I list below the behavioral properties of morphological processes which chapters 4 and 5 argued reflect the formal structure of the TUHL:

1. The organization of morpho(phono)logical processes into disjunctive *vs.* conjunctive rule blocks arises out of the boolean structure of AND/OR nets.

2. The cross-classification of roots into sets of entries and sets of forms does not require the addition of morphology specific mechanisms, such as morpholexical rules (Lieber 1980) or stem sets (Anderson 1992).

3. The presence of both regular, but not productive, and productive subpatterns of a single morphological process (such as '-ity' suffixation in English) reduces to the difference between partially extensionally defined and strictly intensionally defined categories.

4. "Storage of output" effects discussed in Bybee 1988 can be accommodated, since no ontological difference is postulated between

representations and rules; analyzability of a form does not preclude its listing.

5. The internal realization of inflectional categories in compounds is a consequence of the bi-dimensional classification of roots independently motivated by stem selection facts and a general Head-Feature Principle. No recourse to a morphology specific principle is required, as in Stump 1991.

6. Multiple exponence or portmanteaux are no embarassment since morphological constituent structure categories are distinguished from phonological affixation processes.

This laundry list of benefits should not obscure the preliminary nature of this work. Much remains to be done. For one thing, the TUHL architecture was only applied to a few examples. How easy it will be to scale up to large portions of natural languages' lexicons remains to be demonstrated. Until such large lexicons are built, the TUHL success should be greeted with a certain dose of scepticism. Secondly, the TUHL cannot currently account for several general properties of morphological processes. I name but two here.

It is common for one member of inflectional paradigms to be unmarked phonologically. In fact, it is so common cross-linguistically that several scholars have suggested that it should follow from an adequate characterization of morphological processes. Word formation should be formulated in such a manner that when inflectional features are not marked phonologically, forms automatically "skip" the rules or constructions otherwise needed to realize them. For example, Zwicky 1991 suggests a general convention to the effect that when no Word Formation Rule refers to a particular feature specification, the base form serves as the output. The fact that 'bird' can realize the [+SG] feature specification would then follow from this universal default. Similarly, Inkelas and Orgun 1995 proposes that forms to which no suffix is added do not, by default, undergo the phonological rules which are associated with the suffix. The lexical architecture outlined in this book cannot in its current form account for this well-established notion of morphological economy.

The similarity between the bases of forms such as 'aggression' and 'aggressive' are not either explicitly represented in the current TUHL, as pointed out in chapter 5. Unfortunately, to represent this shared information among the two derived forms while insuring the ungrammaticality of the base form '*aggress', we would need to say that the root which is the base of 'aggressive' and 'aggression' *must* occur as the daughter of a local morphological tree. Such constraints cannot be expressed within the description languages that typically underlie HPSG grammars. Koenig 1998 discusses in more detail the issue and suggests a modification of these languages that would allow for the inclusion of such statements. As in the case of morphological economy, what intuitively seems a salient trait of morphological processes cannot be presently expressed.

Thirdly, the view of categorization which forms the basis of the TUHL probably requires extension. This book uses a strict categorization scheme: a category α is a subcategory of β only if it bears all properties of β. The current TUHL only describes lexical relations that obey this scheme. But several scholars, particularly Cognitive Linguists, have suggested that a more complex view of (lexical) categorization is needed. Borrowing a distinction from Langacker 1987, I take for granted in this book that schematization and extension are two complementary categorization methods, so that a study of the consequences of underspecification in a schematization-based approach to categorization was a legitimate research program. Although plausible, this assumption needs to be further discussed in view of the copious research in lexical semantics which demonstrates that the semantic values attached to constructions and lexical items do not cluster arbitrarily, but are motivated by general cognitive mechanisms relating sets of conceptual structures. (See *inter alia* Brugman 1981/1988a, Lakoff 1987, Casad and Langacker 1985, Goldberg 1995, Sweetser 1990, and Zubin and Köpcke 1986.) How these additional relationships interact with the strict categorization scheme I adopted remains unclear at present. One possibility is that they describe principles of network extension, whereas strict categorization of the kind discussed in this book describes generalizations over existing nodes in the network. At present, this hypothesis is nothing more than a suggestion.

A

Type declarations

I list in this appendix declarations for current HPSG sorts which are relevant to the issues discussed in this book. I also list the declarations for the new categories I have introduced, as well as the abbreviations I have used; note that the index lists the pages on which each notion is first introduced. I begin with types from HPSG II, except for the definition of *category* where I adopt the proposal of chapter 9 of Pollard and Sag 1994. The value of each attribute F in the declaration of a type τ constitutes the most general type of value of F for any token of type τ.

A.1 HPSG II type declarations

Signs in HPSG encompass both words and phrases and are made up of three kinds of information: phonological, syntactic/semantic, and quantificational (represented in the QSTORE and RETRIEVED attributes). Syntactic and semantic information, in turn, consists of local and non-local information. The former encodes syntactic/semantic information relevant to local trees, the latter encodes information relevant to unbounded dependencies (long-distance extraction, relatives, and questions). See (1) and (2).[1]

(1)   *sign:* $\begin{bmatrix} \text{PHON(OLOGY)} & \textit{list(phonstring)} \\ \text{SYNSEM} & \textit{synsem} \\ \text{QSTORE} & \textit{set(quantifier)} \\ \text{RETRIEVED} & \textit{list(quantifier)} \end{bmatrix}$

(2)   *synsem:* $\begin{bmatrix} \text{LOCAL} & \textit{local} \\ \text{NONLOCAL} & \textit{nonlocal} \end{bmatrix}$

---

[1] Figures in this appendix include the full names of attributes; abbreviated names used in the rest of the book typically appear outside of the parentheses that surround part of the attribute name.

Three kinds of properties pertain to local trees: local syntactic properties (recorded in the value of the CATEGORY attribute), local semantic properties (recorded in the value of the CONTENT attribute), and local contextual properties (information relative to various background conditions and deictic information, recorded in the CONTEXT attribute). Non-local information is split into unbounded dependencies still unresolved at the node under consideration (recorded in the value of the INHERITED attribute) and unbounded dependencies that terminate at the local tree under consideration (recorded in the value of the TO-BIND attribute of the head of the local tree). Both kinds include information about the "extracted" element in a SLASH attribute as well as information relevant to pied-piping (in the REL and QUE attributes). The type declarations at issue are given in (3)-(5).

$$(3) \quad local: \begin{bmatrix} \text{CAT(EGORY)} & category \\ \text{CONT(ENT)} & content \\ \text{CONTEXT} & context \end{bmatrix}$$

$$(4) \quad nonlocal: \begin{bmatrix} \text{TO-BIND} & nonlocal1 \\ \text{INHERITED} & nonlocal1 \end{bmatrix}$$

$$(5) \quad nonlocal1: \begin{bmatrix} \text{SLASH} & set(local) \\ \text{REL} & set(ref) \\ \text{QUE} & set(npro) \end{bmatrix}$$

Local syntactic information (or category information) consists of three kind of properties, head features, valence and argument-structure features, and presence or absence of a marker, as indicated in (6). The first class of properties pulls together that information which is shared between the mother and the head-daughter of an endocentric local tree (the sharing is insured through a universal Head Feature Principle, see (32) below). The second class of properties basically records the subcategorization information of words and phrases. The ARG-ST list records the "potential" complements, specifiers, and subjects of words, whereas the VALENCE attributes, namely SUBJ, COMPS, and SPR, record the actual subjects, complements, or specifiers for which a word or phrase subcategorizes. It is members of the latter lists which are realized through phrase-structural schemata. Once realized these elements are taken off the relevant lists (through a universal Valence Principle, see (33) below). Finally, the MARKING attribute records whether a phrase requires a marker of some sort or not (for example whether a sentence is preceded by 'that').

(6) *category:*
$$\begin{bmatrix} \text{HEAD} & head \\ \text{VAL(ENCE)} & \begin{bmatrix} \text{SUBJ} & list(synsem) \\ \text{COMPS} & list(synsem) \\ \text{SPR} & list(synsem) \end{bmatrix} \\ \text{ARG-ST} & list(synsem) \\ \text{MARKING} & marking \end{bmatrix}$$

The head properties of words and phrases vary with the nature of the head. All major (substantive) syntactic heads are marked for whether they are predicative or serve as modifiers. Only nouns are marked for the ability to bear case, only verbs for a verb form, auxiliary, and inverted status, and only prepositions for prepositional form status. Finally, only functional syntactic heads record the syntactic and semantic properties of what they specify through the attribute SPEC. The relevant type declarations are diagrammed in (7)-(11).

(7) *substantive:*
$$\begin{bmatrix} \text{PRD} & boolean \\ \text{MOD} & mod\text{-}synsem \end{bmatrix}$$

(8) *functional:* $\begin{bmatrix} \text{SPEC} & synsem \end{bmatrix}$

(9) *noun:* $\begin{bmatrix} \text{CASE} & case \end{bmatrix}$

(10) *verb:*
$$\begin{bmatrix} \text{VFORM} & vform \\ \text{AUX} & boolean \\ \text{INV} & boolean \end{bmatrix}$$

(11) *preposition:* $\begin{bmatrix} \text{PFORM} & pform \end{bmatrix}$

This book has nothing to say about the contextual information included in words or phrases and I therefore leave out its description. As for semantic information, HPSG distinguishes two basic kinds of semantic information, entities and eventualities (corresponding to the types *nom-object* and *psoa* or parametrized state of affairs). Nominal semantic information consists of an index, corresponding to the nominal's discourse referent and a set of restrictions that constrain the interpretation of this referent. Each index is marked for so-called ϕ-features, namely person, gender, and number (see (13)). States-of-affairs consist of a list of quantifiers and a nucleus which encodes the situation type described by the word or phrase. See (12)-(14).

(12) *nom-object:*
$$\begin{bmatrix} \text{INDEX} & index \\ \text{RESTR} & set(psoa) \end{bmatrix}$$

(13) *index:*
$$\begin{bmatrix} \text{PERS(ON)} & person \\ \text{NUM(BER)} & number \\ \text{GEND(ER)} & gender \end{bmatrix}$$

(14) *psoa:*
$$\begin{bmatrix} \text{QUANTS} & list(quantifier) \\ \text{NUC(LEUS)} & qfpsoa \end{bmatrix}$$

Now that I have defined the properties of words and phrases which can be encoded at each node of a local tree, let me turn to the description of how phrase-structural information is encoded. In keeping with its attribute-value representational scheme, phrase-structural information is encoded in HPSG through features rather than through a set of $\bar{\text{X}}$ rules or principles. Information directly off the leftmost bracket of an AVM corresponds to properties of the mother node in more conventional tree-based representations. Information regarding the daughters of a local tree are encoded as values of the DAUGHTERS attribute. Phrases differ as to their internal constituency which is indicated in the particular kinds of *con-struc* they include. Headed phrases , for example, are distinguished by the presence of two kinds of daughter, a head daughter and a list of complement daughters (where complements include subjects). The former is the value of HEAD-DTR, the latter that of COMP-DTRS. Head-complement phrases require the syntactic/semantic information of each complement daughter to be (token) identical to a member of the COMPS list of the head-daughter phrase, whereas head-subject phrases require the syntactic/semantic information of the complement daughter to be (token) identitical to the value of the head-daughter's SUBJ attribute. A subset of the relevant categories are defined in (15)-(18). (17) describes the head-complement schema whereas (18) describes the head-subject schema.

(15)   *phrase:* $\left[\text{DAUGHTERS(DGHTRS)} \; \textit{con-struc}\right]$

(16)   *head-struc:* $\begin{bmatrix} \text{HEAD-DTR} & \textit{sign} \\ \text{COMP-DTRS} & \textit{list(phrase)} \end{bmatrix}$

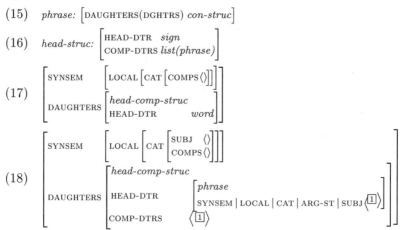

(17)

(18)

A.2   New or revised types

Now that the definitions of all the relevant types from HPSG II have been presented, I turn to the new types I introduced in chapters 3 and 4. These new types concern the internal constituency of words as well as the modifications necessary to the HPSG II types they require. The first new type of objects is the category of complex lexemes, that is, those lexemes which have an internal morphological structure. This internal constituency is recorded in the value of the μ-STRUC attribute. As was the case with phrases, the daughter of a morphological tree is recorded in the value of a DAUGHTER attribute (abbreviated as DGHTR in the text). For complex lexemes that are not composite words, the internal constituency of complex lexemes is quite degenerate; it consists of this single daughter. For composites, an additional daughter is added (see the DAUGHTER2 attribute, abbreviated as DGHTR2 in the text). Diagrams (19)-(21) present the definitions of categories that pertain to morphological constituent structure.

(19)   complex-lexeme: $\left[\mu\text{-STRUC } \mu\text{-struc} \right]$

(20) μ-struc: $\left[\text{DAUGHTER } lexeme \right]$

(21)   composite-μ-struc: $\left[\text{DAUGHTER2 } lexeme \right]$

The representation of the phonology of lexemes discussed in chapter 4 differs significantly from what it is in HPSG II. The type declaration for *phon* is altered accordingly. First the value of the PHON attribute is changed. It consists of a form and a list of affixes. Furthermore, the value of the FORM attribute does not consist of a list of segments, but rather a list of $\alpha\beta$ elements which are defined as the combination of lexical and surface segments (recorded in the values of the LEX and SURF attributes respectively). Affixal material, for its part, consists of a list of prefixes and a list of suffixes, each defined as a list of phonological strings. Finally, phonological strings are defined, as in HPSG II, as lists of phonemes: the type *phonstring* stands for the type *list(phoneme)*, defined in (26). Other types are defined in (22)-(24).

(22)   phon: $\begin{bmatrix} \text{FORM} & list(\alpha\beta) \\ \text{AFF(IXES)} & \textit{affix-lists} \end{bmatrix}$

(23)   affix-lists: $\begin{bmatrix} \text{SUFF(IXES)} & list(phonstring) \\ \text{PREF(IXES)} & list(phonstring) \end{bmatrix}$

(24) $\alpha\beta$: $\begin{bmatrix} \text{SURF(ACE)} & phoneme \\ \text{LEX(ICAL)} & phoneme \end{bmatrix}$

(25)   phonstring $\equiv$ list(phoneme)

(26)   list(phoneme): $\begin{bmatrix} \text{FIRST } phoneme \\ \text{REST } list(phoneme) \end{bmatrix}$

I have also changed some of the definitions of types provided in HPSG II so as to reflect new properties of lexemes introduced in chapters 3 and 4. The first change concerns the syntactic category of lexemes (by

contrast to that of phrases). I adopt the distinction between argument
structure and valence information currently in use in HPSG, but ARG-ST
information is further divided into semantic arguments and additional
arguments. The old list of arguments is redefined as the sequence union
of these two lists.[2]

$$(27) \quad \textit{lex-category:} \quad \begin{bmatrix} \text{HEAD} & \textit{head} \\ \text{VAL(ENCE)} & \begin{bmatrix} \text{SUBJ} & \textit{list(synsem)} \\ \text{COMPS} & \textit{list(synsem)} \\ \text{SPR} & \textit{list(synsem)} \end{bmatrix} \\ \text{ARG-ST} & \textit{arg-st} \\ \text{MARKING} & \textit{marking} \end{bmatrix}$$

$$(28) \quad \textit{arg-st:} \quad \begin{bmatrix} \text{SEM-ARG} & \boxed{1} & \textit{list(synsem)} \\ \text{ADD-ARG} & \boxed{2} & \textit{list(synsem)} \\ \text{ARG-LIST} & \boxed{1} \bigcirc \boxed{2} \end{bmatrix}$$

Two new head properties have been added, the LEXEME attribute
(abbreviated LXM) and the μ-FEATURES attributes. I assume both properties are common to functional and substantive heads. The revised
declaration for the category *head* is given in (29).

$$(29) \quad \textit{head:} \quad \begin{bmatrix} \text{LXM} & \textit{lex-prop} \\ \mu\text{-FEAT(URES)} & \mu\textit{-prop} \end{bmatrix}$$

The LEXEME attribute gathers strictly morphological attributes that
serve to identify lexemes or lexeme classes. Two of its features are LEX-ID
(for LEXICAL-IDENTITY) and the (declension/conjugation) CLASS attribute for those languages for which it is relevant. Latin verbs also
include a THEME-V attribute. The μ-FEATURES attribute groups together all of a head's other morphologically relevant properties, including VFORM and CASE, which are direct properties of the HEAD feature
in HPSG II. The definition of the verbal subcategory of morphological
features, or μ-verb-prop, for example, is given below. (Note that the
type of the AGR attribute value is *index*. The definition in (13) therefore
applies.)

$$(30) \quad \begin{bmatrix} \mu\textit{-verb-prop} \\ \text{VFORM} & \textit{vform} \\ \text{AGR} & \textit{index} \end{bmatrix}$$

Finally, I added the attribute DESIG-ARG to the semantic content
of verbal categories (whose denotata are parametrized states of affairs,

---

[2]Three lists L_1, L_2, and L_3 stand in a sequence union relation if the third list
includes all members of the first two as well as respect the order among their elements. If L_1 and L_2 are $< a, b >$ and $< c, d >$ respectively, $L_3 = < a, b, c, d >$ or
$L_3 = < c, a, d, b >$, and so forth stand in a sequence union relation with L_1 and L_2.

or *psoa* in short). This attribute encodes the notion of a verb's logical subject. The revised definition of the *psoa* category is given in (31).[3]

(31) *psoa:* $\begin{bmatrix} \text{QUANTS} & \textit{list(quantifier)} \\ \text{NUCLEUS} & \textit{nucleus} \\ \text{DESIG-ARG} & \textit{entity} \end{bmatrix}$

A.3   Some HPSG principles

Aside from an articulated network of categories, an HPSG-style grammar relies on a few universal principles; I only discuss in this appendix those which pertain to the issues raised in the book.

(32) HEAD-FEATURE PRINCIPLE
      In a headed phrase (phrases of type *headed-phrase* in the analysis of phrases proposed in Sag 1997), the head properties of the phrase's mother are the head properties of the phrase's head. More technically, the values of the paths:

      SYNSEM|LOCAL|CATEGORY|HEAD
      and
      DAUGHTERS|HEAD-DAUGHTER|SYNSEM|LOCAL|CATEGORY|HEAD

      are (token) identical.

(33) VALENCE PRINCIPLE
      In a headed phrase, the value of the head's valence features (the values of SUBJ, COMPS, and SPR) are the concatenation of the mother's valence features with the list of SYNSEM values of the relevant daughters (the subject daughter for SUBJ, the complement daughters for COMPS, and the specifier daughter for SPR).

(34) LEXICAL AMALGAMATION OF SLASH
      Words amalgamate the SLASH values of all their arguments (that is, of members of their ARG-LIST).

(35) (DEFAULT) SLASH INHERITANCE PRINCIPLE
      In a headed phrase, the values of the SLASH attribute of a phrase is the value of the SLASH attribute of its head-daughter.

To model endocentric morphological trees, I added the following principle in chapter 5 (adapted from Krieger and Nerbonne 1993):

(36) MORPHOLOGICAL HEAD FEATURE PRINCIPLE
      In a headed morphological structure— that is, for complex lexemes whose μ-STRUC value is of type *headed-μ-struc*— the value of the head feature of the mother is token-identical to the value of the head feature of the head daughter or:

---

[3] The category *entity* subsumes quantifier-free parametrized states of affairs (or *qf-psoa*) and nominal objects.

μ-STRUC|DGHTR|SYNSEM|LOCAL|CATEGORY|HEAD =
SYNSEM|LOCAL|CAT|HEAD.

Finally, (37) states the blocking principle I have adopted in chapters 4 and 5.

(37) a. MORPHOLOGICAL BLOCKING PRINCIPLE

A L-category l_1 of type *word* is ungrammatical if it contains (or one of its subconstituents contains) a basic type τ_1 that unilaterally subsumes a *lexical competitor* τ_2 (type and phonological information aside).

b. Two basic categories of an AND/OR net are *lexical competitors* iff:

1. They are maximally specific types of the net (they do not have subtypes in the net);
2. They are mutually exclusive (they belong to an OR division in the net);
3. One unilaterally subsumes the other (is informationally less specific than the other), when their phonological and own type information is left aside.

(38) illustrates how the valence principle interacts with the SUBJ, COMPS, SPR lists. The AVM describes (part of) the information-structure associated with a transitive VP such as 'likes Glen'. Note that the value of the SYNSEM of the sole complement is token-identical to the member of the COMPS list (see the tag ③). Once the complement is realized it is taken off the mother node's COMPS list.

$$
(38) \begin{bmatrix} \text{SYNSEM} & \begin{bmatrix} \text{LOCAL} \mid \text{CAT} & \begin{bmatrix} \text{VAL} & \begin{bmatrix} \text{SUBJ} & ① \\ \text{COMPS}\langle\rangle \\ \text{SPR} & ② \end{bmatrix} \end{bmatrix} \end{bmatrix} \\ \text{DAUGHTERS} & \begin{bmatrix} \textit{head-comp-struc} \\ \text{HEAD-DTR} & \begin{bmatrix} \text{SYNSEM} \mid \text{LOCAL} \mid \text{CAT} & \begin{bmatrix} \text{VAL} & \begin{bmatrix} \text{SUBJ} & ① \\ \text{COMPS}\langle ③ \text{ NP}\rangle \\ \text{SPR} & ② \end{bmatrix} \end{bmatrix} \end{bmatrix} \\ \text{COMP-DTRS}\left\langle \begin{bmatrix} \textit{phrase} \\ \text{SYNSEM} ③ \end{bmatrix} \right\rangle \end{bmatrix} \end{bmatrix}
$$

A.4 Abbreviations

Let me now summarize some of the abbreviations used throughout the book.

1. NP abbreviates:

$$
\begin{bmatrix}
\text{LOCAL} & \begin{bmatrix}
\text{CATEGORY} & \begin{bmatrix}
\text{HEAD} & noun \\
\text{VALENCE} & \begin{bmatrix}
\text{SUBJ} & list(synsem) \\
\text{COMPS} \langle\rangle \\
\text{SPR} & \langle\rangle
\end{bmatrix}
\end{bmatrix}
\end{bmatrix}
\end{bmatrix}
$$

In other words, NP stands for the syntactic and semantic information of a nominal constituent which does not subcategorize for a complement or specifier (this constituent might still subcategorize for an external subject, though).

2. NP$_{\boxed{1}}$ abbreviates the syntactic and semantic information of an NP whose semantic index has a value tagged $\boxed{1}$. As mentioned in chapter 2, properly speaking tags always come in pairs and simply indicate that two path values are identical. The use of a single tag in the following diagrams is therefore merely abbreviatory.

$$
\begin{bmatrix}
\text{LOCAL} & \begin{bmatrix}
\text{CONTENT} & \begin{bmatrix} \text{INDEX} \ \boxed{1} \end{bmatrix} \\
\text{CATEGORY} & \begin{bmatrix}
\text{HEAD} & noun \\
\text{VALENCE} & \begin{bmatrix}
\text{SUBJ} & list(synsem) \\
\text{COMPS} \langle\rangle \\
\text{SPR} & \langle\rangle
\end{bmatrix}
\end{bmatrix}
\end{bmatrix}
\end{bmatrix}
$$

3. NP$_{it}$ abbreviates the syntactic and semantic information of an NP whose semantic index is of type it (a subtype of expletive nominal index in HPSG).

$$
\begin{bmatrix}
\text{LOCAL} & \begin{bmatrix}
\text{CONTENT} & \begin{bmatrix} \text{INDEX} \ it \end{bmatrix} \\
\text{CATEGORY} & \begin{bmatrix}
\text{HEAD} & noun \\
\text{VALENCE} & \begin{bmatrix}
\text{SUBJ} & list(synsem) \\
\text{COMPS} \langle\rangle \\
\text{SPR} & \langle\rangle
\end{bmatrix}
\end{bmatrix}
\end{bmatrix}
\end{bmatrix}
$$

4. VP abbreviates:

$$
\begin{bmatrix}
\text{LOCAL} & \begin{bmatrix}
\text{CATEGORY} & \begin{bmatrix}
\text{HEAD} & verb \\
\text{VALENCE} & \begin{bmatrix}
\text{SUBJ} & \langle synsem \rangle \\
\text{COMPS} \langle\rangle \\
\text{SPR} & \langle\rangle
\end{bmatrix}
\end{bmatrix}
\end{bmatrix}
\end{bmatrix}
$$

Thus VP stands for the syntactic and semantic information of a verbal constituent which does not subcategorize for a complement or specifier, but does subcategorize for a subject.

5. VP:$\boxed{1}$ abbreviates the syntactic and semantic information of a VP whose semantic content is tagged $\boxed{1}$.

$$
\begin{bmatrix}
\text{LOCAL} & \begin{bmatrix}
\text{CONTENT} & \boxed{1} \\
\text{CATEGORY} & \begin{bmatrix}
\text{HEAD} & verb \\
\text{VALENCE} & \begin{bmatrix}
\text{SUBJ} & \langle synsem \rangle \\
\text{COMPS} \langle\rangle \\
\text{SPR} & \langle\rangle
\end{bmatrix}
\end{bmatrix}
\end{bmatrix}
\end{bmatrix}
$$

6. S[*fin*] abbreviates the syntactic and semantic information of finite clauses or:

$$
\begin{bmatrix}
\text{LOCAL} & \begin{bmatrix}
\text{CONTENT} & \boxed{1} \\
\text{CATEGORY} & \begin{bmatrix}
\text{HEAD} & \begin{bmatrix} verb \\ \text{VFORM } finite \end{bmatrix} \\
\text{VALENCE} & \begin{bmatrix} \text{SUBJ} & \langle\rangle \\ \text{COMPS} & \langle\rangle \\ \text{SPR} & \langle\rangle \end{bmatrix}
\end{bmatrix}
\end{bmatrix}
\end{bmatrix}
$$

7. $\begin{bmatrix} \text{SYNSEM} \mid \text{LOCAL} \mid \text{CAT} \mid \text{HEAD } noun \end{bmatrix}$

abbreviates:

$$
\begin{bmatrix} \text{SYNSEM} & \begin{bmatrix} \text{LOCAL} & \begin{bmatrix} \text{CAT} & \begin{bmatrix} \text{HEAD } noun \end{bmatrix} \end{bmatrix} \end{bmatrix} \end{bmatrix}.
$$

The same convention applies to any path to an attribute A_n of the form:

$$
\begin{bmatrix} A_1 \mid A_2 \ \ldots \ \mid A_n \ value \end{bmatrix}.
$$

Bibliography

Abeillé, Anne. 1990. Lexical and syntactic rules in a tree adjoining grammar. In *Proceedings of the 28th ACL meeting*, 292–298. Pittsburgh.

Anderson, Stephen. 1969. *West Scandinavian vowel systems and the ordering of phonological rules*. Doctoral dissertation, MIT, Cambridge, Mass.

Anderson, Stephen. 1992. *A-Morphous Morphology*. Cambridge: Cambridge University Press.

Andrews, Avery. 1990. Unification and morphological blocking. *Natural Language and Linguistic Theory* 8:507–557.

Archangeli, Diana. 1984. *Underspecification in Yawelmani phonology and morphology*. Doctoral dissertation, MIT, Cambridge, Mass.

Aronoff, Marc. 1976. *Word Formation in Generative Grammar*. Cambridge, Mass.: MIT Press.

Bach, Emmon. 1976. An extension of classical transformational grammar. In *Problems of Linguistic Metatheory (Proceedings of the 1976 Conference)*, 183–224. Michigan State University.

Barsalou, Lawrence. 1993. Flexibility, Structure, and Linguistic Vagary in Concepts: Manifestations of a Compositional System of Perceptual Symbols. In *Theories of Memory*. 29–101. Lawrence Erlbaum.

Barsalou, Lawrence, and Jesse Prinz. 1997. Mundane Creativity in Perceptual Symbol Systems. In *Creative thought: An investigation of conceptual structures and processes*, ed. Thomas B. Ward, Steven M. Smith, and Jyotsna Vaid. 267–307. Washington D.C.: American Psychological Association.

Berwick, Robert. 1991. Principles of principle-based parsing. In *Principle-Based Parsing: Computation and Psycholinguistics*, ed. Robert et al. Berwick. 1–37. Dordrecht: Kluwer.

Bird, Steven, and Mark Ellison. 1994. One-Level Phonology: Autosegmental Representations and Rules as Finite Automata. *Computational Linguistics* 20:55–90.

Bird, Steven, and Ewan Klein. 1994. Phonological Analysis in Typed Feature Systems. *Computational Linguistics* 20:455–491.

Blevins, James P. 1995. Syncretism and Paradigmatic Opposition. *Linguistics and Philosophy* 18(2):113–152.

Bloomfield, Leonard. 1933. *Language*. Chicago: Chicago University Press. 1984 reprint.

Bobrow, Robert, and Bonnie Webber. 1980. Knowledge representation for syntax/semantics processing. In *Proceedings of the 1st National Conference on Artificial Intelligence*. 316–323. Morgan Kaufmann.

Bochner, Harry. 1993. *Simplicity in Generative Morphology*. Berlin: Mouton de Gruyter.

Bowermann, Melissa. 1987. Commentary: Mechanisms of Language Acquisition. In *Mechanisms of language acquisition*, ed. MacWhinney. 443–466. Hillsdale, N.J.: Erlbaum.

Brachman, Ronald, and James Schmolze. 1985. An Overview of the KL-ONE Knowledge Representation System. *Cognitive Science* 9:171–216.

Bresnan, Joan, and Jonni Kanerva. 1989. Locative inversion in Chicheŵa: A Case Study of Factorization in Grammar. *Linguistic Inquiry* 20:1–50.

Bresnan, Joan, and Ronald Kaplan. 1982. Introduction: Grammars as Mental Representations of Language. In *The Mental Representation of Grammatical Relations*. xvii–lii. Cambridge, Mass.: MIT Press.

Bresnan, Joan, and Sam Mchombo. 1995. The Lexical Integrity Principle: Evidence from Bantu. *Natural Language and Linguistic Theory* 13:181–254.

Briscoe, Ted, Ann Copestake, and Alex Lascarides. 1995. Blocking. In *Computational Lexical Semantics*, ed. P. St. Dizier and E. Viegas. Cambridge: Cambridge University Press.

Brugman, Claudia. 1981/1988a. *The Story of Over: polysemy, semantics, and the structure of the lexicon*. New York: Garland.

Brugman, Claudia. 1988b. *The Syntax and Semantics of Have and its complements*. Doctoral dissertation, University of California at Berkeley.

Bybee, Joan. 1985. *Morphology: a Study of the Relation between Meaning and Form*. Amsterdam: Benjamins.

Bybee, Joan. 1988. Morphology As Lexical Organization. In *Theoretical Morphology*. 119–141. San Diego: Academic Press.

Bybee, Joan, and Carol Moder. 1983. Morphological classes as natural categories. *Language* 59:251–270.

Bybee, Joan, and Dan Slobin. 1982. Rules and schemes in the development and use of the English past tense. *Language* 58:265–289.

Carpenter, Bob. 1991. The Generative Power of Categorial Grammars and Head-Driven Phrase Structure. *Computational Linguistics* 17:301–313.

Carpenter, Bob. 1992. *The Logic of Typed Feature Structures*. Cambridge: Cambridge University Press.

Carpenter, Bob, and Carl Pollard. 1991. Inclusion, disjointness and choice: The logic of linguistic classification. In *Proceedings of the 29th ACL meeting*, 9–16. Berkeley.

Casad, Eugene, and Ronald Langacker. 1985. "Inside" and "outside" in Cora Grammar. *International Journal of American Linguistics* 51:247–281.

Chomsky, Noam. 1965. *Aspects of the Theory of Syntax.* Cambridge, Mass.: MIT Press.

Chomsky, Noam. 1981. *Lectures on Government and Binding.* Dordrecht: Foris.

Chomsky, Noam. 1982. *Some Concepts and Consequences of the Theory of Government and Binding.* Cambridge, Mass.: MIT Press.

Copestake, Ann, and Ted Briscoe. 1995. Semi-productive polysemy and sense extension. *Journal of Semantics* 12:15–67.

Daelemans, Walter, Koenraad De Smedt, and Gerald Gazdar. 1992. Inheritance in natural language processing. *Computational Linguistics* 18:205–218.

Davis, Anthony. 1996. *Lexical Semantics and Linking in the Hierarchical Lexicon.* Doctoral dissertation, Stanford University, Stanford.

Davis, Anthony, and Jean-Pierre Koenig. 1997. Linking as constraints on word classes in a hierarchical lexicon. Manuscript, State University of New York at Buffalo.

Di Sciullo, Anna-Maria, and Edwin Williams. 1987. *On the Definition of Word.* Cambridge, Mass.: MIT Press.

Fillmore, Charles. 1982. Frame Semantics. In *Linguistics in the Morning Calm,* ed. The Linguistic Society of Korea. 111–137. Seoul: Hanshin Publishing Co.

Fillmore, Charles. 1985. Frames and the Semantics of Understanding. *Quaderni di Semantica* 6:22–53.

Fillmore, Charles, and Paul Kay. (Forthcoming). *Construction Grammar.* Stanford: CSLI Publications.

Fillmore, Charles, Paul Kay, and Catherine O'Connor. 1988. Regularity and idiomaticity in Grammatical Constructions: the case of *Let alone*. *Language* 64:501–538.

Flickinger, Daniel. 1987. *Lexical rules in the hierarchical lexicon.* Doctoral dissertation, Stanford University.

Flickinger, Daniel, and John Nerbonne. 1992. Inheritance and complementation: A case study of *easy* adjectives and related nouns. *Computational Linguistics* 18:269–310.

Fodor, Jerry. 1983. *The Modularity of Mind.* Cambridge, Mass.: MIT Press.

Godard, Daniele, and Ivan Sag. 1995. Reflexivization and intransitivity: The case of French. Annual Meeting of the Linguistics Society of America.

Goldberg, Adele. 1991. On the Problems of Lexical Rules Accounts of Argument Structure. In *Proceedings of the Annual Cognitive Science Society Conference.* Chicago.

Goldberg, Adele. 1992. *Argument Structure Constructions.* Doctoral dissertation, University of California at Berkeley, Berkeley.

Goldberg, Adele. 1995. *Constructions: A Construction Grammar Approach to Argument Structure*. Chicago: Chicago University Press.

Gordon, Peter. 1985. Level-ordering in lexical development. *Cognition* 21:73–93.

Green, Georgia. 1996. Modeling grammar growth: Universal grammar without innate principles or parameters. Manuscript.

Grimshaw, Jane. 1982. On the Lexical Representation of Romance Reflexive Clitics. In *The Mental Representation of Grammatical Relations*, ed. Joan Bresnan. 87–148. Cambridge, Mass.: MIT Press.

Gropen, Jess, Steve Pinker, Michael Hollander, Richard Goldberg, and Ronald Wilson. 1989. The learnability and acquisition of the dative alternation in English. *Language* 65:203–257.

Gross, Maurice. 1975. *Méthodes en Syntaxe*. Paris: Hermann.

Gupta, Prahlad, and David Touretzky. 1994. Connectionist models and linguistic theory: Investigations of stress systems in language. *Cognitive Science* 18:1–50.

Hankamer, Jorge. 1989. Morphological parsing and the lexicon. In *Lexical Representation and Process*, ed. William Marslen-Wilson. 392–408. Cambridge, Mass.: MIT Press.

Inkelas, Sharon. 1989. *Prosodic constituency in the lexicon*. Doctoral dissertation, Stanford University, Stanford.

Inkelas, Sharon, and Orhan Orgun. 1995. Level ordering and economy in the lexical phonology of Turkish. *Language* 71:763–793.

Inkelas, Sharon, and Orhan Orgun. (In press). Level (non)ordering in recursive morphology: evidence from Turkish. In *Morphology and Its Relation to Phonology and Syntax*, ed. Steven Lapointe, Diane Brentari, and Patrick Farrell. Stanford. CSLI Publications.

Jackendoff, Ray. 1975. Morphological and semantic regularities in the lexicon. *Language* 51:639–671.

Jaeger, Jeri, Alan Lockwood, David Kemmerer, Robert Van Valin, Brian Murphy, and Hanif Khalak. 1996. A positron emission tomographic study of regular and irregular verb morphology in English. *Language* 72:451–497.

Jurafsky, Daniel. 1991. *An On-line Model of Human Sentence Interpretation: A Theory of the Representation and Use of Linguistic Knowledge*. Doctoral dissertation, University of California at Berkeley, Berkeley.

Jurafsky, Daniel. 1996. A Probabilistic Model of Lexical and Syntactic Access and Disambiguation. *Cognitive Science* 20:137–194.

Karttunen, Lauri. 1993. Finite-State Constraints. In *The Last Phonological Rule*, ed. John Goldsmith. 173–194. Chicago: Chicago University Press.

Kenstowicz, Michael. 1994. *Phonology in Generative Grammar*. Cambridge, Mass.: Blackwell.

Kim, John, Steven Pinker, Alan Prince, and Sandeep Prasada. 1991. Why No Mere Mortal Has Ever Flown Out to Center Field. *Cognitive Science* 15:173–218.

King, Paul. 1989. *A Logical Formalism for Head-Driven Phrase Structure Grammar*. Doctoral dissertation, University of Manchester, Manchester.

King, Paul. 1994. An expanded logical formalism for Head-driven Phrase Structure Grammar. Technical report. Tübingen. Seminar für Sprachwissenschaft Technical Report.

Kiparsky, Paul. 1973. "Elsewhere" in phonology. In *A Festschrift for Morris Halle*, ed. Stephen Anderson and Paul Kiparsky. 93–106. New York: Holt, Rinehart, and Winston.

Kiparsky, Paul. 1982a. From Cyclic Phonology to Lexical Phonology. In *The Structure of Phonological Representation I*, ed. Harry van der Hulst and Norval Smith. Dordrecht: Foris.

Kiparsky, Paul. 1982b. Lexical morphology and phonology. In *Linguistics in the Morning Calm*. 3–91. Seoul: Hanshin.

Kiparsky, Paul. 1985. Some consequences of Lexical Phonology. *Phonology Yearbook* 2:83–136.

Koenig, Jean-Pierre. 1993. Linking Constructions vs. Linking Rules: Evidence from French. In *Proceedings of the 19th annual meeting of the Berkeley Linguistics Society*, ed. Joshua Guenter, Barbara Kaiser, and Cheryl Zoll, 217–231. Berkeley. Berkeley Linguistics Society.

Koenig, Jean-Pierre. 1994. *Lexical Underspecification and the Syntax/Semantics Interface*. Doctoral dissertation, University of California at Berkeley, Berkeley.

Koenig, Jean-Pierre. 1995. Mapping constructions as word-templates: evidence from French. In *Grammatical Relations: Theoretical approaches to Empirical Questions*, ed. Clifford Burgess, Katarzyna Dziwirek, and Donna Gerdts. 249–270. Stanford: CSLI Publications.

Koenig, Jean-Pierre. 1998. Inside-out constraints and Description Languages for HPSG. In *Lexical and Constructional Aspects of Linguistic Explanation*, ed. Gert Webelhuth, Jean-Pierre Koenig, and Andreas Kathol. 265–279. Stanford: CSLI Publications.

Koenig, Jean-Pierre, and Daniel Jurafsky. 1994. Type Underspecification and On-line Type Construction in the Lexicon. In *Proceedings of WCCFL XIII*, 270–285. Stanford. CSLI Publications.

Koenig, Jean-Pierre, Orhan Orgun, and Daniel Jurafsky. 1996. Constraint-based Morphology. Paper presented at the Third International Head-Driven Phrase-Structure Grammar conference, Marseille, France.

Koskenniemi, Kimmo. 1983. Two-level Morphology: A General Computational Model for Word-Form Recognition and Production. Technical report. Helsinki: Department of General Linguistics, University of Helsinki.

Koskenniemi, Kimmo. 1997. Representations and Finite-State Components in Natural Language. In *Finite-State Language Processing*, ed. Emmanuel Roche and Yves Schabes. 99–116. Cambridge, Mass.: MIT Press.

Krieger, Hans-Ulrich, and John Nerbonne. 1993. Feature-Based Inheritance Networks for Computational Lexicons. In *Inheritance, Defaults, and the*

Lexicon, ed. Ted Briscoe, Valeria de Paiva, and Ann Copestake. 90–136. Cambridge: Cambridge University Press.

Krieger, Hans-Ulrich, Hannes Pirker, and John Nerbonne. 1993. Feature-based allomorphy. In *Proceedings of the 31st meeting of the ACL*, 140–147. Columbus.

Lakoff, George. 1970. *Irregularity in Syntax*. New York: Holt, Rinehart, and Winston.

Lakoff, George. 1977. Linguistic Gestalts. In *Papers from the 13th Regional Meeting of the Chicago Linguistic Society*, 236–287. Chicago. Chicago Linguistic Society.

Lakoff, George. 1987. *Women, Fire and Dangerous Things*. Chicago: The University of Chicago Press.

Lakoff, George. 1993. Cognitive Phonology. In *The Last Phonological Rule*, ed. John Goldsmith. 117–145. Chicago: Chicago University Press.

Lakoff, George, and Henry Thompson. 1975. Introducing cognitive grammar. In *Proceedings of the 1st annual meeting of the Berkeley Linguistics Society*, 295–313. Berkeley. Berkeley Linguistics Society.

Lambrecht, Knud. 1994. *Information Structure and Sentence Form*. Cambridge: Cambridge University Press.

Langacker, Ronald. 1987. *Foundations of Cognitive Grammar, vol.1*. Stanford: Stanford University Press.

Langacker, Ronald. 1991. *Foundations of Cognitive Grammar, vol. 2*. Stanford: Stanford University Press.

Lascarides, Alex, Ted Briscoe, Nicholas Asher, and Ann Copestake. 1996. Order independent and persistent typed default unification. *Linguistics and Philosophy* 19:1–90.

Levin, Beth. 1993. *English Verb Classes and Alternations*. Chicago: Chicago University Press.

Levin, Beth, and Malka Hovav Rappaport. 1994. A preliminary analysis of causative verbs in English. In *The Acquisition of the Lexicon*, ed. Lila Gleitman and Barbara Landau. 35–77. Cambridge, Mass.: MIT Press.

Lieber, Rochelle. 1980. *The Organization of the Lexicon*. Doctoral dissertation, MIT.

Lieber, Rochelle. 1992. *Deconstructing Morphology*. Chicago: Chicago University Press.

Lukatela, Georgije, B. Gligorijevic, A. Kostic, and M T. Turvey. 1980. Representation of inflected nouns in the internal lexicon. *Memory and Cognition* 8:415–423.

Marcus, Gary, Ursula Brinkman, Harald Clahsen, Richard Wiese, et al. 1995. German inflection: the exception that proves the rule. *Cognitive Psychology* 29:189–256.

Marr, David. 1982. *Vision*. San Francisco: Freeman.

Matthews, Peter. 1974. *Morphology*. Cambridge: Cambridge University Press.

McCawley, James. 1968. Concerning the base component of a transformational grammar. *Foundations of Language* 4:243–269.

Mchombo, Sam. 1993. A formal analysis of the stative construction in Bantu. *Journal of African Languages and Linguistics* 14:5–28.

Meurers, Detmar, and Guido Minnen. 1997. A Computational Treatment of Lexical Rules in HPSG as Covariation in Lexical Entries. *Computational Linguistics* 23:543–568.

Michaelis, Laura. 1993. *Toward a Grammar of Aspect: The Case of the English Perfect Construction*. Doctoral dissertation, University of California at Berkeley, Berkeley.

Michaelis, Laura, and Knud Lambrecht. 1996. Toward a construction-based theory of language function: The case of nominal extraposition. *Language* 72:215–247.

Miller, Philip. 1991. *Clitics and Constituents in Phrase Structure Grammar*. Doctoral dissertation, Rijksuniversiteit, Utrecht.

Miller, Philip, and Ivan Sag. 1997. French clitic movement without clitics or movement. *Natural Language and Linguistic Theory* 15:573–639.

Mohanan, Karuvannur. 1986. *The Theory of Lexical Phonology*. Dordrecht: Reidel.

Norvig, Peter, and George Lakoff. 1987. Taking: A study in lexical network theory. In *Proceedings of the 13th annual meeting of the Berkeley Linguistics Society*. Berkeley. Berkeley Linguistics Society.

Orgun, Orhan. 1994. Monotonic cyclicity and Optimality Theory. In *NELS 24*. 461–474. Department of Linguistics, University of Massachusetts: GLSA.

Orgun, Orhan. 1995. Flat vs. branching structures in morphology: The case of suspended affixation. In *Proceedings of the 21st annual meeting of the Berkeley Linguistics Society*. Berkeley. Berkeley Linguistics Society.

Pesetzky, David. 1982. *Paths and Categories*. Doctoral dissertation, MIT, Cambridge, Mass.

Pinker, Steven. 1989. *Learnability and Cognition: the acquisition of argument structure*. Cambridge, Mass.: MIT Press.

Pinker, Steven, and Alan Prince. 1988. On language and connectionism: Analysis of a Parallel Distributed Processing model of language acquisition. *Cognition* 28:73–193.

Pinker, Steven, and Alan Prince. 1991. Regular and Irregular Morphology and the Psychological Status of Rules of Grammar. In *Proceedings of the 17th annual meeeting of the Berkeley Linguistics Society*, ed. Laurel Sutton and Christopher Johnson, 230–251. Berkeley. Berkeley Linguistics Society.

Pollard, Carl. 1991. Sorts in unification-based grammars and what they mean. Manuscript, Ohio State University.

Pollard, Carl, and Ivan Sag. 1987. *Information-based Syntax and Semantics, vol.1*. Stanford: CSLI Publications.

Pollard, Carl, and Ivan Sag. 1994. *Head-Driven Phrase-Structure Grammar*. Chicago: Chicago University Press.

Pulleyblank, Douglas. 1986. *Tone in Lexical Phonology*. Dordrecht: Reidel.

Pullum, Geoffrey, and Arnold Zwicky. 1991. A Misconceived Approach to Morphology. In *Proceedings of WWCFL 10*, ed. Dawn Bates. 387–398. Stanford: CSLI Publications.

Quillian, M. Ross. 1968. Semantic memory. In *Semantic information processing*, ed. Marvin Minsky. 216–270. Cambridge, Mass.: MIT.

Rappaport, Malka Hovav, and Beth Levin. 1992. -er nominals: implications for the theory of argument structure. In *Syntax and Semantics vol.26*, ed. Tim Stowell and Eric Wehrli. San Diego: Academic Press.

Reape, Mike. 1994. Domain Union and Word Order Variation in German. In *German in Head-Driven Phrase Structure Grammar*, ed. John Nerbonne, Klaus Netter, and Carl Pollard. 151–197. Stanford University: CSLI Publications.

Riehemann, Susanne. 1993. Word Formation in Lexical Type Hierarchies. Master's thesis, University of Tübingen, Tübingen.

Ruwet, Nicolas. 1982. Le datif épistémique en français et la Condition d'opacité de Chomsky. In *Grammaire des insultes et autres études*. 172–204. Paris: Seuil.

Sag, Ivan. 1991. Linguistic Theory and Natural Language Processing. In *Natural Language and Speech*, ed. Ewan Klein and Frederik Veltman. 69–83. Berlin: Springer-Verlag.

Sag, Ivan. 1997. English relative clauses. *Journal of Linguistics* 33:431–483.

Sag, Ivan, and Daniele Godard. 1994. Extraction of *De*-Phrases from the French NP. In *NELS 24*. 519–541. Department of Linguistics, University of Massachusetts: GLSA.

Selkirk, Elisabeth. 1982. *The Syntax of Words*. Cambridge, Mass.: MIT Press.

Selkirk, Elisabeth. 1984. *Phonology and Syntax*. Cambridge, Mass.: MIT Press.

Shieber, Stuart. 1986. *An introduction to Unification-based approaches to grammar*. Stanford: CSLI Publications.

Shih, C.-L. 1986. *The Prosodic Domain of Tone Sandhi in Chinese*. Doctoral dissertation, University of California at Los Angeles.

Spencer, Andrew. 1988. Arguments for morpholexical rules. *Journal of Linguistics* 24:1–30.

Sproat, Richard. 1992. *Morphology and Computation*. Cambridge, Mass.: MIT Press.

Steriade, Donca. 1995. Underspecification and markedness. In *A handbook of phonological theory*, ed. John Goldsmith. 114–174. Cambridge, Mass.: Blackwell.

Stump, Gregory. 1991. A paradigm-based theory of morphosemantic mismatches. *Language* 67:675–725.

Stump, Gregory. 1993. How Peculiar is Evaluative Morphology? *Journal of Linguistics* 29:1–36.

Stump, Gregory. (In press). Comments on Inkelas and Orgun's paper. In *Morphology and Its Relation to Phonology and Syntax*. Stanford. CSLI Publications.

Sweetser, Eve. 1990. *From Etymology to Pragmatics*. Cambridge: Cambridge University Press.

Talmy, Leonard. 1985. Lexicalization patterns: Semantic structure in lexical forms. In *Language Typology and Syntactic Description, vol.3*, ed. Timothy Shopen. 57–149. New York: Cambridge University Press.

Wasow, Thomas. 1977. Transformations and the lexicon. In *Formal Syntax*, ed. Peter Culicover, Tom Wasow, and Adrian Akmajian. 327–360. New York: Academic Press.

Wilensky, Robert. 1983. *Planning and understanding: a computational approach to human reasoning*. Reading, Mass.: Addison-Wesley.

Williams, Edwin. 1981. On the notions "lexically related" and "head of a word". *Linguistic Inquiry* 12:245–274.

Williams, Edwin. 1994. Remarks on lexical knowledge. In *The Acquisition of the Lexicon*, ed. Lila Gleitman and Barbara Landau. 7–34. Cambridge, Mass.: MIT Press.

Wittenburg, Kent. 1993. F-PATR: Functional constraints for unification-based grammars. In *Proceedings of the 31st meeting of the ACL*, 216–223. Columbus.

Zubin, David, and Klaus-Michael Köpcke. 1986. Gender and Folk Taxonomy: The Indexical Relation between Grammatical and Lexical Categorization. In *Categorization and Noun Classification*, ed. Colette Craig. 139–180. Philadelphia: Benjamins North America.

Zubizarreta, Maria-Luisa. 1987. *Levels of Representation in the Lexicon and in the Syntax*. Foris: Dordrecht.

Zwicky, Arnold. 1985. Heads. *Journal of Linguistics* 21:1–20.

Zwicky, Arnold. 1986. The general case: basic form versus default form. In *Proceedings of the 12th annual meeting of the Berkeley Linguistics Socitey*, ed. Vassiliki Nikiforidou, Mary VanClay, Mary Niepokuj, and Deboraj Feder, 305–314. Berkeley. Berkeley Linguistics Society.

Zwicky, Arnold. 1989. What's become of Derivations? Defaults and Invocations. In *Proceedings of the 15th annual meeting of the Berkeley Linguistics Socitey*, ed. Kira Hall, Michael Meacham, and Richard Shapiro, 303–320. Berkeley. Berkeley Linguistics Society.

Zwicky, Arnold. 1991. Some Choices in the Theory of Morphology. In *Formal Grammar: Theory and Implementation*, ed. Robert Levine. 327–371. Vancouver: University of British Columbia.

Name Index

Subject Index

(Italicized page numbers refer to definitions of technical terms and abbreviations.)

$\alpha\beta$ elements, *103*, 106, 108, 117
affixes, 97–98
as heads, 162–178
AND/OR nets, 135–142, 161, 174, 175, 178
conjunctive *vs.* disjunctive application of rules, 80–82
AND/OR trees, 20–24
ARG-ST list, 29, 67, *188*, 192
attribute-value matrix, *16–18*
AVM, *see* Attribute-Value Matrix

blocking, *see* Elsewhere Condition, 117–130, 194
Breton compounds, 154–160

CATEGORY, *188*
category abstraction, 4, 161
category and types, 18n
CCLR, *see* Complement Clitic Lexical Rule
CELR, *see* Complement Extraction Lexical Rule
CG, *see* Construction Grammar
Chicheŵa inchoativization, 163–166
CLASS, *192*
class and categories, 18n
COGGR, *see* Cognitive Grammar
Cognitive Grammar, 3, 5, 15

competence and performance, 7, 129
complement clitic lexical rule, *32*, 36
complement extraction lexical rule, *31*
complex lexeme, *92–101*, 107, 116, 133, 135, 157, 191, 193
COMPS list, 29, 62, *188*, 190, 193, 194
conjunctive type construction, *21*, 62–64, 82
on-line, *see* On-Line Type Construction
conjunctive *vs.* disjunctive rule application
stem selection, 135–150
conjunctive *vs.* disjunctive rule application, *see* AND/OR nets
conjunctively *vs.* disjunctively ordered rule blocks, 40, 136, 174
constituent structure morphology, *see* morphology, constituent-based, 56–58, 85
constraint satisfaction, 7
Construction Grammar, 3, 5, 7, 14, 15, 121
constructions, 6, 7, *14*, 53, 55
morphophonology, 102–117
morphosyntax, 92–101
CONTENT, *188*